D1271375

Participants

Bulgaria	**Zahari Staikov** **Sasha Todorova** **Krastu Petkov** *Bulgarian Academy of Sciences*
Federal Republic of Germany	**Klaus Bartölke** *University of Wuppertal*
Hungary	**Tamás Rozgonyi** **Antal Gyenes** *Hungarian Academy of Sciences*
Ireland	**John Hurley** *National Institute for Higher Education* **Noirin O'Broin** *The Economic and Social Research Institute*
Mexico	**Germán Otálora-Bay** *Institute of Technology and Higher Education*
Romania	**Ion Drăgan** **Septimiu Chelcea** **Petre Cristea** **Pompiliu Grigorescu** **Stefan Stefănescu** **Cătălin Zamfir** *University of Bucharest*
(Vienna)	**Gunilla Vyskovsky** *European Coordination Centre for Research and Documentation in Social Sciences*

Other Contributors

Austria	**Georg Wieser** *University of Vienna*
Israel	**Menachem Rosner** *University of Haifa*
Italy	**Mino Vianello** *University of Rome*
Yugoslavia	**Bogdan Kavčič** *University of Ljubljana*

Authority and Reward in Organizations

An International Research

Codirected by
Arnold S. Tannenbaum
and Tamás Rozgonyi

Coordinated by the
European Coordination Centre
for Research and Documentation
in Social Sciences

Survey Research Center
Institute for Social Research
The University of Michigan

1986

Library of Congress Cataloging-in-Publication Data

Authority and reward in organizations.

  Bibliography: p.
  1. Organizational behavior—Case studies.
I. Tannenbaum, Arnold.
II. Rozgonyi, Tamás. III. European Coordination
Centre for Research and Documentation in Social
Sciences. IV. University of Michigan. Survey
Research Center.
HD58.7.A96 1986   302.3'5   86-20120
ISBN 0-87944-309-X

ISR Code Number 4676

Published in 1986 by:
Institute for Social Research
The University of Michigan, Ann Arbor, Michigan

6 5 4 3 2 1
Manufactured in the United States of America

Acknowledgments

The research reported in this book represents the collaborative effort of colleagues from Eastern and Western Europe, Mexico, and the United States. We are grateful to the Ford Foundation for a grant that permitted Arnold Tannenbaum to participate in this collaboration. Thanks to the grant, he was able to join his colleagues in developing the technical plan of the research and to work with them in his capacity as codirector, along with Tamás Rozgonyi, in carrying out the plan. While on a fellowship provided by the German Marshall Fund of the United States, Tannenbaum did a large part of the editing of this book and wrote several chapters. We offer our sincere thanks to the German Marshall Fund for this support.

The research was carried out under the aegis of the European Coordination Centre for Research and Documentation in Social Science (Vienna Centre), which provided substantial administrative and financial support. We acknowledge the help of Vienna Centre project coordinators Risto Kolari and Helmut Ornauer, who helped launch the project, and Gunilla Vyskovsky, who contributed to the preparation of this volume. We are grateful also to Daniel Denison for his helpful reactions to an earlier draft.

Contents

Chapter 9
Summary and Conclusions
Arnold S. Tannenbaum and Tamás Rozgonyi   **233**

Appendix A
History of the Project
Gunilla Vyskovsky   **245**

Appendix B
Questionnaire   **249**

Bibliography   **273**

1

Introduction

Arnold S. Tannenbaum and Tamás Rozgonyi

Complex work organizations are an essential component of modern society; indeed, they help to define what we mean by modern society (Inkeles & Smith, 1974). Organizations create the goods and services that we identify with modernity and that contribute to affluence. But organizations entail costs as well as benefits to members. Furthermore, these costs and benefits are not distributed equally or randomly among members; rather, they derive systematically from the structure of the organization and are therefore distributed in ways that correspond to that structure. Thus, organization is more conducive to the welfare of some members than of others, depending on their location in "organizational space." Hierarchy is one aspect of structure that helps to define that space.

The research described in the following chapters is an attempt to replicate, in industrial organizations from a diverse group of societies, earlier research concerning the effect of hierarchy on the reactions and adjustments of members. The present research examines some of these effects in socialist countries of Eastern Europe, including Bulgaria, Hungary, and Romania, as well as in countries of Western Europe and Latin America, including the Federal Republic of Germany, Ireland, and Mexico. The earlier work suggested that persons at upper levels compared to those at lower echelons are likely to experience greater satisfaction, involvement, and motivation in their jobs; stronger identification with and loyalty to their organization; and greater satisfaction of needs for self-esteem and self-actualization. Significant perceptual, ideological, and cognitive differences also distinguish persons of different rank.

Ordinarily, such effects of hierarchy are not purposely designed into an organization; nor are they intentionally fostered by leaders. On the contrary, many leaders bemoan the lack of morale and the

1

poor motivation at lower levels (unlike the state of affairs at the top), and they regret the "communications gap" and the unfortunate inclination of persons of low rank to take a view of organizational life so different from their own view. Thus, hierarchy has unintended and dysfunctional effects (in addition to the functional ones), including the relatively poor motivation and lesser feeling of responsibility on the part of many workers at the bottom and the potential conflict between persons at relatively high levels and those below. Hierarchy also poses a moral dilemma in societies that espouse equality, democracy, and other humanistic values.

Official responses to the functional and moral problems of hierarchy vary from one society to another. Some of the countries in this research have formal policies to counteract the inequality and oligarchy implicit in hierarchy and to mitigate some of the undesirable effects that are especially apparent at lower levels of organizations. The Federal Republic of Germany's system of *Mitbestimmung*, for example, legally requires that workers have the opportunity to influence decisions in their enterprise through a council of elected representatives and/or through a supervisory board that includes representatives of management and labor. In Ireland, "joint consultation" is formally employed in many firms, and workers are elected to the board of directors of some state-owned enterprises. In many Western societies, legally sanctioned collective bargaining provides a means for the participation of workers through negotiation with management about issues that are related directly to workers' welfare. In socialist countries, pay differentials between persons of different rank are formally limited (although not eliminated) as a way of moving organizations toward an egalitarian ideal. In Bulgaria, the law also specifies that management bodies include worker representatives to solve the social problems associated with production. In Romania, a General Assembly of the Working People, in which all categories of personnel are represented, is formally empowered to decide general and economic issues of the firm. These policies will be described in more detail in the following chapters, as we examine the hierarchical distribution of authority and reward along with some of the reactions and adjustments of members reported by persons at different levels.

Authority and Reward

Students of organization have sought to explain the motivation, satisfaction, and other reactions of organization members. The explanations have not always been consistent with one another, yet they share a common implication: The conditions of organization that are conducive to the motivation and satisfaction of members are among the conditions that prevail at the upper more than at the lower levels of the organizational hierarchy. Models of job enrichment (Herzberg, 1966) and of job redesign (Hackman & Oldham, 1976), for example, along with models of the autonomous work group, sociotechnical systems, and participative management (Davis, 1972; Engelstad, 1972; Rubenowitz, 1974) tell us (by implication if not explicitly) that the conditions that motivate workers and contribute to a feeling of satisfaction are precisely those that distinguish the upper levels from those below. These conditions include the greater authority—and therefore greater control—exercised by persons at upper levels, along with other rewarding features of work, extrinsic as well as intrinsic, such as higher pay and status and the opportunity to use complex skills and to exercise discretion. In addition, a number of demographic characteristics distinguish upper-level persons from those below: In general, upper-level persons are older and more senior in their company and have more formal education. These demographic correlates of hierarchy, like authority and reward, also have implications for the motivation and satisfaction of people at work.

Authority[1]

Authority in an organization is the formal right to exercise control or influence over what goes on in an organization. Classical theories of organization prescribe a hierarchical distribution of authority and control. While some contemporary theories propose to modify the rigidity of those hierarchical arrangements, most contemporary views still implicitly accept a distribution of control that is essentially hierarchical. That control is in fact distributed hierarchically in organizations is perhaps among the best-documented facts of organizational life. Organization members themselves are unequivocal in reporting this distribution; it has been documented through research in many and varied organizations, including business, industrial, and military organizations; cooperatives; municipal agencies; schools; colleges; religious institutions; and even, with some exceptions, voluntary organizations. It has been found in organizations of developed and developing countries as well as in capitalist and socialist societies. Although managers and rank-and-file workers may differ in the details of their perceptions of how much authority and influence different groups exercise in their organization, they do not disagree that persons at higher levels in the hierarchy exercise more control than persons at lower levels do (IDE, 1981; Tannenbaum & Cooke, 1979).

People generally want—or at least say they want—to exercise control or influence in their work situation. Exactly how much influence is desired may vary from one individual to another, but most people prefer having some say in their work situation to being powerless. When members of organizations are asked how much authority and influence they have and how much they would like to have, the prevailing response is what Porter (1962a, 1962b) has referred to as a "perceived need deficiency": People want more than they think they have. Furthermore, the deficiency is greater near the bottom of the organization than near the top.

It seems reasonable to expect that, in most cultures, the exercise of influence (or the perception that one has influence) is rewarding and therefore a source of satisfaction. Studies of participative decision making support the contention that workers who have the opportunity to exercise influence through participation are likely to be more satisfied (if not necessarily more productive) than workers who do not have that opportunity (Locke & Schweiger, 1979). Furthermore, the satisfaction associated with the exercise of influence is not confined to developed countries or to cultures with a prevailing "Protestant work ethic." Peruvian workers described by Whyte and Williams (1963), for example, expressed distrust toward their company management and reacted negatively to American-style "human relations" techniques of supervision, but nonetheless reported satisfaction with their supervisor to the extent that they saw themselves and their co-workers as having influence "about how things are done in [their] work group" (p. 5). Similarly, black clerical workers in South Africa, whom Orpen and Ndlovu (1977, p. 32) describe as "the object of legalized and social discrimination which forces them to occupy inferior positions in society," report satisfaction with their jobs to the extent that they feel they can influence decisions that affect their work. In one exception, the kibbutz factory, the exercise of authority and influence does not relate to job satisfaction, although it does correlate with the sense of responsibility that members report in their work situation (Tannenbaum et al., 1974). Strong egalitarian norms in the kibbutz may create ambivalence in some members toward the exercise of authority. One might surmise, then, that while exercising authority may not make kibbutz members happy, it does make them responsible.

Other Rewarding Features of Work

The exercise of authority or control is a reward implicitly associated with rank, but it is by no means the only rewarding feature that varies with hierarchical position. Work near the bottom of the hierarchy in industrial plants is not, in general, likely to be the most rewarding. It is relatively repetitious, routinized, and fractionated; it allows relatively little use of discretion; and it provides few opportunities to learn new things or to use one's ideas and skills—conditions that are frustrating and alienating to many people (Argyris, 1964). The relationship of these features of work to job satisfaction has been widely documented. Rousseau (1977), for example, in a review of research in the United States on job design, found support for the notion that a job is satisfying to the extent that it provides an employee with the opportunity to use a number of different skills or to make decisions related to the work process (which is more likely to occur at the top of the hierarchy than at the bottom). (See also Rousseau, 1978; Srivastva et al., 1975.)

A national sample survey in the United States showed that in the work force as a whole, people who reported that their jobs allowed them autonomy in matters that affected their work or made "enriching" demands on them (e.g., that one learn new things, have a high level of skill, be creative, and do a variety of different things) were likely to be more satisfied with their jobs than were people who did not report such characteristics (U.S. Department of Labor, 1971; see also Friend & Burns, 1977). Emery and Phillips (1976), comparing skilled and unskilled urban workers in Australia, showed that the unskilled perceived themselves to have little freedom, variety, or opportunity to learn on their jobs and felt correspondingly little satisfaction with and enthusiasm for their jobs; administrative and professional personnel, on the other hand, reported substantially more "positive" reactions. Zdravomyslov and Iadov (1964), agreeing essentially with Herzberg's (1966) theory, concluded from their study of young Soviet workers that the most important determinant of job satisfaction is the job's content. Routine or unvarying jobs are less satisfying than complex jobs that require discretion and decision making on the part of workers. Such characteristics of work seem to help define the advantage experienced by people at the top and explain the greater satisfaction or motivation that is more likely to be found at upper levels in the organization.

Social status or prestige is a further reward associated with rank. The respect and recognition accorded to people in prestigious positions undoubtedly contribute to a sense of self-esteem and satisfaction and, therefore, to a positive adjustment in the work situation. For example, in a study of 2,000 American managers, Porter (1962b) found that managers at higher levels had higher self-esteem than those below them did. Weaver (1977) concluded, on the basis of data from a national survey in the United States, that occupational prestige is a more important determinant of job satisfaction than is work autonomy, authority, or income.

The prestige or status of occupations is remarkably similar in all complex societies, even though the societies differ in culture and political system (Treiman, 1977). For example, Inkeles and Rossi (1956) report correlations mainly above 0.90 among the status of occupations as ranked by persons in Japan, Britain, New Zealand, the United States, and the Soviet Union. The lowest correlation, that between the USSR and Japan, is 0.74. Furthermore, the occupational status hierarchy seems to be reasonably stable historically. From an examination of records of several ancient and now defunct societies as well as many contemporary ones, Treiman (1977) concluded that the ranking of occupations in the ancient societies was very much like that in contemporary societies. Sarapata found, in a longitudinal analysis, that the status structure has remained fairly stable in Poland, although he detected a slight flattening that entailed a small increase in the prestige accorded to occupations at the lower end, accompanied by a very slight increase at the upper end (Sarapata, personal communication). The occupational status hierarchy in complex societies is apparently determined largely by very general characteristics that all societies have in common, rather than by idiosyncratic features of culture (Treiman, 1977). According to these studies, people in all countries who are at relatively high levels in an organizational hierarchy (factory managers and engineers, for example) enjoy substantially greater prestige than workers at the bottom of the hierarchy enjoy. Prestige may be more important to people in some societies, such as the Italian, than in others, such as the American (Tannenbaum et al., 1974), but the prestige *structure* is similar among these societies.

High pay is a further reward of rank, although analyses in a number of countries indicate that level of pay has little bearing on attitude toward the company or on job satisfaction. In a study of over 2,500 young Soviet workers, Zdravomyslov and Iadov (1964) found that while many workers attached importance to wages, level of pay per se did not affect satisfaction with work. Unskilled manual workers earned relatively high wages compared to other workers, but they were the least satisfied with their jobs. Reasonably enough, however, level of pay does have implications for satisfaction with *pay* (if not for satisfaction with job) in most countries where these relationships have been studied. An interesting exception occurs among the young Soviet workers studied by Zdravomyslov and Iadov (1964): Unskilled manual workers whose jobs were routine and monotonous were more dissatisfied with their wages than were skilled workers whose pay was lower. This is consistent with the finding of Tannenbaum and others (1974) that the character of the job affected satisfaction with pay, even though the amount of pay did not affect satisfaction with the job. Persons who reported having opportunities to use their skills or to learn new things on their job were more satisfied with their pay than were persons who did not report such opportunities, even though they received the same level of pay. "Enriching" qualities of work apparently enhance the feeling of satisfaction with one's economic compensation as well as with the job itself.

Demographic Correlates of Hierarchy

A number of demographic characteristics are usually associated with rank. People at upper levels, on the average, have more years of formal education, are older, and have greater seniority in the company than people at lower levels. Education per se, however, is not likely to explain the greater job satisfaction or the more favorable attitude toward the company felt by people at upper levels. On the contrary, education appears to have a *negative* impact on job satisfaction and on attitude toward the company. Other things being equal, more educated people are less satisfied with their jobs or with their company than less educated people are, probably because for many people education creates skills that are not utilized and expectations that are not met (Lawler, 1971; Mann, 1953; Morse, 1953; Tannenbaum et al., 1974).

Age, however, often does have a positive effect on attitude toward the company and on job satisfaction, according to analyses in a number of countries. The finding that older workers have a more positive attitude toward their companies fits the notion that older people are more conservative than younger people. This relatively "favorable adjustment" of older workers occurs despite their less happy adjustment in certain aspects of nonwork life, in the United States at least (Gurin, Veroff, & Feld, 1960; Morse, 1953) — which emphasizes the special importance work has for them. Crozier (1971) and Marenco (1959), noting a similar relationship between age and job satisfaction in France, explained it in terms of a "classic pattern": Younger workers enter a job with some enthusiasm, but soon they are disillusioned and their attitudes decline sharply. In time, however, they adjust to the realities of organizational life, learn how to cope with some of the difficulties of the job, and develop a tolerance for the frustrating aspects of organization that younger people find disturbing. Hence, there is a steady growth of positive attitude with age after that initial decline. Age and seniority, therefore, may be among the correlates of job satisfaction that are associated with hierarchical rank.

Thus, hierarchy implies demographic differences among members in addition to differences in authority and reward. As a consequence of these differences, organizational hierarchy creates a distribution of personal reactions among members that is also hierarchical. This is the general hypothesis to which the following chapters are addressed.

The Research

The data presented in the following chapters were collected through a common questionnaire that was translated from English into the languages of the respective countries. To check the accuracy of the translation and ensure the uniformity of the instrument, each translation was retranslated into English by an independent translator and adjusted as needed. The questionnaire is presented in Appendix B.

The design of the research followed a similar but not identical format in all of the countries. The plan called for the selection of 10 plants in each country, matched across countries in size, type of industry, and type of technology. A total of at least 35 persons, representing all levels, was to be selected from each plant. The procedure for sampling respondents had two objectives.[2] One was to have equal numbers of respondents at each hierarchical level within each plant, insofar as possible. (Thus, we did not draw a simple random sample, because that would have provided very few persons at middle and upper levels.) We established a sampling rate that was proportional to rank: The top manager in each plant was to be selected with certainty, while persons at successively lower levels were assigned correspondingly lower probabilities of selection. A second sampling objective was to maintain the integrity of the organization's hierarchical chains. For example, starting with the selection of the top person, respondents at successively lower levels were to be included for selection only if their immediate superior were selected. This procedure ensured that workers would be compared to their *own* supervisors and managers and not to superiors in other groups or departments.

Several deviations occurred when the general plan was implemented. The selected plants in the socialist countries are substantially larger, on the average, than those in the other countries, which reflects the generally larger average size of plants in the socialist countries. (Gyenes and Rozgonyi present a brief analysis of these differences in Chapter 6.) The types of industries and technologies in the selected plants also differ somewhat among countries, reflecting in part differences in the prevalence and availability of given industries. In Hungary, 11 plants rather than 10 were included. Furthermore, the number of respondents and the rate at which they were selected varies among the plants, although in all plants, persons at upper levels had a greater probability of inclusion than did persons at lower levels. Moreover, the authors of the following chapters define in slightly different ways the hierarchical categories—top, middle, and bottom—that they employ in their analyses. The top category in Romania, for example, includes the top manager along with his immediate subordinates, and a couple of plants in Mexico include more than one person in the top category. In all of the other plants, however, the top category includes only one person, and in all cases, regardless of how many persons are included, each person placed in the top group is higher in rank than each person placed in the middle group, just as each person in the middle group is hierarchically above persons classified in the bottom group. Finally, analysis procedures may differ among countries. Tests of statistical significance were not performed in all countries, and the regressions presented do not in all cases employ identical predictors.

These variations from a common plan limit the inferences we might draw about differences between countries, since variations in the data might very well be the result of variations in methodology. The variations should not seriously limit the possibility of inferences about *similarities* between countries, however. If similarities should appear—and the reader will see that they do—they are not likely to be explained away by variations in the way the research was carried out. They will testify instead to the generality and potential importance of certain facts about hierarchy in organizations.

Plan of the Chapters

Chapter 2 summarizes the other results of an earlier study that served partly as a model for the present work. That study, carried out in industrial organizations of Italy, Austria, the United States, Yugoslavia, and the kibbutzim of Israel, noted some common effects as well as some differences between these societies in the extent to which hierarchy expresses itself. All of the societies showed hierarchical gradients of authority and reward and of members' reactions and adjustments, but the gradients were less steep in the socialist Yugoslav and kibbutz plants than in the Italian, Austrian, and American organizations. This is consistent with the hypothesis that organizations designed on the basis of socialist ideological principles will be characterized by less-marked differences between levels.

Chapters 3–8 present the data of the study. Both the research and the analyses were conducted separately in each country by the authors of the respective chapters. Nonetheless, the chapters follow a similar format. We have tried to avoid unnecessary repetition in each chapter concerning common features of the rationale, design, and analyses. Chapter 3 presents some details of these common features that are not repeated in the remaining chapters; therefore, the reader might find the discussion in Chapter 3 helpful in understanding the remaining chapters.

Each chapter includes three main sections plus conclusions. The first section describes the cultural and political circumstances that are relevant to hierarchy in the industrial organizations of the country, as well as some facts about the plants in the study that are relevant to the design of the research. In each country, there is some concern about the hierarchical distribution of authority and reward, whether that concern is expressed formally through official ideology and law, informally through cultural norms, or both. *Mitbestimmung* in the Federal Republic of Germany, the election of employees to the boards of state enterprises in Ireland, and the effort to apply Marxist principles in the socialist countries are all expressions of this concern. Although approached differently by the different countries, hierarchy is a salient issue for all of them.

The second and third sections of each chapter present and discuss the data that were collected through the questionnaire. The data from all of the plants in each country were combined, and respondents were divided into three hierarchical groups—top, middle, and bottom. The top group consists of the managers (one in each plant) who have no superior in the plant. (In Romania, this group also includes the direct subordinates of each top person.) The bottom group includes only rank-and-file workers—persons who have no subordinates. The middle group consists of all who are between the top and the bottom.

Much of the data are presented as averages for these groups computed from the five-point scales of the questionnaire (see Appendix B). Hierarchical gradients can be seen in systematic differences between groups—in the increasing (or decreasing) scores from the bottom group to the top. In some chapters, statistical tests have been performed on these differences.

The second section in each chapter presents two sets of data based on the questionnaire. The first concerns demographic and economic correlates of hierarchy—the age, sex, education, seniority, and salary of the persons at the respective levels. Salary is a major reward of membership in most work organizations, of course, and the data of all countries show a gradient for this variable (as for most of the other variables of this section). Our proposed limitation against comparing data between countries applies less to salary, perhaps, than to measures of attitude and perception. The variance in salary is very small between enterprises within each socialist society, because the salaries of occupations in these societies are regulated centrally; as a matter of policy, wages for given categories of personnel do not vary much even among plants that differ in size, type of industry, profitability, or geographic region. Thus, while the data show gradients of salary in the plants of all countries, the gradients are much less steep in the socialist countries than in the others.

The second set of data of the second section, which is based primarily on self-reports or reports about one's superior, documents hierarchical gradients of authority and reward in the plants of each country. Included here, in addition to measures of authority and influence, are measures of "enriching" qualities of the respondent's job, such as the extent to which the job provides opportunities for the respondent to use his or her skills, learn new things, and decide his or her own work pace. This section is also concerned with behavior of the respondent's superior that may be rewarding to subordinates, such as supportiveness.

The third section of each chapter is concerned with several kinds of reactions and adjustments of members, such as "morale" (for example, satisfaction with job); personal adjustment (for example, feelings of alienation); "motivation" (for example, the initiative the respondent takes on the job or the respondent's feeling of responsibility in the plant); and perceptions about how the organization operates and how it should operate (for example, how decisions in the plant are made and how they should be made). The gradients of authority and reward documented in the previous sections lead us to expect gradients of these reactions and adjustments. According to our general hypothesis, persons at upper levels, who have more authority and receive greater rewards than those below, are also likely to be more satisfied and motivated in the organization and to feel less alienated than those below. Persons near the top are also likely to differ from those below in how they "see" or interpret events in their organization and in what they want for their organization.

This section of each chapter (except the Mexican chapter) will describe the results of several standardized regression analyses. The regressions explored how members' reactions and adjustments to their work situations might be explained by some of the measures of authority and reward, as well as by demographic characteristics and the position of each member in the hierarchy. These analyses by themselves, of course, do not prove causality, but they illustrate similarities between countries in some of the "predictors" of members' reactions and adjustments to their work situations—reactions and adjustments such as job satisfaction, work motivation, and feelings of alienation—despite the cultural and political differences between countries.

Two measures of hierarchical position are included in the regressions. One defines the level of the respondent in terms of his or her distance from the bottom of the hierarchy. Rank-and-file workers have a score of 1 on this measure, their immediate supervisors have a score of 2, and so on to the top of the organization. The second measure defines the length of the hierarchical chain in which the respondent is located, since some chains have more levels than others (Tannenbaum et al., 1974, p. 19ff.). A person with a score of 1 in a chain of seven levels is thus distinguishable from a person with a score of 1 in a chain of three levels.

The final chapter of the volume summarizes the findings from the previous chapters and offers our conclusions. The distribution of authority and reward has substantial ideological, theoretical, and practical relevance in many countries. This study may be the first in which colleagues from Eastern European and Western countries have worked together to explore this topic empirically. We were not able to maintain completely uniform standards; therefore, the inferences we can draw from the data are limited, especially with regard to differences between countries. Nonetheless, the results do provide some clues to those differences; they also illustrate some differences in the ways researchers in different places are inclined to view the issues of this research and to interpret the findings. In addition, the data suggest generalizations that transcend culture and politics and that persist despite variations in method and approach. They show a connection in all of the countries between hierarchy and the reactions and adjustments of organization members.

Notes

[1]The following brief review draws from Tannenbaum (1980).

[2]For details of the general model of sampling, see Tannenbaum et al. (1974, p. 14ff.).

2

Hierarchy in Organizations: The Earlier Project

Arnold S. Tannenbaum, Bogdan Kavčič, Menachem Rosner,
Mino Vianello, and Georg Wieser

This chapter summarizes the results of an earlier study that served as a model for the present research. The same questionnaire was employed in the two studies (see Appendix B). The earlier study was conducted in ten industrial plants in each of five societies—Italy, Austria, the United States, Yugoslavia, and the kibbutzim of Israel. We were able in the earlier work more than in the present research to match plants well among societies and to maintain a high degree of control and uniformity of methodology. In the earlier work, therefore, we felt it reasonable to compare the data among societies, whereas the possibility of such comparisons is limited in the present study.

Ideology and Formal Structure of the Plants

Plants in Yugoslavia and the kibbutzim of Israel are designed on the basis of socialist ideological principles, while in Italy, Austria, and the United States, they operate as "free enterprises." Thus, plants from the different societies differ from one another in several aspects of formal structure.

The first aspect, and the most important from a socialist standpoint, is ownership. In kibbutzim, the means of production are owned by the members of the kibbutz, including the workers of the factory; in Yugoslavia, the means are owned by society, which delegates the responsibility of ownership to the "workers' collective," consisting of all members of the enterprise.[1] The prerogatives of such ownership are limited by law only in that the workers' collective is responsible for maintaining and enhancing the value of

This chapter is excerpted, with revisions, from Arnold S. Tannenbaum, Bogdan Kavčič, Menachem Rosner, Mino Vianello, and Georg Wieser, *Hierarchy in Organizations: An International Comparison* (San Francisco, 1974), by permission of Jossey-Bass, Inc., Publishers.

the enterprise. In the United States, Austria, and Italy, on the other hand, the plants are owned primarily by one or a few persons, by families, or by shareholders who are not employed in the plant, although several of the plants in the Austrian "sample" are state-owned.

The second aspect of structure that distinguishes the plants of these societies from one another is formal decision making. In the plants of Yugoslavia and of the kibbutzim, ultimate decision-making power resides formally with the total membership. In Yugoslavia, for example, the workers' council, which is elected by all of the members of a plant, is empowered to make basic policy decisions about investments, the distribution of profits, and the hiring and firing of the manager, among other matters. Similarly, major decisions about a kibbutz plant are made either through meetings of all persons who work in the plant or through meetings of the kibbutz community in which workers from the plant may participate. In the "free enterprise" societies, on the other hand, ultimate decision-making power in the plants resides with the owners, whose power may be tempered by restraints imposed by unions, laws, and social norms.

A third aspect that distinguishes the plants is the reward system. The kibbutz was conceived as an egalitarian society that would be guided by the principle "From each according to his abilities, to each according to his needs." Therefore, it is designed to avoid stratification of authority, status, and other social and economic rewards among members. Members receive no wages beyond a small cash allowance for personal expenses. They eat their main meals in a communal dining room and, regardless of their work assignment or their performance in it, have equal access—barring some differences based on seniority—to many facilities, goods, and services, such as housing, clothing, laundry, utilities, food for home consumption, cigarettes, appliances, education, recreation, and vacation travel. The ideological base of Yugoslav plants is also egalitarian, although the formal structure of rewards in these plants is not as egalitarian as in the kibbutz plants. Wages, for example, are distributed according to rank and function, although differences are limited. Medical and other benefits are available equally to all members. Plants in the United States, Austria, and Italy, on the other hand, have a highly differentiated system in which monetary and other rewards are distributed according to rank and function.

At least in formal design, the distribution of authority and reward is more egalitarian in socialist plants than in "free enterprise" ones. In actual operation, however, plants may not function precisely according to their formal plan. Nonetheless, our data do indicate differences in the actual operation of the plants that correspond in some degree to the differences in formal design.

Authority and Reward in the Two Types of Plants

Kibbutz plants in particular stand out in our study of authority and reward. According to respondents, kibbutz members participate substantially in decisions related to the plant as well as to their own work. Participation appears also to characterize relations between superiors and subordinates. Superiors are helpful and supportive to their subordinates and responsive to their ideas and suggestions. Kibbutz plants are also characterized by a relatively flat, power-equalized distribution of control—although managers do exercise more control than workers do in these plants, as in the typical industrial organization of other societies. Furthermore, the character of control and the bases of power in the kibbutz plants reflect a participative managerial style. Members cooperate with their superiors' attempts to influence them more because of a sense of commitment to the organization than because of fear of reprisal or hope for material benefit. Social approval and disapproval, by co-workers as well as supervisors, are the rewards and sanctions for good and bad work. Nonetheless, although highly participative, kibbutz plants are neither as participative as their formal charter implies nor as members would like them to be. Such discrepancy between the ideal and the reality as members see it occurs in the organizations of all societies, although it is smaller in the kibbutz than in other places.

The Yugoslav plants in this study also correspond to the participative model, according to the reports of members, although not as closely as the kibbutz plants do. Interpersonal relations between supervisors and subordinates, in particular, do not appear to be as supportive in the Yugoslav plants as they do in some of the others. Nonetheless, on measures of participative decision making, the Yugoslav plants as a group rank second only to the kibbutz plants, and the Yugoslav plants show a hierarchical distribution of control that is less steep than that in any other group of plants. The relatively participative character of Yugoslav plants reported by respondents in this research corresponds to the findings of a study in 12 countries of Europe by the Industrial Democracy in Europe group (IDE, 1981). The Yugoslav plants in that study were found to have "a more (but not entirely) even distribution of influence across organizational levels than the other countries" (IDE, 1981, p. 155).

The American, Austrian, and Italian organizations were not found to be as participative as the kibbutz or Yugoslav plants in terms of most criteria; nor are they meant to be. The Italian plants are the least participative; members reported that workers have little say about decisions concerning the plant or about their own work and that superiors are not very likely to invite the ideas and suggestions of subordinates or to provide the helpful, supportive relations that imply a participative style. The distribution of control in Italian plants is sharply hierarchical, as it is in the Austrian and American plants; yet the *total amount* of control exercised by the hierarchical groups of the Italian plants is less than in any of the other plants. Thus, while the Italian plants are the least participative, they are not necessarily the most authoritarian; after all, the "authorities," including the managers, do not exercise a very high degree of control in these organizations compared to the control exercised by their counterparts in the other organizations. The low level of participation in the Italian plants compared to the others is accompanied by the greatest discrepancy between the amount of participation members prefer and the amount they perceive to exist.

The American and Austrian plants resemble the Italian in degree of nonparticipation, but they are not as extreme as the Italian in most respects. The American organizations, particularly, diverge from the nonparticipative extreme. This is especially apparent in the area of informal superior/subordinate relations; American superiors are relatively responsive to and supportive of their subordinates. Managers are highly influential in the American plants but workers are not without influence, according to respondents. Although the American plants clearly show a hierarchical distribution of control, the total amount of control exercised by the hierarchical groups, including workers as well as managers, is greater in the American plants than in the other plants.

Thus, the kibbutz and Yugoslav plants are formally more participative than the American, Austrian, and Italian plants, according to members, and the distribution of control that members reported is somewhat less hierarchical in the former set of plants than in the latter, even though a hierarchical distribution is apparent in all places. The data of this study make it difficult to escape the implication, even in the highly participative kibbutz plants, that authority and influence increase substantially with rank. Furthermore, other rewarding aspects of a person's role, such as pay (except in kibbutz plants, where members are not paid), congenial working conditions, and enriching qualities of the job, also clearly increase with rank, but like the hierarchical gradients of authority and influence, the gradients of these rewards tend to be less steep in the kibbutz and Yugoslav plants than in the plants of the other societies.

Reactions and Adjustments of Members

The gradients of authority and reward that are apparent in all of the plants are accompanied by gradients of the reactions and adjustments of members. Persons at upper levels, compared to those below, are predictably more satisfied with their jobs and their salaries; they are more favorably disposed toward the company and feel more responsible and motivated in their work; they are in a number of respects "better adjusted"; and they see the organization in ways that conform in some degree to a more positive stereotype. These tendencies illustrate a widely recognized principle of organization: Positive reaction to and support for the system by members increase with hierarchical ascent.

There are qualifications to this principle, however. The steepness of gradients differs among countries: Hierarchy has less impact on the reactions and adjustments of members in some systems than in others. Such differences in the impact of hierarchy are predictable, in part, from the differences in formal participativeness and underlying ideology that separate the five countries. Ideology defines the general rules and rationalizations by which an organization is to be governed. Ideology may be formally or legally established, as in the kibbutz and Yugoslav systems, or it may exist only as an implicit philosophy, based on tradition or the contemporary realities of power in a society. Ideology manifests itself concretely, however, in the nature of the organizational hierarchy—in the gradients of authority and reward and, consequently, in the gradients of reactions and adjustments of members.

Kibbutz and Yugoslav organizations are designed on the ideological basis of egalitarianism. They are formally more participative than the conventional industrial bureaucracy, and they deemphasize hierarchy through a relatively egalitarian distribution of authority and reward. Consequently, the reactions and adjustments of members are also less sharply graded. American organizations are not very participative formally, but because of a tradition of egalitarianism in the United States, there is some informal participation in these organizations that is at least greater than that in the Italian and Austrian plants. Therefore, the gradients are generally less sharp in the American plants than in the Italian and Austrian ones.

The impact of hierarchy, measured in terms of the steepness of these gradients, is more apparent with respect to some reactions and adjustments than to others. Gradients are steeper, for example, for members' satisfaction with job and pay than for their general psychological adjustment or their perception of the participativeness of their organization. The former reactions more than the latter are clearly affected by conditions associated with position. For example, the satisfaction a member will derive from his or her job is affected by the psychologically enriching opportunities that a job may provide, which are closely tied to rank in the hierarchy. The *general* adjustment of a member, on the other hand, is undoubtedly affected by numerous circumstances in addition to opportunities on the job, many of which are unrelated to position in the hierarchy. Similarly, perceptions of participativeness or other aspects of the way the organization functions, which do not differ very sharply between persons of different rank, are determined by many conditions beyond hierarchy itself, not the least of which are the realities being perceived. Furthermore, some of the objects of perception do not have the strong value connotations for members that lead them to distort their perceptions in a way to conform to or rationalize a value position. Nonetheless, aspects of an organization such as its degree of participativeness are ambiguous realities; perceptions of these aspects may be affected by the respondent's values. There may be systematic bias based on values, therefore, in the responses of persons at upper levels who, in some organizations at least, were more likely than those below to report, for example, that their plant conforms to a participative decision-making pattern.

The steepest gradients are those of authority and reward. Authority and many rewarding conditions, such as high pay or enriching qualities of a job, are explicitly or implicitly *assigned* to positions and become part of the meaning of hierarchy itself. On the other hand, reactions and adjustments such as satisfaction with the job or feelings of alienation are not so much a part of hierarchy as they are a consequence of the authority, reward, and other conditions that help to define hierarchy. Hierarchy, abstracted from these conditions, has relatively little psychological impact on members. Persons at upper levels are not more satisfied with their pay than those below simply because they have high rank, but rather because they receive high pay. Upper-level persons are not more satisfied with their jobs than lower-level persons simply because they are high in the hierarchy, but rather because their jobs afford greater opportunity for self-actualization. When these conditions were defined out of the hierarchy statistically through regression procedures, little difference in reaction and adjustment between persons of different rank remained. And when these conditions are in some measure defined out of the hierarchy in actuality, as in the formally participative system, the effects of hierarchy are at least reduced.

Kibbutz plants have eliminated gradients based on financial reward, and they formally limit the gradient of authority, even if they do not eliminate it. Superiors do not have the right to promote or fire a subordinate, to award benefits, or to impose penalties, which are the underpinnings of authority in other systems. Furthermore, kibbutz plants have formal procedures for all members to influence important decisions. Hence, differences in authority between ranks are formally limited. It may be easier, however, to limit the authority and rewards assigned to leaders than to limit the problems they face. Thus, while some rewards are equalized, responsibility is not. In fact, compared to our original expectation, the gradient of "responsibility felt by members" is surprisingly steep in kibbutz plants. Such a gradient implies greater commitment and concern on the part of leaders than on the part of workers. Hence, some leaders may feel the "negative balance of rewards" that is said to characterize leadership roles in the kibbutzim (Talmon, 1972): Leaders are not rewarded a great deal more than rank-and-file workers, but they feel a good deal more responsible than do the members. The tendency, unique to kibbutz plants, for upper-level personnel to suffer more peptic ulcers than lower-level persons may suggest evidence for the existence of this negative balance. The Yugoslav manager also appears to fare poorly in terms of a number of reactions and adjustments when compared to managers of other plants, although the Yugoslav worker does not do badly compared to his or her counterparts elsewhere. The cost/benefit balance of high rank, calculated in terms of some of the adjustments considered in this chapter, is less favorable in the Yugoslav and kibbutz plants than in the others. Despite this disadvantage, however, leaders in the kibbutz and Yugoslav plants are "better off" than their rank and file on many of the indicators studied here. There is a limit to how far organizations can go in mitigating the inevitable consequences of hierarchy.

Conclusions

All plants show some degree of hierarchical effect. Considering the diversity of ideology and formal structure among the plants, this suggests a universality of the effect. In fact, the similarities between countries are as important as the differences, and the systems are impressively alike even with respect to some of the relationships underlying the effects of hierarchy. For example, regression analyses suggest that in all countries, regardless of ideological base, the authority and the enriching opportunities that a job provides, along with certain valued physical qualities of the job, help explain a member's satisfaction with that job. Education also affects job satisfaction, but the impact of education is negative in all countries. The kibbutz worker does not differ in this respect from the Italian worker or from the worker in other systems. The more educated the worker, the less likely he or she is to be satisfied with his or her job, holding rank and other hierarchical conditions constant. Such consistency between systems is not easily explained by chance; we can be reasonably confident that we are dealing with a fairly general feature of organizational life. Furthermore, some *patterns* of relationships are similar among the countries. For example, salary has no bearing on job satisfaction in any country, although it does, quite reasonably, affect satisfaction with pay in at least three of the four countries where members are paid. (The result in the fourth country is in the same direction as the other three, although it is not significant statistically.) Authority and influence are clearly associated with a sense of responsibility in all countries, but education is not associated with a sense of responsibility in any country (holding rank constant). The impact of education is intriguing because of its conflicting value implications in all countries. Educated members feel less alienated than their coworkers of the same rank, but they are also more dissatisfied with their jobs than are their co-workers. Education in this sense is a mixed blessing.

Thus, while the data showed some differences among the five countries, they also showed impressive similarities that testify to basic commonalities among them. Some principles of organization and human adjustment transcend culture and ideology.

Hierarchy has both intended and unintended consequences, some of which we have observed and tried to understand through the research summarized in this chapter. Other variables unconnected to hierarchy may provide a more substantial basis for explaining the reactions and adjustments we have investigated, but hierarchy has special importance because it is consciously designed and formally established in an organization. In principle we have some choice concerning the character of hierarchy. Furthermore, the fact that hierarchy is a *structural* feature of organization adds to the significance of its consequences. Hierarchy implies clustering of persons who share a common adjustment—although hierarchy is not the only basis for such clustering. Intentionally, hierarchy organizes the behavior of members so that the behavior is appropriate to the organization's purposes. Intentionally or not, hierarchy also arranges and systematizes members' satisfaction and dissatisfaction, motivation, and adjustment. Hierarchy organizes the feelings of members as well as their behavior, and it does so more substantially in some systems than in others.

Notes

[1]The Yugoslav system of workers' self-management has undergone changes since its inception in 1950, and important constitutional changes were introduced in 1974 and 1976. The description here applies to the period of this research, which occurred prior to 1974. See Kavčič and Tannenbaum (1981); IDE (1981); Secretariat of Information of the SFR of Yugoslavia Assembly (1977).

3

Federal Republic of Germany

Klaus Bartölke[1]

Introduction

Codetermination

Two fundamental questions have to be asked when the problem of democracy in corporations is discussed (Steinmann, 1969, p. 1ff.):

What interests should a corporation serve?

What can be done to ensure that these interests guide the decisions of the organization?

In the Federal Republic of Germany, the established answers to these questions are that the interests of both the employees and the owners should be served and that codetermination (*Mitbestimmung*) as a representative, institutionalized form of participation is the way to ensure that the interests of the employees will help guide the organization's decisions. *Mitbestimmung* means that law rather than collective bargaining or managerial benevolence alone determines how the interests of the respective groups are satisfied and how conflicts are resolved. Thus, in principle, the opportunity for workers to influence certain decisions does not depend on the readiness of the owners to accept or support the decisions. The labor movement in particular has questioned the idea that the ethical standards of those in power can be relied on and that return on investment as a basis for decisions always serves the interests of the employees. In a system of codetermination, power is not legitimated simply by ownership; nor is it assumed that the interests of members will be served by reliance on the owners' sense of morality or on mutual trust, common interests, and responsibilities. Codetermination does assume at least one interest common to both parties, however: survival of the organization as a whole.

Codetermination is the result of a historical development that is explained here only briefly. As in other countries, early industrialization in Germany led to the exploitation of a large part of the work force. Many economic theorists and social philosophers saw in this exploitation a disproof of the claim that economic decisions based solely on private property—an outcome of unrestricted economic liberalism—lead to the highest welfare of all. This disproof was the common ground upon which unions and labor-oriented political parties worked for more or less radical changes, with rather different concepts and strategies (Böhme, 1968, p. 96ff.). The labor movement struggled not only against the employers but also against legislation and other governmental actions that were seen as acting mainly on behalf of those in economic power.

At the beginning of World War I, a coalition for a conflict-free war economy was formed. One practical outcome of the coalition (which was not unanimously supported) was the formation of workers' committees in plants that had more than 50 employees. The end of the war brought the breakdown of the monarchic constitution, accompanied by the formation of soldiers' and workers' councils that were designed to achieve revolutionary changes toward democracy in all social institutions. This system of councils included procedures of direct and indirect democracy. The majority of Social Democrats, however, desired a less revolutionary reform; they preferred that the owners share power with the councils rather than allowing the councils to be predominant (Anthes et al., 1972, p. 61ff.). This development, which in the view of many interpreters did not really affect the power structure, began in 1920 but came to a complete stop with the Third Reich because of the demise of the independent labor movement. In fact, the Hitler government proscribed codetermination in all its forms.

At the end of World War II, there was widespread interest in fundamental anti-capitalist reforms, because capitalism was seen as one of the roots of fascism. The labor movement played an important role in the rebuilding of firms and of the economy, and there was a strong consensus within society for improving labor's power base against the interests of the entrepreneurs (Deppe et al., 1970, p. 69). By the end of the 40s, however, when the Federal Republic of Germany had strengthened its connections with Western states, approaches to far-reaching reforms were blocked, mainly by the United States, in order to prevent the country from becoming communist or socialist. Unions were prepared to strike, however, and consequently codetermination was established in the coal-mining and steel industries (Anthes et al., 1972, p. 80ff.).

Four assumptions underlie the arguments for codetermination in the Federal Republic of Germany. First, true democracy cannot be achieved without economic democracy. Second, a power structure in Germany without codetermination would not be legitimate because it would be based on force. Third, the need for self-fulfillment is basic to human nature; therefore, all persons should have opportunities for self-fulfillment. Fourth, the alienation suffered by workers because of their work cannot be undone outside of work (Bartölke & Wächter, 1974, p. 66ff.).

This philosophy does not accept a distribution of power based on force and on the submission (Burns, 1967, p. 120) of those who are disadvantaged simply because of their perceived powerlessness and their failure to perceive alternatives to their powerlessness (Habermas, 1973, p. 132). The concept of codetermination rejects Michels' "iron law of oligarchy." It asserts that the potential of members in organizations to take action and make decisions can be developed, and that although a stratified social structure favors oligarchy and bureaucracy, it does not inevitably produce them (Naschold, 1973, p. 13).

Two levels of codetermination should be distinguished. The first level, which involves the "supervisory board" (*Aufsichtsrat*), is not treated here because it is irrelevant to the plants studied.[2] The second level is found in plants with at least five employees over 18 years of age and at least three employees who have worked in the plant for 6 months or more. Legal regulations regarding this level are contained in the Workers' Constitution Act of 1972 (*Betriebsverfassungsgesetz*), which applies to all of the plants in this study; it became effective sometime before the beginning of the field work. The law is outlined here, although all of its provisions were not realized in practice at the time the data were collected.

The workers' council in a plant is a representative body, elected by the employees, with a number of members that depends on the number of employees in the plant. The law requires plants with 21 to 50 employees over 18 years of age to have three representatives on the council; plants with 51 to 150 employees must have five; plants with 151 to 300 employees, seven; plants with 301 to 600 employees, nine; and plants with 601 to 1,000 employees, eleven. There is a provision that neither white-collar nor blue-collar workers will absolutely dominate the council. In plants of 300 employees or more, one or several members of the council—depending on the size—are paid their normal salary while working exclusively for the council.

Two principles stated in the law underlie the rights given to the workers' council. The first is that the council and the management must behave cooperatively toward one another. The second is that the employees will not strike to deal with plant-specific problems. Strikes are only allowed in connection with industrywide, collective bargaining processes. In the case of conflict within plants, a Unification Committee (*Einigungsstelle*), which consists of an equal number of persons from both sides and one neutral person, must be convened.

The workers' council can exercise varying degrees of influence in four areas: social affairs, the organization of work, personnel affairs, and business affairs.

In social affairs, the workers' council can initiate action concerning such matters as rules of discipline in the plant, regulation of working hours, the pay structure, timing of vacation, the form of the suggestion system, and the installation of instruments designed to control the performance of workers. Furthermore, the council's agreement must be obtained for decisions regarding these matters.

With respect to the organization of work, the council must be informed and consulted if management intends to introduce changes in the design of jobs or of the work environment. Furthermore, the council has a right to countermand changes if they are not in accordance with generally accepted ergonomic principles about job design and the humanization of work. However, these principles are often ambiguous and this itself leads to conflicts.

With respect to personnel affairs, the council has a veto on decisions about selection, placement, and discharge, and it has the right to take part in personnel planning and training and development activities. In addition, the agreement of the council is necessary in deciding the principles of performance appraisal, the kind of information required from applicants, and the use of psychological tests.

Codetermination cannot really be said to exist in business affairs. The workers' council has a right to be informed through a special committee that acts only as a consultant to management. If the plant is to be closed, however, a plan for mitigating or compensating economic disadvantages for the workers (*Sozialplan*) must be developed in cooperation with the council.

In addition to defining the role of the council, the law specifies the rights of individual workers: A worker must be given specifications of the job and its role operations and may make suggestions and grievances on such matters. A worker may also have access to his or her personnel file. A worker's comments about his or her performance appraisal must be included in the file (Fitting, 1974, p. 183ff.; Rüthers, 1973, p. 139ff.).

Many plants do not actually conform to the 1972 act. Many small plants do not even have councils (Presse- und Informationszentrum des Bundestages, 1972). Nonetheless, the large majority of workers is represented on councils, and progress is being made, particularly through the work of the unions, toward full implementation of the law.

Characteristics of Plants Studied

The field work for this study was done from February to September of 1972. The plants studied are spread throughout the country. Because of a general reluctance of managers and owners to participate, and because the research design restricted the selection of plants to those that met several requirements, as many as 200 firms had to be contacted in order to obtain the participation of 10. Table 3.1 describes some of the characteristics of the plants that were selected in the final "sample." Table 3.2 shows the composition of the respondents within plants.

At the beginning of the field work we tried to obtain more precise information about the effectiveness of the plants than just the often vague data about development of gross sales that is presented in Table 3.1. Company personnel were very reluctant to provide this information, however, so we abandoned our attempt to obtain it. The information about gross sales can be interpreted here as a reasonable indicator of the viability of the plants, although it is not possible to compare the plants on these figures because of differences in the respective environments. This interpretation appears to be sound when differences between industries in the growth of gross sales are taken into account. For example, from 1970 to 1972 the average growth of the plastics industry was 14 percent; non-ferrous foundry industry, -7.5 percent; food industry, 7.5 percent; metal works industry, 7 percent; and wood manufacturing industry, 18 percent.[3]

Table 3.3 shows more detail about the selected branches of industry (figures are for 1972). Only plants with more than 10 employees are included.

Only about 10 percent of the plants in the Federal Republic of Germany are as large as the plants we designate as "large" in this study. About a third of all plants fall within the size range of the "small" plants we have selected (Statistisches Bundesamt, 1974, p. 222). The plants in this study cannot be called atypical, however, since a large number of employees are in plants of these types of industry.

Correlates of Hierarchy

Economic and Demographic Characteristics

This section presents data about the salary, education, age, seniority in the plant, and sex of top management, middle manage-

Table 3.1
CHARACTERISTICS OF PLANTS

	Number of Employees	Number of Levels	Union Membership	Absenteeism (1971)	Turnover (1971)	Location	Age	Ownership	Average Growth of Gross Sales Last Five Years	Growth Expectation for Coming Five Years	Technology
Plastics Large	250	5	35%	6%	5%	Rural	50	Part of a concern, economically independent	30%	Similar	Large batch and mass production
Small	50	4	4	2	6	Rural	10	Private property	20	Higher	Large batch and mass production
Foundry Large	742	5	90	10	12	Urban	12	Part of a concern	Good	Good	Large batch and mass production
Small	71	4	35	5	40	Rural	33	Family owned	Relatively positive	Positive	Unit and small batch

Table 3.1 (continued)

	Number of Employees	Number of Levels	Union Membership	Absenteeism (1971)	Turnover (1971)	Location	Age	Ownership	Average Growth of Gross Sales Last Five Years	Growth Expectation for Coming Five Years	Technology
Canning											
Large	605	5	73%	10%	21%	Rural	50	Part of a concern	Very good	Very good	Large batch and mass production
Small	70	4	65	4	10	Rural	150	Family owned	Very low	Very low	Large batch and mass production
Metal works											
Large	454	5	1	4	25	Rural	17	Family owned	20%	15%	Unit and small batch
Small	84	4	14	7	29	Urban	100	Family owned	5	Higher	Unit and small batch
Furniture											
Large	333	7	1	9	20	Rural	3	Part of a concern, economically independent	Good	15%	Large batch and mass production
Small	50	5	40	5	30	Urban	40	Family owned	Satisfactory	Not pessimistic	Unit and small batch

Table 3.2

RANK AND SEX OF RESPONDENTS

	Top and Middle Managers		Rank and File	
	Number	Percentage Female	Number	Percentage Female
Plastics				
Large	18	5%	16	50%
Small	5	20	29	77
Foundry				
Large	19	0	15	0
Small	7	13	26	7
Canning				
Large	17	5	15	56
Small	12	15	22	50
Metal works				
Large	16	0	19	28
Small	10	40	21	64
Furniture				
Large	16	0	14	29
Small	10	0	24	16

ment, and rank-and-file persons.

The results presented in Table 3.4 clearly indicate support for the supposition that the average salary, level of education, age, seniority, and percentage of persons who are male are likely to be greater at upper levels in the hierarchy than at lower levels. One minor exception—the lack of difference in seniority between middle and bottom groups—is due to opposing results in large and small plants: Seniority is definitely associated with hierarchy in small plants, but in the large ones it is higher in the middle than at the top. This may be attributable to the fact that in the small plants we studied, all top persons were owners or co-owners, whereas only in one of the large plants was the top person an owner. Large plants also rely more heavily on direct performance criteria for promotion decisions than do small plants (Bartölke, 1975, p. 58ff.).

Table 3.3

CHARACTERISTICS OF THE SELECTED INDUSTRIAL BRANCHES AND OF
ALL INDUSTRIES IN THE FEDERAL REPUBLIC OF GERMANY

	Number of Plants	Employees in Thousands	Gross Sales in Billion DM	Wages and Salaries in Billion DM
Plastics	1,988	181	11,205	3,905
Non-ferrous foundry	319	30	1,484	519
Food	5,018	478	65,888	8,116
Metal works	3,715	412	23,624	6,723
Wood manufacturing	2,910	237	15,909	2,795
All industrial branches	55,796	8,340	596,014	147,480

Source: Statistisches Bundesamt (1974, pp. 219, 226, 228).

Codetermination obviously has not eliminated the correlation between demographic characteristics and hierarchical level. This is
especially apparent in the distribution of salaries, which is a critical
issue in industrial relations. The ratio of highest to lowest salaries
in the Federal Republic of Germany plants comes close to ratios
reported for comparable American plants (Tannenbaum et al.,
1974, p. 106ff.).[4]

Role Characteristics

In his description of kinds of variables, Rosenberg (1968) distinguishes those variables with "qualities inherent in the nature of an
organism" as "immanent" (p. 18). The authority/influence of a person, the opportunities provided by a job, and a job's physical
qualities are considered immanent variables in hierarchy under existing societal conditions (Cartwright, 1965, p. 2; Evans, 1963,
p. 468; Tannenbaum, 1968b, p. 45).

Authority and influence. An authority/influence index was built
from two questions, one concerning the respondent's authority
(cf. Q.1g, Appendix B) and the other concerning his or her influence
(cf. Q.26d, Appendix B). Questions were answered on five-point
scales from 1 (little or no authority or influence) to 5 (a very great
deal of authority or influence). Since authority/influence is likely to

Table 3.4

ECONOMIC AND DEMOGRAPHIC CHARACTERISTICS OF MEMBERS

	Top Management (n = 9–10)	Middle Management (n = 114–130)	Rank and File (n = 174–208)
Salary[a] (average DM per month)	4,799	1,728	867
Education[b] (average years)	5.1	4.6	4.2
Age (average years)	50	40	36
Plant seniority[c] (average years)	5.9	5.9	4.6
Sex (percentage female)	—	7.7%	39.4%

[a]Averages exclude the salary of 25 part-time employees who are only to be found at the bottom of the hierarchy.

[b]Education is measured on a scale where 1 = less than four years, 2 = 4 to 6 years, 3 = 6 to 8 years, 4 = 8 to 10 years, 5 = 10 to 12 years, and 6 = more than 12 years of education.

[c]Plant seniority is measured on the following scale: 1 = under 6 months, 2 = 6 months to 1 year, 3 = 1 to 2 years, 4 = 2 to 3 years, 5 = 3 to 6 years, 6 = 8 to 10 years, 7 = 10 to 20 years, and 8 = 20 years or more.

be distributed unequally in organizations, it is also likely that organization members will desire an amount of it that is different from the amount they perceive to exist. Therefore, questions were asked concerning the preferred as well as the actual state.[5] The data are presented in Figure 3.1.

With respect to both actual and preferred authority/influence, the data clearly support the hypothesis of hierarchical differences between groups. Predictably, the preferred distribution is more equalitarian than the actual. One might wonder, however, why the respondents, who include rank-and-file workers, do not come closer in their preference to the ideal of power equalization. Perhaps it is because people adapt to the realities of their situations, as aspiration theory suggests.

In general, organization members value the opportunity to exercise authority/influence. The discrepancy between preferred and actual authority/influence changes systematically in magnitude and

Figure 3.1
HIERARCHICAL DISTRIBUTION OF AUTHORITY/INFLUENCE
BASED ON SELF-REPORTS

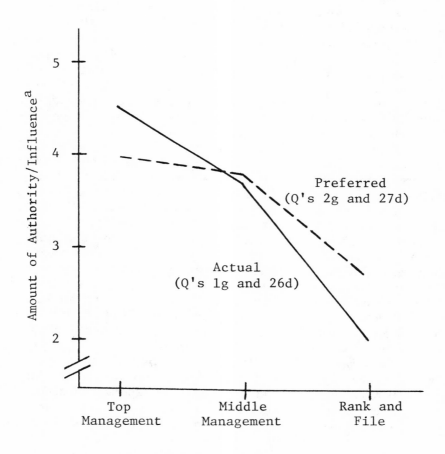

--Position in Hierarchy--

[a]Analysis of variance indicates difference
between groups for actual and preferred
authority/influence is significant at the
.01 level of confidence.

direction as one moves from the bottom to the top of the hierarchy. Persons at the bottom of the hierarchy have little opportunity to exercise authority/influence—substantially less than they want. We see in Figure 3.1 an expression of the deprivation that they feel. Persons at the top, on the other hand, say they have more than they want (Kaufmann, 1974, p. 29ff.; Nick, 1974, p. 35ff.).

The preference of top persons for less authority/influence might be explained by their inclination to give a socially acceptable response. (The Workers' Constitution Act was being discussed publicly during the time of the study.) Managers may also be expressing a desire to reduce their work load and responsibilities. In any case, the data of Figure 3.1 show that members prefer a less hierarchical structure, not a structure without hierarchy.

Distribution of control (control graph). To measure the distribution of control in each plant, respondents were asked how much influence each of the three groups—top management, all other managers, and workers as a group—actually have in the plant and how much influence each of these groups *should* have. Figure 3.2 presents data based on the responses of all respondents.

The data show clearly that members both perceive and prefer a hierarchical distribution of control. Furthermore, the discrepancies between perceived and preferred control are greater at the bottom than at the top, probably because the description of a desired state is affected by the actual situation and by what respondents believe is realistically possible (Tannenbaum et al., 1974, p. 62). The desired distribution thus is flatter and the desired total amount of control (as indicated by the average height of the curve) higher.[6]

Participativeness and supportiveness of superior. Differences between hierarchical groups in authority/influence and control imply different roles; different roles imply different expectations about the exercise of influence. Since such differences are found in the superior-subordinate relationship, an index was constructed to describe the behavior of superiors toward their subordinates.[7]

The data presented in Table 3.5, with the exception of Question 44, indicate highly significant differences between levels. (The top group as defined is not relevant because it has no superiors in the plant.) This is consistent with the notion that managerial personnel are more likely than persons at the bottom of the hierarchy to be offered opportunities for participation and to be supported, or at least to feel that they are. There may be two related reasons for this. First, middle managers are perceived by their superiors to perform more complex and less structured tasks than persons at the bottom perform. Second, middle managers have more education and experience than bottom persons have. The former are therefore con-

Figure 3.2
DISTRIBUTION OF CONTROL AS REPORTED BY ALL MEMBERS

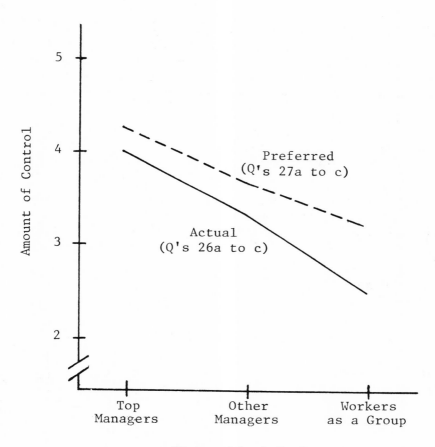

--Hierarchical Scale--

sidered more important to the effectiveness of the plant and are treated with more respect and consideration.

Table 3.5

PARTICIPATIVENESS AND SUPPORTIVENESS OF SUPERIOR

	Middle Management (n = 121)	Rank and File (n = 198–199)
Q.41. Does your immediate superior ask your opinion when a problem comes up that involves your work?	4.1	3.5**
Q.42. Is your immediate superior inclined to take into account your opinion and suggestions?	4.1	3.5**
Q.43. Is your immediate superior friendly and easily approached if there are problems?	4.1	3.8**
Q.44. Does your immediate superior make people under him feel free to take their complaints to him?	3.9	3.9
Q.46. Do you have trust in your immediate superior?	4.2	3.9**
Average	4.1	3.7**

**The difference between groups is significant at the .01 level of confidence.

Bases of superior's power. Given the differences in participativeness and supportiveness of superiors of persons at the middle and at the bottom of the hierarchy, one might expect that persons at these respective levels will react differently to the attempts of their superiors to influence them. Accordingly, respondents were asked why they acceded to such attempts. The "bases of power" as conceptualized by French and Raven (1959, p. 150ff.) provide a framework for examining these reasons. The bases include (1) expert, (2) reward, (3) referent, (4) coercive, and (5) legitimate power. A sixth base, which comes close to what Cartwright (1965) refers to as "ecological control" and Mary Parker Follett (1942) calls "control by the situation," was added to French and Raven's bases. The statements that correspond to these bases are presented in Table 3.6.

Table 3.6

BASES OF THE SUPERIOR'S POWER AS REPORTED BY SUBORDINATES

Q.47. When you do what your immediate superior requests you to do on the job, why do you do it?	Middle Management (n = 116–120)	Rank and File (n = 187–190)
I respect his competence and judgment.	3.8	3.7
He can give special help and benefits.	2.9	3.2**
He's a nice guy.	3.0	3.4**
He can penalize or otherwise disadvantage me.	2.0	2.2
It is my duty.	4.2	3.9**
It is necessary if the organization is to function properly.	4.5	4.0**

**The difference between groups is significant at the .01 level of confidence.

The significant differences between groups lead to an interesting conclusion: The rank-and-file group assigns greater importance to reward and referent power, whereas the middle management group perceives legitimate power and control by the situation as more relevant. This might mean that persons in the middle adhere more strongly to bureaucratic procedures—to formal ingredients of the organization—but it may also mean that they are more involved in organizational processes. Social or informal aspects are comparatively more important for persons at the bottom than for persons in the middle. This is an indication of greater commitment by persons at upper levels to the logic underlying hierarchical structures and to the ideology of efficiency.

The similarity in the relative importance assigned to the bases is also striking. Both groups perceive legitimate power and control by the situation to be most important. This may result partly because these two bases can be interpreted as measuring the degree of acceptance of general values of socio-economic life. They show that acceptance is generally high (although, understandably, it is higher for persons at upper levels than for those at lower levels). Furthermore, these are "impersonal" bases of control. Acceding to the control of the impersonal structure may be more "rational" and less threatening psychologically than acceding to the control of people.[8] Coercion is especially unacceptable to respondents as a basis of a superior's power, although ironically—as will be shown later (Tables 3.17 and 3.18)—punishment as a basis of control is more likely than reward to occur in these plants.

Enriching qualities of the job. Some jobs more than others give organization members the opportunity to use their skills, learn new things, do interesting work, and set their own work pace. Given the nature of jobs in hierarchical organizations, these opportunities might be expected to decline with hierarchical descent. Accordingly, we asked questions about each of the above opportunities and computed an index for each person that defines the average amount of such opportunity that the job provides.[9] A parallel set of questions asked what opportunities the respondent would *like* to have, and an index was constructed from these.[10] As shown in Figure 3.3, the results demonstrate the predicted hierarchical pattern. Furthermore, the discrepancy between the actual and preferred qualities is greater at the bottom than at the top, although it is similar for middle management and rank-and-file levels. This similarity contradicts the conjecture that discrepancies grow from top management to rank and file. When these results are compared to those for authority/influence (shown in Figure 3.1), it seems that influence is more closely bound to hierarchy than are enriching qualities of the job (see also Tannenbaum et al., 1974, pp. 98ff. and 103ff.).

Physical qualities of the job. The last role characteristic to be investigated involves qualities of work that are ordinarily considered favorable (for example, clean, mental, and varied). A seven-point scale was used to determine the extent to which respondents' jobs were, for example, tiring or not tiring, physical or mental, clean or dirty, and routine or varied. Table 3.7 presents the index computed from the responses.[11]

As expected, top management jobs have more favorable physical qualities than middle management and rank-and-file jobs do, but again, the hierarchical differentiation is less marked than for

Figure 3.3

ENRICHING QUALITIES OF THE JOB BASED ON SELF-REPORTS

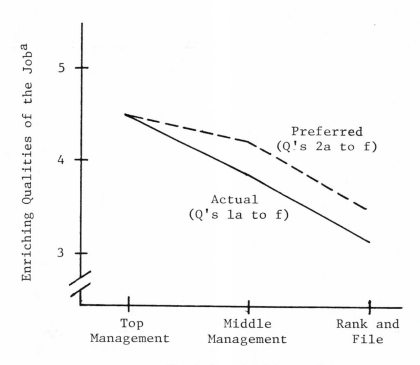

--Position in Hierarchy--

[a]Analysis of variance indicates difference between groups for actual and preferred enriching qualities of the job is significant at the .01 level of confidence.

Table 3.7

PHYSICAL QUALITIES OF THE JOB

	Top Management (n = 9–10)	Middle Management (n = 117–120)	Rank and File (n = 190–197)
Tiring (1)			
— not tiring (7)	4.7	4.5	4.4
Healthful (7)			
— unhealthful (1)	5.4	4.3	4.3
Physical (1)			
— mental (7)	6.3	5.5	4.2**
Dirty (1)			
— clean (7)	6.3	4.8	3.8**
Heavy (1)			
— light (7)	3.6	4.1	4.0
Same tasks during the day (1) — different tasks during the day (7)	6.8	6.0	4.8**
Dangerous (1)			
— safe (7)	5.8	5.3	4.9
Average (Q.3)	5.6	4.9	4.4**

**The difference between groups is significant at the .01 level of confidence.

authority/influence. However, there are sharp differences between levels for qualities that have to do with the extent to which a job is "industrial" (for example, physical/mental, dirty/clean, and routine/varied). The one exception to the general direction of the results in Table 3.7 involves the item "heavy-light." The term is ambiguous in German, meaning "difficult vs. easy" as well as heavy vs. light in the purely physical sense.

In general, the data show that respondents perceive the existence of hierarchy; it is a psychological fact of life for them. Hierarchical differences in authority/influence are especially apparent in their view of organizational life.

Reactions and Adjustments

The aspects of work described in the previous section are likely to have implications for the reactions and adjustments of organiza-

tion members. This section explores how the reactions and adjustments of hierarchical groups differ from one another and how the
aspects of role just described might help to explain those differences.
The reactions and adjustments fall into four areas: morale, motivation, personal adjustment, and perceptions.

Morale

Three aspects of morale have been measured. We refer to the
first as job satisfaction; the index used measures satisfaction with
activities at work compared with activities outside of work, satisfaction with company, and satisfaction with the job itself.[12] Second is
satisfaction with pay, which is measured by a single question. The
third aspect, attitude toward company leadership, is measured by
an index consisting of three questions: Do you think the responsible
people here have a real interest in the welfare of those who work
here? Do the responsible people in this plant improve working conditions only when forced to? When a worker in this plant makes a
complaint about something, is it taken care of?[13] The results of
these measures are presented in Table 3.8.

Table 3.8

MORALE

	Top Management (n = 10)	Middle Management (n = 121)	Rank and File (n = 199–200)
Job satisfaction (Q.8, 9, 10)	4.4	3.9	3.5**
Satisfaction with pay (Q.59)	3.9	3.2	3.1**
Attitude toward plant leadership (Q.24, 25, 28)	4.1	3.7	3.4**

**The difference between groups is significant at the .01 level of confidence.

These data definitely support the hypothesis of hierarchical differences, as do those of many studies (e.g., Argyris, 1973, p. 141ff.;
Bartölke, 1974, p. 309ff.; Bruggemann, Grosskurth, & Ulich, 1975,
p. 20ff.; Israel, 1972, p. 251ff.; Lawler, 1973, p. 11ff.; Neuberger,
1974, passim; Oetterli, 1971, p. 110ff.; Tannenbaum, 1966,

p. 17ff.; Tausky, 1970, p. 111ff.; Vroom, 1970, p. 91ff.).

Table 3.9 shows the result of a standardized multiple regression that attempts to predict each measure of morale on the basis of the aspects of hierarchy that have been discussed in the previous section.

Table 3.9

THE RELATIVE IMPORTANCE OF THE PREDICTORS OF MORALE

Multiple R	Job Satisfaction .56*		Satisfaction with Pay .39*		Attitude toward Plant Leadership .50*	
Predictors	Beta	Rank	Beta	Rank	Beta	Rank
Enriching job qualities	.30*	1	.06	7	.15*	4
Authority/ influence	.12	5	.11	6	.30*	1
Physical job qualities	.25*	2	.13*	4	.13*	5
Education	−.13*	4	−.05	8	−.06	7
Age	.17*	3	.13	5	.26*	2
Plant seniority	−.01	9	−.02	9	−.15*	3
Length of chain	.03	8	−.19*	3	−.02	8
Level in hierarchy	−.04	6	−.37*	2	−.07	6
Salary	.04	7	.38*	1	.02	9

*The coefficient is significant at the .05 level of confidence or better.

Enriching job qualities and physical job qualities are the most important factors for explaining job satisfaction. The finding that enriching and physical qualities of a job rank first and second, respectively, while salary ranks close to last, could be interpreted as support for the argument that intrinsic factors are more important than extrinsic ones for job satisfaction. Furthermore, education is negatively related to job satisfaction, a result that is consistent with a previous finding: More-highly educated persons are not as satisfied as less-educated persons when such factors as salary, hierarchical level, age, and job opportunities are controlled. This is consistent with equity theory: Education is an "input" that should be associated with an equivalent "output" if a person is to experience equity (Adams, 1965, p. 276). Hence, increases in education without increases in rank, salary, and other rewards are likely to be accompanied by dissatisfaction. Age, on the other hand, is positively related to job satisfaction, which is consistent with research in the Federal Republic of Germany indicating that older persons have lower aspiration levels than younger persons do (Bruggemann, Grosskurth, & Ulich, 1975, p. 116ff.).[14]

It is not surprising that salary is the best predictor of satisfaction with pay. The negative relationship between hierarchical level and satisfaction with pay can also be interpreted on the basis of equity theory: Variations in rank without corresponding variations in pay (as under the controlled conditions of this regression analysis) will be perceived as inequitable. The negative relationship for length of chain is reasonable on the same basis: Persons who are high in a hierarchy, with comparatively many levels below them, might consider their salary to be too low, whereas persons at the bottom of tall hierarchies might perceive their pay to be relatively high. A tentative explanation for the positive relationship between favorable physical qualities of a job and satisfaction with pay might be that, salary being controlled, better job qualities are perceived as an additional "output" (Lawler, 1971, p. 221ff.; Tannenbaum et al., 1974, p. 141ff.).

Attitude toward company leadership is best explained by authority/influence and age. Older persons and those who perceive themselves to have great influence—a valued characteristic—tend to have positive attitudes toward the management of their plant. Similarly, persons who perceive their jobs to have enriching qualities and favorable physical qualities are also likely to have positive attitudes toward management. Seniority, however, is associated negatively with attitude toward management. Persons who are similar to others in age, hierarchical level, education, and salary, but who have greater seniority, tend to have negative feelings about management. It may be that those who have seniority consider it to be an important contribution; if that seniority is not honored, a feeling of inequity will result.

To summarize a rather heterogeneous picture, four variables seem to have relatively great importance for morale: physical job qualities, enriching job qualities, age, and authority/influence.

Motivation

The variables to be treated in this section—feeling of responsibility for the system, motivation to perform on the job, initiative, feeling of responsibility for one's own job, and aspirations to advance in the organizational hierarchy—are likely to be more directly related to effectiveness of the organization than are the variables of the previous section that define morale. The components of motivation have to do with members' involvement in or identification with the plant and their jobs, their acceptance of organizational goals, and the likelihood that they will put effort into achieving those goals.

Responsibility for the system was measured by an index composed of items concerning responsibility for the success of one's work group, one's department, and the plant as a whole.[15] Responsibility for one's own work has been treated independently, because it has been suggested earlier (Bartölke, 1969, p. 113) that one might identify with one's job while being indifferent to larger parts of the system and vice versa. In fact, product-moment correlations show that there are highly significant positive relationships between the first three system-oriented responsibility items, but that responsibility for one's own work does not relate positively to the others.

Motivation on the job was measured by the question "In your kind of job, is it usually better to let your superior worry about introducing better or faster ways of doing your work?" Initiative was measured by the question "How often do you try out on your own a better or faster way of doing the work?"

Aspirations to advance in the hierarchy (referred to as mobility aspirations) were measured by a question that asked whether respondents would or would not accept a higher position that would involve difficulties such as added obligations and responsibilities, frequent criticism, or problem employees.[16] This question was not asked of top managers. Table 3.10 presents the relevant data.

The results show, in general, the expected hierarchical differences (Bartölke, 1969, p. 75ff.; Katz & Kahn, 1966, p. 336ff.; Lawler, 1973, p. 11ff.; Morse & Reimer, 1956, p. 120ff.; Neuberger, 1974, p. 49ff.; Tannenbaum, 1966, p. 38ff.; Wächter, 1973, p. 49ff.). The exceptions concern responsibility for one's own work and initiative (as in trying out better and faster work methods on one's own). Apparently, responsibility to and engagement in one's own work is still a strong norm in the Federal Republic of Germany. Persons at *all* levels in the hierarchy indicate feeling a great amount of such responsibility and initiative, thus lending support to the stereotype that Germans are generally hard-working and committed to fulfilling tasks assigned to them.

The data on mobility aspirations (Table 3.11) show a definite hierarchical pattern. An average of 60 percent of the middle management respondents and 35 percent of the rank-and-file

Table 3.10

MOTIVATIONAL ASPECTS

	Top Management (n = 9–10)	Middle Management (n = 112–121)	Rank and File (n = 182–200)
Responsibility for the system[a] (Q.11a, b, c)	5.0	4.4	3.7**
Responsibility for own work (Q.11d)	5.0	4.8	4.5
Motivation on the job (Q.6)	–	3.9	3.2**
Initiative[b] (Q.7)	5.1	4.9	4.5

[a]Index based on measures of responsibility for success of work group, department, and plant.

[b]Measured on a six-point scale.

**The difference between groups is significant at the .01 level of confidence.

respondents indicated that they would accept a higher position despite certain inherent difficulties. The interpretation of the difference between management and rank and file, however, is not so obvious. Does it reflect inherent personality differences between persons at middle and bottom levels—differences that, in fact, *determined* those persons' positions? Or is the difference due to the fact that middle managers (most of whom have already been promoted) have experienced success, while rank-and-file personnel (who have not been and probably will not be promoted) may have had their hopes frustrated?

The feeling of responsibility for one's own work does not seem to be explained very well by the predictors in Table 3.12. Nor are the hierarchical differences large for this variable, as we have seen. In the Federal Republic of Germany, feeling responsible for one's work may depend more on personal values developed through socialization than on the conditions defined in Table 3.12—with the exception that the authority/influence a person has may have a significant effect on the sense of responsibility he or she feels (Bartölke, 1969, p. 87).

Responsibility for the system is best explained by individual in-

Table 3.11

UPWARD MOBILITY ASPIRATION

Q.48. Imagine you were offered the following possibilities within this plant. Would you accept them or not?	Percentage Who Would Accept a Higher Position Despite Difficulties	
	Middle Management (n = 114–118)	Rank and File (n = 187–191)
Move to a higher position involving:		
Additional obligations and responsibilities	64%	47%**
Training requirements	62	37**
Frequent criticism	56	29**
"Problem" employees	40	18**
More work worries	76	52**
Average	60	35**

**The difference between groups is significant at the .01 level of confidence.

fluence and enriching job qualities. Education is the third most important variable, which might mean that higher education leads to a stronger sense of responsibility for organizational matters, because education is related to knowledge about the interdependencies of plant operation.

Motivation appears to be best explained by the positive effects of enriching qualities of the job, education, salary, and seniority. The importance of enriching job qualities gives support to theories of motivation that focus on intrinsic aspects of work. The effects of education may be that more-educated persons are not as likely as less-educated persons to depend on their superior. Also, when enriching qualities of the job, individual influence, education, seniority, and salary are controlled, it is clear that increasing age is connected with diminishing motivation; this may be because needs have been satisfied or aspiration levels adapted.

Enriching job qualities and authority/influence account for most

Table 3.12

THE RELATIVE IMPORTANCE OF THE PREDICTORS OF MOTIVATIONAL ASPECTS

Predictors	Responsibility for System .60* Beta	Rank	Responsibility for Own Work .36* Beta	Rank	Motivation .56* Beta	Rank	Initiative .38* Beta	Rank	Mobility Aspirations .55* Beta	Rank
Enriching job qualities	.27*	2	.08	5	.33*	1	.37*	1	.16*	7
Authority/influence	.31*	1	.31*	1	-.01	6	.23*	2	.30*	1
Physical job qualities	.03	7	.00	9	-.05	7	-.15*	5	-.08	8
Education	.11*	3	.05	7	.20*	3	.02	9	.17*	6
Age	.08	4	-.08	4	-.31*	2	.04	8	-.25*	4
Plant seniority	.04	5	.07	6	.12*	5	.04	7	-.04	9
Length of chain	-.03	7	-.08	3	.02	9	-.15	4	-.20*	5
Level in hierarchy	-.03	7	-.10	2	.05	8	-.22	3	-.26*	3
Salary	-.01	9	.03	8	.19*	4	-.13	6	.28*	2

*The coefficient is significant at the .05 level of confidence or better.

of the variance in initiative. Like responsibility for one's own work, however, initiative is not very well explained.

Mobility aspirations are positively related to authority/influence, salary, education, and enriching qualities of the job. In comparable situations, those who experience higher authority/influence and more enriching job qualities, have more years of personal education, or receive a higher salary strive more for higher positions. In other words, those who are relatively successful already want to be even more successful. Age, level, and length of chain are negatively connected with mobility aspirations. The negative relationship of age and (taking into account the controls) level might best be explained by the satisfaction of one's own needs or the adaptation of one's aspiration level. The phenomenon of mobility aspirations diminishing with length of chain might be explained by two aspects of hierarchy: Persons at higher levels and in longer chains have more levels below them than persons in shorter chains; therefore, they may have more fully satisfied their status needs. Those at lower levels of the longer chains work mainly in the production departments of the plants; they may be either unwilling to move upward or discouraged about trying to because of the obstacles they have encountered in past attempts.

To summarize, authority/influence, enriching job qualities, and education contribute positively to motivation. The negative associations of age with these values show either changes of values or resignation as one grows older.

Personal Adjustment

We explored two measures of personal adjustment: alienation and psychological adjustment. Alienation was measured with an index of ten items that refer to powerlessness, meaninglessness, normlessness, social isolation, and self-estrangement.[17] Our index of psychological adjustment consists of nine items designed to measure such criteria as depression, resentment, and self-esteem.[18] A high score on the index of psychological adjustment implies "good" adjustment—for example, low depression, low resentment, and high self-esteem. For alienation, however, a high score implies "poor" adjustment; that is, high alienation. As Tables 3.13 and 3.14 show, both indices are associated with hierarchy in the expected way, one increasing and the other decreasing with hierarchical ascent.

Psychological adjustment is considered to be one indicator of mental health (Bass & Barrett, 1972, p. 96ff.; Secretary of Health, Education, and Welfare, 1973, p. 81ff.; Strauss, 1974, p. 91ff.).

Table 3.13

PSYCHOLOGICAL ADJUSTMENT[a]

Q.49. How true are the following statements?	Top Management (n = 10)	Middle Management (n = 118–119)	Rank and File (n = 192–198)
I feel depressed.	4.4	3.9	3.8
Other people are always more lucky than I.	4.2	3.9	3.5
I often feel bored.	4.7	4.6	4.2
I seem not to get what is coming to me.	4.2	3.2	3.1**
Usually everything I try seems to fail.	4.5	4.4	4.1
Things seem hopeless.	5.0	4.6	4.3*
I feel resentful.	5.0	4.3	4.2**
I sometimes feel that my life is not very useful.	4.9	4.6	4.2
It seems to me that I am a failure.	5.0	4.7	4.5
Average	4.7	4.4	4.1**

[a] A high score implies disagreement with the item and, therefore, "good" adjustment.

*The difference between groups is significant at the .05 level of confidence.

**The difference between groups is significant at the .01 level of confidence.

Table 3.14
ALIENATION[a]

Q.52. How true are the following statements?	Top Management (n = 9–10)	Middle Management (n = 117–118)	Rank and File (n = 189–194)
It is not possible to rely on others.	2.7	3.0	3.1
Today it is practically impossible to find real friends because everyone thinks only of himself.	2.7	3.0	3.2
Men like me cannot influence the course of events; only men in high positions can have such influence.	2.4	2.9	3.7**
I have never had the influence over others that I would have liked.	2.0	2.4	2.8*
Public affairs are so complicated that one cannot help but be confused by them.	2.4	2.5	2.9
Despite the many advances science has made, life today is too complicated.	2.6	2.6	3.2
I can never do what I really like because circumstances require that I do otherwise.	2.2	2.4	2.7
Life is so routinized that I do not have a chance to use my true abilities.	1.7	2.3	2.7**
Life seems to be moving on without rules or order.	1.7	2.1	2.5**
Nowadays it is hard to know right from wrong.	2.2	2.5	3.1**
Average	2.3	2.6	3.0**

[a]A high score means agreement with the item and, therefore, high alienation.

*The difference between groups is significant at the .05 level of confidence.

**The difference between groups is significant at the .01 level of confidence.

The results of the multiple regression analysis for this measure, shown in Table 3.15, are reasonable: The more favorable the physical qualities of the job and the higher the education, hierarchical level, and salary (as aspects closely related to status), the better the psychological state of the individual.

Table 3.15
THE RELATIVE IMPORTANCE OF THE
PREDICTORS OF PERSONAL ADJUSTMENT

Multiple R	Psychological Adjustment .45*		Alienation .54*	
Predictors	Beta	Rank	Beta	Rank
Enriching job qualities	.11	6	−.26*	1
Authority/influence	−.13	5	−.12	4
Physical job qualities	.14*	3.5	−.16*	3.5
Education	.15*	2	−.16*	2.5
Age	−.02	8	.10	5
Plant seniority	−.01	9	.02	7.5
Length of chain	.08	7	.00	9
Level in hierarchy	.22	1	.02	7.5
Salary	.14	3	−.04	6

*The coefficient is significant at the .05 level of confidence or better.

Similarly, the data on alienation agree with arguments that are often expressed in the literature (Blauner, 1964, p. 2). Persons whose jobs offer them enriching opportunities, authority/influence, and favorable physical qualities and who have higher education are less likely to be alienated than are those whose jobs do not have these characteristics.

Two correlates of hierarchical position—the education level of members and the physical qualities of their job—appear to be most important in explaining the two indices of personal adjustment. The relatively low variance explained jointly by all predictors in the regression, however, shows that personal adjustment is by no means solely determined by those predictors. Circumstances outside the work organization are also likely to be important determinants of adjustment.

Perceptions

Managers, because of their authority, the rewards they receive, and the special responsibility they feel, are likely to see organizational life in a different light than rank-and-file members do.

> [Management personnel] are the ones who, by virtue of their official position and the authority that goes with it, are in a position to "do something" when things are not what they should be and, similarly, are the ones who will be held to account if they fail to "do something" or if what they do is, for whatever reason, inadequate. (Becker, 1970, p. 19)

This section explores the notion that role affects perception, examining how persons of different rank differ in the way they perceive decision making, control, rewards, penalties, and the benefits of and requirements for advancement within their organization.

Decision making. The degree to which the organization allows or encourages members to participate in decision making (referred to in the study as the participativeness of the organization) is measured through selected items from an instrument developed by Likert (1961, p. 222ff.). These items are outlined in Table 3.16. The questions allow a comparison between the level of participativeness that members perceive and the level that they would prefer.

It is apparent that persons at higher levels perceive their organization to be more participative than do persons at lower levels. In fact, persons at upper levels do "participate" more than those at lower levels; therefore, they are inclined to see the whole organization as relatively participative. Furthermore, the authority and responsibility that persons at upper levels have lead them to think of their organization in socially acceptable terms. According to contemporary norms, organizations in the Federal Republic of Germany *should be* participative; therefore, in the view of top managers, they *are* participative—at least more so than in the view of less influential workers at the bottom of the hierarchy.

The preferred level of participativeness is also higher than the perceived level, as indicated by the fact that all discrepancies are positive (Likert, 1967, p. 26ff.; Tannenbaum et al., 1974, p. 51ff.). The preferred level does not differ significantly between groups, however, which results in a greater discrepancy between actual and preferred participation at the bottom than at the top. This is attributable to the inclination of upper-level persons to perceive their organization to be as participative, or nearly as participative, as they would like it to be.

Respondents express a somewhat greater desire to be asked for their opinion about matters that affect them and to participate in job-related matters than to participate in plant matters. One might therefore infer that members actually perceive participation in deci-

Table 3.16

PERCEPTIONS AND PREFERENCES ABOUT THE PARTICIPATIVENESS
IN THE PLANTS, MEASURED IN TERMS OF LIKERT'S MODEL

	Perceptions by:[a]		
	Top Management (n = 8–10)	Middle Management (n = 119–121)	Rank and File (n = 193–200)
Q.34. Actual participation by workers in job decisions	3.0	2.5	2.4*
Q.35. Preferred participation by workers in job decisions	3.2	3.1	3.3
Discrepancy Q.35 − Q.34	0.2	0.6	0.9*
Q.36. Actual participation by workers in plant decisions	2.9	2.2	2.1**
Q.37. Preferred participation by workers in plant decisions	3.1	3.0	3.0
Discrepancy Q.37 − Q.36	0.2	0.8	0.9*
Q.39. Actual extent to which opinions are asked of those who are affected by decisions	3.1	2.6	2.3**
Q.40. Preferred extent	3.4	3.5	3.4
Discrepancy Q.40 − Q.39	0.3	0.9	1.1**

[a]The data presented in this table are averages for the respective groups on a four-point scale where "4" implies a high degree of participation.

*The difference between groups is significant at the .05 level of confidence.

**The difference between groups is significant at the .01 level of confidence.

sions about the job as more important than participation in decisions about the larger matters of the plant as a whole.[19] Thus, rank-and-file persons do not seriously challenge the power of those at the top to control far-reaching, plantwide decisions (about technology, for example), even though such plantwide decisions very often have a direct or indirect effect on these members' working conditions, which they *would* like to control more. This seeming paradox may be attributable to the failure of many workers to see the relationship between their immediate environment and the larger environment.

Distribution of control. Distribution of control has already been discussed as one indicator of hierarchically differentiated roles. We examine here how persons of different rank may differ in their perceptions of the distribution of control and in their preferences for that distribution. Figure 3.4 shows actual distribution of control as perceived by the three hierarchical groups in one graph; the preferred distributions of control are presented in three separate graphs. The arrows indicate how preferred distribution differs from the actual distribution perceived by each group.

All of the distributions, both actual and preferred, show a hierarchical pattern, indicating that the average member recognizes and accepts the value of a hierarchical distribution of influence. The differences that appear between groups have to do with total amount of control, the hierarchical gradient of control, and the discrepancies between actual and preferred distribution of control. Persons at lower levels perceive a lower total amount of control than do persons at upper levels. One reason might be that persons at the top of the hierarchy tend to receive biased information that indicates a state of affairs in accordance with their intent, while rank-and-file persons are unaware that they do not always follow management's directives (Katz & Kahn, 1966, p. 245). Thus, persons at the top see their organization as more controlled than do those at the bottom.

Middle managers perceive a steeper hierarchy than do either the top managers or the rank-and-file personnel, whose perceptions of the gradient are very much alike. This holds reasonably well both for perceptions of the actual distribution and for the preferred distribution of control. Persons at middle levels have a unique experience of hierarchical processes because of their double dependency: They both give and receive orders. This seems to support the view that persons in middle managerial positions conform strongly to the hierarchical pattern and see strong hierarchy as necessary for the profitability and survival of the organization. In this respect, they are more inclined to favor the interests of the owners

Figure 3.4

DISTRIBUTION OF CONTROL AS REPORTED BY PERSONS AT THREE HIERARCHICAL LEVELS

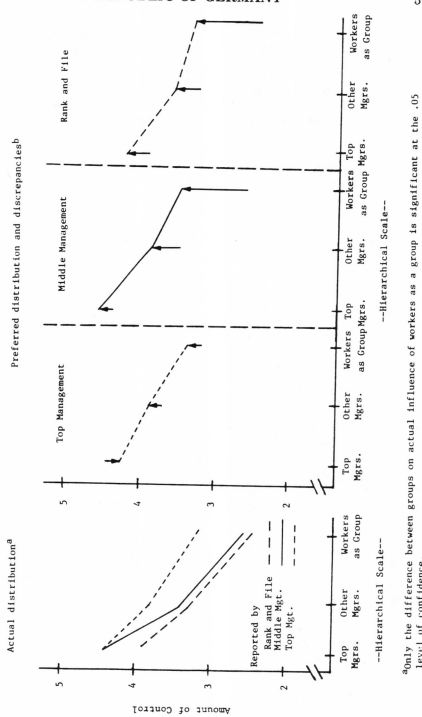

Preferred distribution and discrepancies[b]

Actual distribution[a]

[a]Only the difference between groups on actual influence of workers as a group is significant at the .05 level of confidence.

[b]Length and direction of vertical arrows show the discrepancies between preferred and actual state.

than the interests of the workers. As to the actual distribution, it should be mentioned that the perceptions of the persons in the middle and at the bottom regarding workers as a group are very close to each other—as are the perceptions of top and middle managers about the influence of plant leadership. This high degree of agreement is probably due to the greater amount of information that persons in the middle have about those at the top and the bottom.

Another point should be made in this context. The only statistically significant difference in the data on the distribution of control between groups of respondents concerns the actual influence of workers as a group. Rank-and-file persons perceive workers as having very little influence, whereas top management perceives the workers' influence to be comparatively high. Top persons are likely to view the influence of the workers as threatening, because it limits the influence of the owners and representatives. The workers, on the other hand, desirous of influence, see themselves as relatively powerless.

The preferred total amount of control is generally higher than the actual. Middle managers and rank-and-file persons show the most consistent pattern in that they want those who have the least amount of influence to experience the greatest increase and those with most influence to receive the smallest increase. The decrease in influence of the plant leadership proposed by the top group is surprising, however. The effect is that middle persons desire more influence for the top management than the top management desires for itself.[20] This might be explained by social desirability—the belief of top managers that they should endorse a democratic norm. Their proposal for a decline in influence may also reflect a desire for a reduced work load.

Nevertheless, within all groups the discrepancy is relatively high for preferred and actual influence of workers as a group. It is generally believed that workers should exert influence; most persons, regardless of level, appear to express this socially desirable norm.[21] The discrepancy is lowest in the responses of the top managers, however, and highest in the responses of rank-and-file personnel. This is consistent with public arguments about codetermination, in which representatives of the entrepreneurs claim that the influence of the workers should not be enlarged too much or it will destroy the balance of power between workers and management, and representatives of the unions and the Social Democrats argue for increasing the influence of workers in plants and companies because of the workers' relative powerlessness.

Rewards and sanctions. A basic aim of control is to maintain performance, and one means to reach that aim is to reward good performance and penalize bad. Therefore, we attempted to ascertain the perceptions of respondents concerning the rewards and penalties that workers are likely to receive for exceptionally good or bad work. Respondents were asked to check as many rewards and penalties as applied from the lists shown in Tables 3.17 and 3.18.

Table 3.17

REWARDS FOR GOOD WORK

Q.12. What happens if a member in this organization does an especially good job in his work?	Percentage of Respondents Checking the Response		
	Top Management (n = 10)	Middle Management (n = 121)	Rank and File (n = 197)
His superior will praise him.	80%	61%	46%**
His co-workers will praise him.	10	10	22*
His co-workers will criticize him.	0	7	9
He may be offered a better job at the same level.	0	13	17
He will be given a bonus or higher wage.	70	36	19**
His co-workers will have a high opinion of him.	20	14	11
He will have a better opportunity for advancement.	70	44	27**
His superior will have a high opinion of him.	40	45	36
Nothing will happen.	0	11	21**

*The difference between groups is significant at the .05 level of confidence.
**The difference between groups is significant at the .01 level of confidence.

Table 3.17 shows some striking differences between hierarchical groups. For example, persons at the top are more likely than those at the bottom to say that workers will be praised by their supervisor, that they will be given a bonus, and that they will have a better chance for promotion if they perform well on their job. Persons at the bottom are more likely than those at the top to say that nothing will happen or that a worker might be praised by his own co-workers as a result of good performance.

The data concerning the consequences of bad work (Table 3.18) are similar in their implications to those for consequences of good work. Managers, more than workers, perceive or are prejudiced toward consequences that imply an effectively functioning system: Workers will be criticized by their superiors and will have poorer opportunities for advancement as a consequence of poor work. One apparent exception is the report by 20 percent of the top managers (and only 6 percent of the rank-and-file workers) that co-workers will support a poor performer against criticism, but this difference between groups is not significant statistically.

By and large, managers more than workers have an image of their organization that fits the "professional" model of an effectively functioning administrative system, where good work is given appropriate recognition and reward. Nonetheless, substantial numbers of persons at lower levels do report some of the rewards that management sees as likely. Both managers and workers appear to be saying that among the consequences for good work, the likelihood of supervisory praise and of opportunity for advancement are high compared to the likelihood of other consequences.

The data in Table 3.18 are similar in another respect to those in Table 3.17. Managers and rank-and-file members are close in the relative ranking of consequences that their responses imply. For example, criticism by a superior and poorer chances for promotion are indicated by relatively large percentages of both managers and rank-and-file members.

A comparison of the two tables and of desired consequences for good and bad work (for which data are not reported here) suggests two implications. First, there is some common acceptance of reward and penalty systems and the values on which they are built. Second, some sort of reaction to bad work is more probable than a reaction to good work. For example, "nothing" (last item in the tables) is more likely as a consequence of good work than of bad work—which is very much like the result reported in earlier research (Tannenbaum et al., 1974, p. 71).

A general, if slightly overstated, conclusion can be drawn. The upper-level representatives of the structure are more likely than

Table 3.18

SANCTIONS FOR BAD WORK

Q.14. What happens if a member in this organization does a very poor job?	Percentage of Respondents Checking the Response		
	Top Management (n = 10)	Middle Management (n = 121)	Rank and File (n = 198)
His superior will criticize him.	80%	80%	66%**
His co-workers will criticize him.	40	35	25
His co-workers will support him against criticism	20	3	6
He will be given an inferior job.	10	15	14
His salary will be reduced.	20	31	24
His co-workers will have a low opinion of him.	30	23	16
He will have less good opportunities for advancement.	80	51	41*
His superior will have a low opinion of him.	50	42	32
Nothing will happen.	0	4	7

*The difference between groups is significant at the .05 level of confidence.

**The difference between groups is significant at the .01 level of confidence.

those who are disadvantaged in the structure to perceive consequences that are part of a traditional performance-oriented hierarchical structure. Consequences that are not closely bound to the logic of hierarchy and to what might be called "good management" are perceived as relatively unlikely by the representatives of the structure but as rather important by those who are disadvantaged by it.

Advantages of advancement. Positions of high rank, as we have seen, are more rewarding in a number of ways than positions of low rank. Therefore, advancement in the organization is itself likely to be considered rewarding, although in the view of some members it is not likely to be achieved simply as a consequence of good work. It is of interest, therefore, to learn what managers and workers perceive to be the advantages of high rank and what they believe is required to achieve advancement.

Respondents were asked to rank, from a list of possibilities, the three most important advantages of advancement. Table 3.19 presents this list and the average rank assigned to each. A high score implies high importance.

Table 3.19 shows rather close agreement between groups about the relative importance of high wages, the opportunity to enlarge one's skills, and the opportunity to make decisions; these advantages rank relatively high for all groups. Better opportunities for social contacts and influence outside the plant are assigned low importance. This might be interpreted as an indicator that those advantages of advancement that are closely related to hierarchy itself, such as its "immanent" aspects (Rosenberg, 1968) and, in capitalistic economies, its monetary rewards, are perceived as more important than aspects related to social life, which are considered to be independent of organizational hierarchy.

Criteria for advancement. Table 3.20 presents data about requirements for advancement as perceived by organization members. Only with respect to three of the items—quality of work done, having friends in higher management, and taking initiative—are the groups statistically different. Nonetheless, taken together, the data support the notion that managers are more likely than workers to see virtuous qualities as the bases of advancement—quality and quantity of work done, dependability, creativeness, initiative, and so forth—while workers are more likely than managers to explain advancement in terms that do not attach particular credit to the one who advances—having friends in higher management, political recommendations, elbowing, and seniority. In other words, persons at upper levels are more likely to say that adherence to performance criteria leads to advancement, while persons at the bottom perceive advancement to be based on arbitrary decisions. Workers take a more cynical view than managers do, attributing advancement to criteria that are less justifiable or not immediately related to performance, such as "seniority," "friends in higher management," and "recommendations of a political nature."

Although there appear to be systematic differences between

Table 3.19

PERCEIVED ADVANTAGES ASSOCIATED WITH HIGH POSITION

Q.55. What do you think are the main advantages of moving into a higher position in this plant?[a]	Top Management (n = 10)		Middle Management (n = 110)		Rank and File (n = 180)	
	Score	Rank	Score	Rank	Score	Rank
Prestige or esteem	1.0	7	0.8	7	1.2	5.5
Variety of work	1.3	5.5	0.9	6	1.4	2.5
Independence	1.3	5.5	1.2	5	1.2	5.5
Social contacts	0.3	8	0.3	8	0.6	8
Opportunity to make decisions	1.8	3	1.8	3	1.2	5.5
Opportunity to enlarge skills	2.4	1	2.3	2	1.4	2.5
Opportunity to enlarge knowledge	1.7	4	1.5	4	1.2	5.5
Influence people outside the plant	0.0	9	0.0	9	0.1	9
Higher wages	2.1	2	2.6	1	2.3	1

[a]Respondents were asked to select the three most important items and to rank them from 1 to 3 in the order of their importance. We assigned a score of 0 if the item was not ranked at all, 1 if the item was ranked third, 2 if the item was ranked second, and 3 if the item was ranked first. High scores imply high importance. The data in the column labeled "rank" represent the order of the items according to their scores.

groups, the order of criteria within groups is rather similar. Quality of work done and dependability rank high, and supervisor's opinion, seniority, friends in higher management, elbowing one's way, and recommendations of a political nature rank comparatively low in all groups. This agreement suggests that there are norms common to all members of industrial organizations.

The relative importance of the requirements is not that definite,

Table 3.20

CRITERIA FOR ADVANCEMENT

Q.16. How important is each of the following factors for getting ahead in this company?	Top Management (n = 9–10)		Middle Management (n = 116–121)		Rank and File (n = 171–188)	
	Score	Rank	Score	Rank	Score	Rank
Quality of work done	4.4	1	4.1	2	3.7	2*
Quantity of work done	3.7	6	3.6	9	3.4	7
Supervisor's opinion	3.2	9	3.8	7	3.6	4
Dependability	4.3	2	4.4	1	4.1	1
Creativeness, inventiveness	3.5	7.5	3.6	8	3.2	8
Seniority in the plant	2.2	10	2.6	10	2.9	10
Having friends in higher management	1.7	11	2.3	11	2.7	11*
Having good professional knowledge	3.5	7.5	3.9	4	3.4	6
Taking initiative	4.0	3	4.0	3	3.1	9**
Having outstanding ability to work with people	3.9	4	3.8	6	3.6	3
Loyalty to the company	3.8	5	3.9	5	3.5	5
Recommendations of political nature	1.3	12.5	1.4	13	1.6	13
Elbowing one's way to get ahead	1.3	12.5	1.8	12	1.9	12

*The difference between groups is significant at the .05 level of confidence.

**The difference between groups is significant at the .01 level of confidence.

however. For example, taking initiative is considered relatively important by top and middle managers and rather unimportant by rank-and-file persons, probably because, as shown earlier, the latter have little opportunity to demonstrate initiative; therefore, they are not likely to perceive it as a requirement for advancement. Since ability to work with people is perceived as relatively less important by middle management than by top management and the rank and file, one might speculate that persons in the middle are more responsible for coordinating activities than are persons at other levels, but feel that they are not adequately promoted even though they do a good job in working with people; therefore, they conclude that ability to work with people is unimportant as a criterion for advancement.

Conclusions

Our analysis shows a highly consistent effect of hierarchy that suggests two general conclusions:

1. The authoritative and asymmetrical character of hierarchy (Katz & Kahn, 1966, p. 216ff.) is very well reflected in role characteristics such as authority/influence and enriching qualities of the job, in demographic characteristics, and, consequently, in the reactions and adjustments of members and their perceptions concerning the system.

2. The less favorable situation of rank-and-file persons leads them to prefer a state different from the one in which they find themselves. It is understandable, therefore, that rank-and-file persons more than upper-level persons will want change (Dahrendorf, 1969, p. 41), especially in large plants, as data not presented here show,[22] although that desire for change does not imply a rejection of hierarchy and its consequences but simply a desire for modifications of the organization within a hierarchical framework.[23]

The acceptance of a hierarchical distribution of values shows either that there are some shared values and norms in support of hierarchy (Dahrendorf, 1969, p. 34ff.; Katz & Georgopoulos, 1972, p. 122; Tausky, 1970, p. 120) or that members accept hierarchy as a practical matter, since, after all, they cannot do much about it (Bartölke, 1969, p. 155ff.; Luhmann, 1975, p. 104ff.).

In either case, approval of the power distribution could be considered to imply some legitimation (Blau, 1974, p. 213), even though managers and workers may differ in details about the desired distribution of control and the desired participativeness of the system. But the systematic differences between groups in the preferences that they express indicate at least some difference in norms and values (Ziegler, 1970, p. 62ff.). Such differences are important because organizations as contrived systems (Katz & Kahn, 1966, p. 33ff.) are determined by dominant interests; anything that threatens that dominance threatens the organizational status quo.

The visible threat to the status quo appears to be moderate and does not mean that there will be immediate action for change, especially since lower-level members are dependent on their organization and socialized to accept hierarchical structures. The results of this study do not imply, however, that hierarchy and hierarchical gradients are natural and therefore necessary (Herbst, 1976). The fact that they are common does not make them inevitable. If one accepts that democracy is "power vested in the membership to legislate on policy" (Katz & Kahn, 1966, p. 45; also Bartölke & Wächter, 1974), then the plants studied are perceived by their members to be less than democratic. This perception coincides with that of labor-oriented critics who claim that the industrial relations system introduced in the Federal Republic of Germany in 1972 did not succeed in producing countervailing power for the workers.

Notes

[1]Suggestions and support from D. Flechsenberger, J. Gohl, E. Kappler, P. Nieder, U. Schumann, R. Wilfer, and especially W. Sodeur are gratefully acknowledged.
This research was made possible by a grant from Deutsche Forschungsgemeinschaft.

[2]The impressions about codetermination given by Jenkins (1973, p. 115ff.) mainly concern this aspect prior to the new law. A more detailed description prior to the new law is given by Emery and Thorsrud (1969, p. 42).

[3]Calculated on the basis of Statistisches Bundesamt (1974, p. 215).

[4]A note of caution does seem necessary. The data for the Federal Republic of Germany include averaged monetary bonuses, but the U.S. data do not.

[5]The reliability of the index for actual authority/influence is 0.80; for the desired authority/influence, 0.50. Reliabilities are calculated with a formula given by Nunnally (1967) ("internal scale reliability").

[6]The relevance of this phenomenon is described by Tannenbaum (e.g., 1968c, p. 307ff.).

[7]The reliability of the index is 0.88.

[8]This reasoning comes close to—but is not identical with—statements by Tausky (1970, p. 122ff.).

[9]The reliability of this index is 0.77.

[10]The reliability here is 0.74.

[11]The reliability of the index is 0.74.

[12]The reliability of this index is 0.65.

[13]Due to an error, the last question was excluded from the questionnaire for the person at the top of each plant. The reliability of the index is 0.71.

[14]The explanation given by Quinn, Staines, and McCullough that older persons have better jobs (U.S. Department of Labor, 1974, p. 12) does not apply here because of the controls used.

[15]The reliability of this index is 0.84.

[16]A chi-square test shows that the five items forming the index are strongly associated with each other.

[17]A discussion of these items is given in Bartölke et al. (1976).

[18]The reliabilities of the index are 0.87 for psychological adjustment and 0.82 for alienation.

[19]A similar interpretation is given by Bundesminister für Arbeit und Sozialordnung (1974, p. 203). The importance of this question is generally described, e.g., by Bartölke and Wächter (1974) and Vilmar (1971).

[20]This might be interpreted as support for the results of a study comparing British and German managers, which concluded that German managers prefer centralized decision making (Child & Kieser, 1975). See also Haire, Ghiselli, and Porter (1966), Hofstede (1974), Granick (1972), and Hartmann (1959) as cited by Child and Kieser (1975).

[21]The idea of codetermination in the Federal Republic of Germany is supported by the three major political parties, although there are definite differences in the amount and the form of codetermination that the parties support.

[22]This is probably the case, because unions and workers' councils can generally be expected to be more active in large plants and because large plants seem to exert more pressure for high performance (Bartölke, 1975).

[23]These conclusions are consistent with Tannenbaum et al. (1974).

4

Ireland

John Hurley and Noirin O'Broin

Introduction

Industrial Organizations in Ireland

A short description of the economic and industrial environment in which factories operate in the Republic of Ireland will acquaint readers in other countries with a few facts relevant to a study of hierarchy and decision making in Irish industry.

In a number of respects, such as the recruitment of managers, organizational structure, decision making, and management philosophy, Irish industry is similar to the free enterprise economies in Europe and the United States. Table 4.1 presents the percentage of the work force employed in agriculture, industry, and the services.

Table 4.1
DISTRIBUTION OF EMPLOYMENT

Employment Sector	Percentage of Total Employment
Agriculture	25.5%
Industry	30.0
Services	44.4
Total	100.0

Source: Kennedy and Bruton, 1975, p. 11, Table 1.6.

Size of factories. The average factory employs approximately 60 people, according to the Census of Industrial Production, 1968. The census excluded factories employing less than 3 people, and for this

67

reason the average figure of 60 is likely to be higher than if the census had included all factories. Table 4.2, based on that census, shows that the majority of factories employ fewer than 100 people.

Table 4.2

PROPORTION OF FACTORIES BY NUMBER EMPLOYED

Number Employed	Percentage of Factories
Under 15	41.3%
15–99	45.1
100–499	11.9
500 and over	1.7
Total	100.0

Ownership of factories. There is considerable emphasis in Ireland on decentralization; most of our industries are owned by corporations, partnerships, or individuals. Very few industries are owned by the state; in fact, there is a strong emphasis on private ownership and the rights of individuals to own small farms and small industries. Those industries that are owned by the state tend to be large essential utilities, notably the transport organization (CIE) and the electricity utility (ESB).

Several state agencies operate to encourage corporations and individuals to set up industries, offering expertise, financing, and a thorough knowledge of the local situation. Furthermore, in order to diversify Ireland's mainly agricultural economy and bring in valuable expertise, it has become government policy to use tax concessions to attract foreign plants to Ireland.

Unionization. Table 4.3 compares the degree of unionization in Ireland with that in eight other European countries. The years given are those for which comparable statistics were available.

Industrial disputes. Table 4.4 provides statistics for industrial disputes in Ireland and other European Economic Community countries in 1967–71.

Kennedy and Bruton make the following observations regarding industrial disputes in Ireland:

> The principal cause of Ireland's high loss of man-days was the long duration of disputes .... The number of workers involved per dispute in Ireland was comparatively small. A comparatively small number of lengthy disputes accounts for a high proportion of total man-days lost ...

Table 4.3

DEGREE OF UNIONIZATION IN SELECTED COUNTRIES,
AS PERCENTAGE OF TOTAL WORK FORCE

Country	Year	Degree of Unionization
Belgium	1966	67.6%
Austria	1965	66.1
Ireland	1966	*52.3*
Norway	1966	50.0
Sweden	1968	49.0
Denmark	1968	48.5
United Kingdom	1966	42.0
Federal Republic of Germany	1966	40.0
Switzerland	1968	19.0

Source: Hillery and Kelly, 1974, pp. 26–27.

due (perhaps) to the prevalence of the comparability principle, so that key bargains, because of their repercussions, are negotiated with more intransigence than an isolated claim would warrant. The multiplicity of unions and employers involved in some negotiations has also been blamed for delay in settling disputes. Inter-union rivalry itself has been a cause of some complex and prolonged disputes. Moreover, workers in Ireland typically do not give delegated authority to their union representatives to conclude a settlement so that each new offer involves a ballot of the membership before acceptance. The ability of workers to take up temporary jobs in the United Kingdom can also delay a speedy settlement. (Kennedy & Bruton, 1975, pp. 90–91)

Joint consultation. A study by Murphy in 1969 showed that, of 53 firms employing between 100 and 500 people, 32 percent used some method of joint consultation. The comparable figure for larger firms was 55 percent; for smaller firms, 11 percent. Murphy's continuing research indicates a trend toward increased use of joint consultation.

Joint consultation in Ireland more often takes place through work councils or joint committees composed of both management and employee representatives. Matters that are the subject of negotiation between unions and management are excluded as a rule; the councils or committees limit themselves to seeking improvement in factory amenities such as heating and ventilation, canteens, toilets, protective clothing for workers, safety arrangements, the operation of suggestion schemes, and the sale of goods made in the factory to employees.

Table 4.4

INDUSTRIAL DISPUTES IN SELECTED COUNTRIES

EEC Country	Number of Disputes per 1,000 Employees	Person-days Lost per 1,000 Employees	Number of Workers Involved per Dispute	Number of Days Worker Remains Out of Work
Belgium	3.8	232.5	519	11.8
Denmark	2.1	24.5	703	1.6
France[a]	19.0	201.2	732	1.5
Germany	n.a.	49.0	n.a.	5.9
Ireland	*16.8*	*776.8*	320	14.5
Italy	31.1	1,372.5	1,135	3.9
Netherlands	0.9	21.6	661	3.8
United Kingdom	12.0	338.1	556	5.1
Luxembourg	n.a.	n.a.	n.a.	n.a.

[a]Data for France exclude 1968.

Source: Kennedy and Bruton, 1975, p. 91.

Participation in decision making. Participation in decision making is an important question for Ireland. Membership in the European Economic Community involved the country in a movement toward a form of shared decision making in industry, in order to comply with the requirement that practices should be uniform within the member states. One of the options suggested in the relevant European Economic Community document (EEC, 1975)— the one-board system with employee representation—became part of the Irish Legal Code in April 1977. The Work Participation (State Enterprises) Act of that year provides for the election by the employees of one-third of the boards of certain state-owned bodies.

Characteristics of Plants Studied

The participants in the Irish study are employed in five distinct industries—canning, furniture, plastics, metal works, and foundries. These industries were chosen for the sake of comparability with the work of Tannenbaum and others (1974). A minority of people engaged in manufacturing are employed in these five industries; it

is not claimed that the participants in the Irish study are representative of industrial workers and managers. Tannenbaum and others
had sampled one large and one small plant, each of which was
functioning as an independent unit, from each of these five industries, or ten plants in all. We did the same, as far as we could.
However, as it proved difficult to secure the participation of a small
foundry functioning as an independent unit, a small metal works
was substituted; therefore, there were two small metal works in the
study. The numbers of people employed in the large and small factories in the sample are shown in Table 4.5.

Table 4.5

SIZES OF PLANTS IN SAMPLE

Plant Type	Small Plants		Large Plants	
	Number of Employees	Number of Levels	Number of Employees	Number of Levels
Plastics	60	4	550	6
Foundry	—	—	300	5
Canning	232	6	690	6
Metal works	51 and 55	4 and 5	580	5
Furniture	43	4	435	5

Two of the eight factories are Irish-owned; three are British;
two are American; and one is French. Of the two remaining factories, one is a subsidiary of a state-owned company and one is
owned by a set of partners.

Of the 302 individuals in the study, 10 are top managers, 126
are middle managers and supervisors, and 166 are "rank-and-file"
workers, a term used in the study to denote people with no subordinates.

Correlates of Hierarchy

Economic and Demographic Characteristics

Individuals in top and middle management positions in the Irish
sample differ in a number of important respects from the rank and
file. Table 4.6 shows that upper-level people, on the average, are
older, have more education, have been in the company longer, and

are paid more than lower-level people. There are no women in the top jobs, and so few middle managers are women that they do not register as percentages in the table.

Table 4.6

ECONOMIC AND DEMOGRAPHIC CHARACTERISTICS OF MEMBERS

	Top Management (n = 10)	Middle Management (n = 126)	Rank and File (n = 166)
Salary (average £s per month)	512.1	183.7	100.5
Education[a] (average years)	11.9	10.8	9.8
Age (average years)	46.1	39.5	32.8
Plant seniority (average years)	6.0	5.9	4.8
Sex (percentage female)	0.0	0.0	20.0

[a]Education is measured on a scale where 1 = less than 4 years, 2 = 4 to 6 years, 3 = 6 to 8 years, 4 = 8 to 10 years, 5 = 10 to 12 years, and 6 = more than 12 years of education.

Tannenbaum and others (1974) noted in an earlier study that in the United States, top persons — who were likely to be the owners in the small organizations — were paid more, on the average, than top persons in large organizations. The reverse was true in the Irish study. However, the large plants were either branches of foreign establishments or autonomous companies set up by non-nationals. Only one of the small plants was owned and managed by a foreign establishment; one other, while Irish-owned, was managed by a non-national.

Tannenbaum and others also noted that although few women held management positions, women had a somewhat larger share of management positions in small factories than in large ones. This was attributed to family ownership. None of the small family-owned businesses in the Irish study employed women as managers.

Role Characteristics

Authority and influence. An index of authority and influence was constructed as the average of responses to the following questions:

Q.1g.   In your work to what extent can you have authority over other people?

Q.26d. How much influence do you, personally, actually have on what happens in this plant?

A parallel set of questions designed to measure the amount of authority/influence respondents prefer to have (Q.2g and Q.27d) simply substituted the words "would like to have" and "should have" in the two questions, respectively.

Figure 4.1 shows that authority and influence are distributed hierarchically. Individuals at upper levels perceive themselves as having significantly more authority and influence than those at lower levels perceive themselves as having, which shows that the survey results (based on the perceptions of large numbers of individuals) are directly in line with the actual practice of authority and influence. Furthermore, the discrepancy between the amount of authority and influence individuals actually have and the amount they would like to have is greater at the bottom of the hierarchy than at the top.

It is only at the top level that organization members in the Irish sample do not want more authority or influence than they have. It is rare for reality to exceed one's ambition: The more one has of anything desirable, the more of it one usually wants. The fact that those at the top feel they have more authority and influence than they need while those at the lower levels feel they do not have enough may well be the basis on which some method of sharing responsibility will develop.

At the top and bottom levels of hierarchy, the results for the measure of authority are very similar to those for the measure of influence, as shown in Table 4.7. The people at the top imply that their influence comes close to matching their authority; those at the bottom indicate having little of either; but the amount of authority exercised by individuals in the middle positions is not matched by the amount of influence they exercise. Supervisors and middle managers see a gap between the authority vested in them and the influence or power they command; as a group, they have much less influence than authority. In other words, they have the trappings of power but not the reality. This gap at middle levels, which is also apparent in the data from the Federal Republic of Germany (4.3 as against 3.1) and Hungary (3.8 as against 3.0), suggests the

Figure 4.1
HIERARCHICAL DISTRIBUTION OF AUTHORITY/INFLUENCE
BASED ON SELF-REPORTS

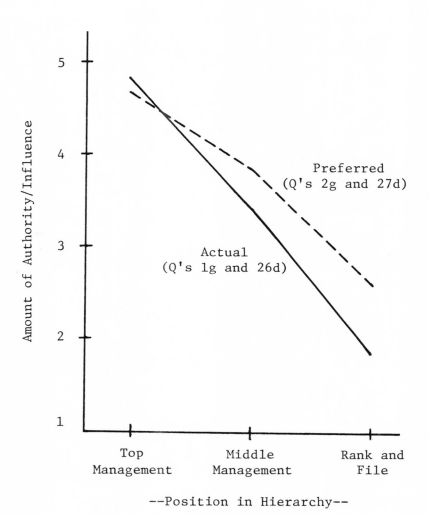

wisdom of considering authority and influence as separate entities for certain types of analyses.

Table 4.7

HIERARCHICAL DISTRIBUTION OF AUTHORITY AND INFLUENCE

	Top Management	Middle Management	Rank and File
Actual authority (Q.1g)	4.9	3.8	1.7
Actual influence (Q.26d)	4.7	3.0	1.9

Distribution of control (control graph). The previous section reported data from each respondent about his or her own personal authority and influence; this section presents data from all respondents about the influence of each hierarchical group. We thus have respondents' judgments about the distribution of control in their plants. Figure 4.2 presents these judgments as averages for all respondents. It also supplies an overall view of the degree of control that respondents think should be exercised by each of the hierarchical groups. Not only is amount of control clearly related to hierarchical level, but individuals also want hierarchical distinctions to be maintained, although they prefer middle management to have somewhat more control and workers substantially more control than these groups do have.

Participativeness and supportiveness of superior. Advocates of participation in decision making argue that it is desirable socially, economically, politically, and psychologically to involve the work force directly in decisions affecting their working lives. Table 4.8 indicates that higher-level superiors are reported to behave more participatively toward subordinates than lower-level superiors do. While superiors of middle managers appear to differ little from superiors of rank-and-file workers in indicators of support such as friendliness and approachability (Q.43) and the freedom they give subordinates to bring complaints to them (Q.44), the former superiors appear distinctly more inclined to ask for subordinates' opinions on work problems (Q.41) and to take account of what the subordinates have to say (Q.42). Superiors at lower levels, however, appear reluctant to carry the practice of participation to that extent. Perhaps the design of higher-level jobs enables more participation to take place between managers and their managerial or supervisory

Figure 4.2
DISTRIBUTION OF CONTROL AS REPORTED BY ALL MEMBERS

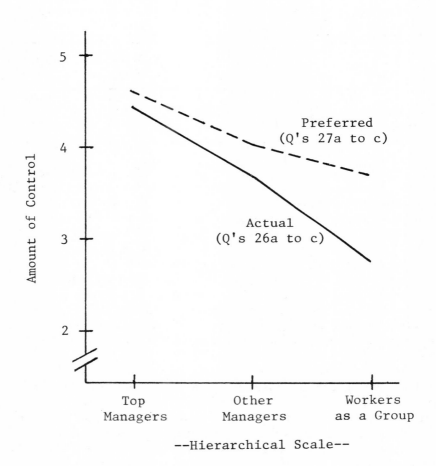

subordinates. Planning and coordinating are considered at present to be the responsibilities of persons at higher levels, whereas the final implementation of decisions falls to the rank and file. This division of functions—planning and coordinating at higher levels and final implementation of decisions at lower levels—means that participation is more likely to occur among those at higher levels in the organization, frequently to the exclusion of the lower-level worker.

Table 4.8

PARTICIPATIVENESS AND SUPPORTIVENESS OF SUPERIOR

	Middle Management	Rank and File
Q.41. Does your immediate superior ask your opinion when a problem comes up that involves your work?	4.4	3.4
Q.42. Is your immediate superior inclined to take into account your opinion and suggestions?	3.9	2.9
Q.43. Is your immediate superior friendly and easily approached if there are problems?	4.3	4.0
Q.44. Does your immediate superior make people under him feel free to take their complaints to him?	4.1	3.8
Q.46. Do you have trust in your immediate superior?	4.1	3.9
Average	4.1	3.6

Bases of superior's power. A person who accepts a job in an organization is generally expected to follow the instructions of his or her immediate superior. But subordinates may attend to the orders of superiors for different reasons corresponding to the bases of power suggested by French and Raven (1959): from a sense of duty (legitimate power), because of the promise of reward or the threat of penalty (reward or coercive power), because their superior is "a nice guy" (referent power), or because they respect the superior's competence and judgment (expert power). Or they may feel that the efficiency of the organization depends on their compliance (Metcalf & Urwick, 1940). Table 4.9 shows the reactions of middle managers and rank-and-file persons to these possibilities.

Table 4.9

BASES OF THE SUPERIOR'S POWER AS REPORTED BY SUBORDINATES

Q.47. When you do what your immediate superior requests you to do on the job, why do you do it?	Middle Management	Rank and File
I respect his competence and judgment.	3.8	3.9
He can give special help and benefits.	2.8	2.7
He's a nice guy.	2.9	2.4
He can penalize or otherwise disadvantage me.	2.3	2.0
It is my duty.	4.3	4.2
It is necessary if the organization is to function properly.	4.4	4.6

Note: The differences between the reactions of middle management and rank and file to the third and fourth statements are significant at the .05 level.

The difference between the answers of management and rank and file is statistically significant with respect to only two of the items: Middle managers indicate more often than the rank and file that they are more likely to carry out their superior's requests because he is "a nice guy" and because he could penalize them if they do not carry out his orders. However, neither managers nor rank-and-file participants give these as the principal reasons for complying with directions. Both of these groups indicate as the more important reasons that to do so is necessary if the organization is to function properly, that it is their duty as subordinates, and that they respect the superior's competence and judgment. The most noticeable feature of Table 4.9 is the agreement among members in different hierarchical levels that these are their main reasons for complying with their immediate superiors' wishes. These reasons are part of the explanation commonly given for the efficiency of bureaucracy as a form of organization.

Enriching qualities of the job. Figure 4.3 indicates that hierarchical level has a substantial impact on the opportunities provided by a job to learn new things; use one's abilities, knowledge, and skills; do interesting work; talk with other people during work time; and decide the pace of work. These are enriching qualities in a job. The correlation between hierarchical level and an index composed of these qualities is .52. The index is also substantially associated with the measure of authority/influence, as can be seen by the correlation of .68.

Members of all levels would like more enriching job opportunities than they perceive themselves to have, although the rank and file display the largest gap between their preference and their experience, as shown in Table 4.10. It is apparent that rank-and-file jobs need to be redesigned to incorporate more of these opportunities.

The scale of authority in the authority/influence index might be compared, because of similar wording, with the index of enriching qualities of the job. Table 4.10 shows that the rank and file perceive themselves to have substantially less authority than enriching job qualities. The other two groups have roughly equal amounts of each. Furthermore, the rank and file prefer that the gap between them and the top of the hierarchy decrease more with regard to enriching qualities than to authority. Indeed, all three hierarchical groups look less for gains in authority than in enriching job qualities, which suggests that authority in their eyes is a mixed blessing. Nonetheless, enriching job qualities are more in evidence among those who have greater authority. The desire of the rank and file to have more of both while at the same time maintaining the gap in authority between the managers and themselves may therefore be somewhat unrealistic. It may not really be possible to enrich a job without introducing an element of authority into it.

Physical qualities of the job. The participants in the study were supplied with a list of adjectives (Q.3) that would enable them to describe their job in terms that have positive or negative connotations—whether, for instance, the job is more or less varied or routine, safe or dangerous, tiring or not tiring, healthful or unhealthful, physical or mental, and clean or dirty. Figure 4.4

Figure 4.3
ENRICHING QUALITIES OF THE JOB BASED ON SELF-REPORTS

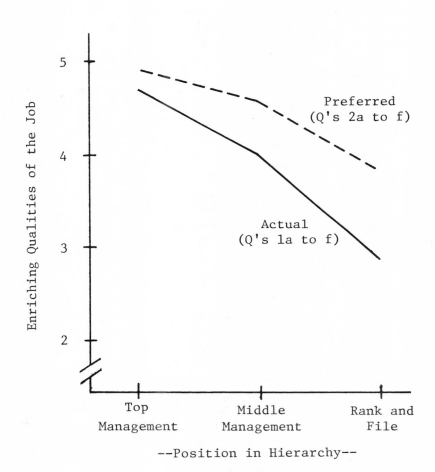

Table 4.10
ENRICHING QUALITIES OF THE JOB AND AUTHORITY
IN JOB—ACTUAL AND PREFERRED

	Actual Situation		Preferred Situation	
	Enriching Qualities	Authority	Enriching Qualities	Authority
Top management	4.6	4.9	4.8	4.6
Middle management	3.9	3.8	4.5	4.0
Rank and file	3.0	1.7	4.0	2.5

presents the results. Most of what are ordinarily considered to be desirable qualities are more often found in top- or middle-level jobs than in jobs at the bottom. For example, managerial jobs are perceived to be cleaner, more varied, more healthful, safer, and more mental (as opposed to physical) than nonmanagerial jobs.. Table 4.11 shows that the lower a person is placed in the organization, the less frequently these desirable qualities of jobs occur, on the average.

Reactions and Adjustments

Morale

Table 4.12 shows that top and middle managers are more satisfied with their jobs and pay than are the rank and file. Managers are also more satisfied with plant leadership and believe that the people in charge are genuinely interested in employee welfare and that the leadership tends to initiate improvements in working conditions and to take care of complaints. Managers' responses to these items, which constitute "attitude toward plant leadership" in Table 4.12, are partly an assessment of their own performance, of course. These reactions, along with the greater satisfaction with job and pay that managers evidence, indicate that they are getting a good deal more psychologically from the system than are rank-and-file members.

Table 4.13 presents the results of a regression analysis that shows the extent to which some of the correlates of hierarchy that we have considered in the previous section contribute to job satisfaction, satisfaction with pay, and attitudes toward company leader-

Figure 4.4

PHYSICAL QUALITIES OF THE JOB AS REPORTED BY THREE HIERARCHICAL LEVELS

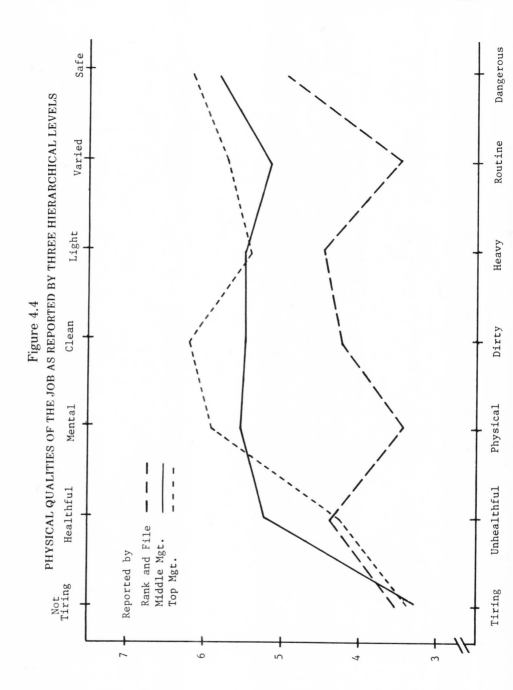

Table 4.11

PHYSICAL QUALITIES OF THE JOB

	Top Management	Middle Management	Rank and File
Average (Q.3)	5.2	5.1	4.0

Table 4.12

MORALE

	Top Management	Middle Management	Rank and File
Job satisfaction (Q.8, 9, 10)	4.8	3.9	3.4
Satisfaction with pay (Q.59)	4.1	3.1	2.8
Attitude toward plant leadership (Q.24, 25, 28)	4.2	3.7	3.2

Note: All differences between groups are significant at the .05 level at least.

ship.

The best single predictor of job satisfaction is the index of enriching qualities of the job. People are more likely to be satisfied to the extent that their jobs include possibilities for them to learn new things, use their skills and abilities, do interesting work, talk with other people while at work, and decide their pace of work—characteristics, it seems, that are very likely to be associated with hierarchical position.

Other factors that appear to be less influential, although significant, in job satisfaction are the age of the individual answering the question, the length of the hierarchy to which he or she belongs, and the physical qualities of the job he or she has been given to do. That job satisfaction increases with age is a common research finding, occurring in other countries of this research and in earlier work

Table 4.13

THE RELATIVE IMPORTANCE OF THE PREDICTORS OF MORALE

Predictors	Job Satisfaction .64**		Satisfaction with Pay .44**		Attitude toward Plant Leadership .58**	
Multiple R	Beta	Rank	Beta	Rank	Beta	Rank
Enriching job qualities	.38**	1	.04	7	.26**	2
Authority/influence	.14	4	.17	3	.33**	1
Physical job qualities	.13**	5	.09	4	.18**	3
Education	.01	9	−.08	5.5	−.11	6
Age	.19**	2	.01	9	.12*	5
Plant seniority	.02	8	−.20**	1	−.14*	4
Length of chain	.15**	3	.03	8	.08	7
Level in hierarchy	−.12	6	.08	5.5	−.05	9
Salary	.08	7	.18	2	−.07	8

*p ≤ .05.
**p ≤ .01.

(Tannenbaum et al., 1974). However, the positive effect of length of hierarchy is not replicated in these other studies, although it is supported by Crozier's (1971) discovery that lower-level office workers value elongated hierarchies for the greater opportunities these afford for increases in status through promotion. Understandably, better working conditions, or "physical qualities of the job" as they are labelled in this study, also increase one's liking for one's work, contribute to the feeling that the work is more interesting than one's outside work activities, and encourage the view that the organization for which one works is a good one. And yet better physical working conditions themselves, as we have measured them, do not have as great an effect on job satisfaction as do enriching qualities of the job, which seems consistent, in principle, with traditional arguments of "human relations."

Satisfaction with pay proved more difficult to predict: only one factor, seniority in the plant, appears to affect it—by decreasing it.

Table 4.13 appears to show that persons who have more authority and influence and who have jobs that provide more enriching opportunities and better working conditions show a more favorable attitude toward company leadership. Older employees also express a more favorable attitude. High seniority in the organization tends, however, to make one more critical of management (under the conditions of this regression analysis in which level in the hierarchy is controlled). More experienced employees may be jealous of less experienced individuals who have been given positions equal to their own. Persons with high seniority may feel that they deserve a higher position and greater rewards than persons with lower seniority deserve. Yet older persons do not seem less satisfied and favorable than do younger persons at a comparable level in the hierarchy—quite the contrary.

Motivation

The motivation of individuals at work is measured here in a number of ways. One set of questions establishes the extent to which individuals feel responsible for the success of their own work, of their own work group, of their department, and of the plant as a whole. Since top managers make decisions affecting the plant as a whole and middle managers are formally assigned responsibility for the efficiency of their work groups and/or departments, it is to be expected that both of these groups would feel more responsible for success in these areas than would the rank and file. Table 4.14 shows that the hierarchical factor clearly influences these reactions; it has the least effect, however, on the degree to which individuals

feel responsible for the success of their own work. Increased commitment to the success of a group, department, or organization appears to follow from being given responsibility and, as we shall see
below, authority with regard to such matters. It could be that enlarging the jobs of the rank and file would increase their commitment in the same way.

Table 4.14

FEELINGS OF RESPONSIBILITY ACCORDING
TO POSITION IN HIERARCHY

Q.11. To what extent do you feel really responsible for the success of:	Top Management	Middle Management	Rank and File
Your own work	4.8	4.7	4.5
Your own work group	4.4	4.5	3.7
Your department	—	4.5	3.6
The whole plant	4.5	3.6	3.0

The information in Table 4.14 about the degree of responsibility
felt by individuals for their own group, department, and plant was
assembled in order to measure the responsibility each person feels
for the total system. Table 4.15 presents this information according
to the level of the individuals in the hierarchy and compares it with
the degree to which the participants feel responsible for their own
work and with two other measures of motivation. The first,
"motivation on the job," was ascertained from replies to the question, "In your kind of job, is it usually better to let your superiors
worry about introducing better or faster ways of doing the work?"
The second, "initiative," was ascertained from replies to the question, "How often do you try out on your own a better or faster way
of doing the work?" Again, hierarchical differences are apparent.
The lower level of motivation and initiative among the rank and file
may reflect an apprehension that contributing ideas to the improvement of work methods might lead to layoffs or to a reduction in
their earnings. Superiors, moreover, might feel uneasy if their subordinates produce ideas that they themselves should have thought
of. Notwithstanding these considerations, rank-and-file participants
indicate that they "sometimes" try out better ways of doing their

work. It is not surprising that managers indicate that they are more likely to take such initiatives. Managers will almost certainly be rewarded for useful and productive innovations, but the outcome for rank-and-file members is less predictable. Their jobs could become more secure due to their plant becoming more productive and competitive. There is also the possibility, however, that innovative ideas could introduce computer-assisted methods and reductions in the numbers of rank-and-file workers employed, while managers' jobs, in spite of many technological changes, are still more secure. This reality could explain the reluctance of the rank and file to try out improved methods of working.

Table 4.15

MOTIVATIONAL ASPECTS

	Top Management	Middle Management	Rank and File
Responsibility for the system[a] (Q.11a, b, c)	4.5	4.2	3.3
Responsibility for own work (Q.11d)	4.8	4.7	4.5
Motivation on the job (Q.6)	—	4.0	3.0
Initiative (Q.7)	4.2	3.8	3.1

[a]Index based on measures of responsibility for success of work group, department, and plant.

Table 4.16 presents the results of regression analyses designed to establish the contribution of some of the correlates of hierarchy to the indices of motivation. It suggests that a sense of responsibility for the total system may be greater in individuals who have jobs with enriching opportunities and in those who can exercise authority and influence. However, none of the nine factors listed in Table 4.16 appears to affect the responsibility individuals feel for the success of their own work. On the other hand, five of these factors seem to affect motivation on the job: Three appear to increase it and two to decrease it. Thus, individuals with a higher rather than a lower position in the hierarchy, with greater rather than fewer enriching job opportunities, and with a longer rather than shorter educational background are less likely to leave it to their superiors to think out better ways of doing their work. The tendency to leave considerations of this kind to superiors may be more noticeable among members of longer rather than shorter hierarchies and among older rather than younger people, even though older people may feel more responsible for the system than younger people do. Perhaps past failures to bring about changes may lead to a disinclination among older people to consider change. Or it may be that older people are more hierarchically oriented; they may think, per- haps as a result of prolonged social conditioning, that it is the business of superiors to initiate and of subordinates to follow the lines laid down for them. A decline in creativity with advancing years cannot be ruled out as another possible reason for the less "motivated" reactions of the older people in the study. In any case, they cannot change their jobs as easily as younger colleagues, whose prospects of future jobs enable them somewhat more to risk the consequences of wrong decisions.

The last column in Table 4.16 suggests that initiative is more likely to come from individuals who have jobs with more rather than fewer enriching opportunities and from those with a longer educational background. Persons in jobs with unfavorable physical qualities, however, appear to show more initiative than persons in "better" jobs, other things being equal. Poor working conditions may lead some persons to try to initiate change.

Mobility Aspirations

Promotion normally involves greater responsibility; it may also entail more worries and expose the promoted person to more criticism. It can be particularly worrisome if subordinates refuse to cooperate or to do their work efficiently. The promoted person may also be expected to undergo training that will entail some sacrifice on his or her part. Table 4.17 shows the extent to which in- dividuals at different hierarchical levels would accept a position of higher rank despite such problems. Managers appear more willing than rank-and-file workers to tackle the difficulties that promotion might bring.

Personal Adjustment

Since lower-level jobs are usually less fulfilling, it was expected that lower-level workers would not be as well "adjusted" psychologi- cally as individuals at higher levels; that is, that they would assent more often to questionnaire statements implying that they felt

Table 4.16

THE RELATIVE IMPORTANCE OF THE PREDICTORS OF MOTIVATIONAL ASPECTS

Predictors	Responsibility for System .53**		Responsibility for Own Work .27*		Motivation .53**		Initiative .47**	
Multiple R	Beta	Rank	Beta	Rank	Beta	Rank	Beta	Rank
Enriching job qualities	.27**	1.5	.13	3	.28**	2	.36**	1
Authority/influence	.27**	1.5	.19	1	.01	8	.03	7
Physical job qualities	.02	6	.08	5	-.00	9	-.13*	2
Education	.01	8	.06	7	.12*	5	.12*	3
Age	.16**	3	.06	8	-.20**	3	.02	8
Plant seniority	.00	9	.01	9	.08	7	.06	5
Length of chain	-.02	7	.06	6	-.14*	4	-.01	9
Level in hierarchy	.02	5	-.14	2	.33**	1	.08	4
Salary	-.12	4	-.09	4	-.09	6	.04	6

*p ≤ .05.
**p ≤ .01.

Table 4.17

UPWARD MOBILITY ASPIRATION

Q.48. Imagine you were offered the following possibilities within this plant. Would you accept them or not?	Percentage Who Would Accept a Higher Position Despite Difficulties	
	Middle Management	Rank and File
Move to a higher position involving:		
Additional obligations and responsibilities	80%	60%
Training requirements	80	60
Frequent criticism	70	40
Problem employees	50	40
More work worries	70	40
Average	70	48

bored, depressed, or resentful, for example, or that they sometimes felt that their lives were not very useful. We refer to an index based on such items as "psychological adjustment." Alienation, a second index of adjustment, is based on questions designed to measure feelings of powerlessness, meaninglessness, normlessness, social isolation, and self-estrangement (Dean, 1961; Seeman, 1959). The correlates of hierarchy, including authority/influence and enriching opportunities, should affect the hierarchical distribution of alienation as well as of psychological adjustment. Tables 4.18 and 4.19 show that with each higher level, adjustment as measured by both indexes does in fact improve. Interestingly, on the alienation questions rank-and-file members expressed feelings of regret that they had "not had the influence over others that I would have liked" and that "men like me cannot influence the course of events." This is in line with the finding in Table 4.17 that 60 percent of rank-and-file workers would accept a higher level position if it were offered to them. Their higher alienation probably reflects the reality that very few rank-and-file workers do in fact move up the hierarchy.

Table 4.18

PSYCHOLOGICAL ADJUSTMENT[a]

Q.49. How true are the following statements?	Top Management	Middle Management	Rank and File
I feel depressed.	4.4	3.9	3.5
Other people are always more lucky than I.	4.6	4.1	3.4
Usually everything I try seems to fail.	4.5	4.6	4.2
Things seem hopeless.	5.0	4.6	4.2
I feel resentful.	4.7	4.4	4.2
I sometimes feel that my life is not very useful.	4.6	4.6	4.2
Average	4.6	4.4	3.9

[a]High score implies disagreement with the item and, therefore, "good" adjustment.

According to the regression analyses of Table 4.20, enriching job opportunities and other "positive" qualities of work seem to explain in part the better psychological adjustment at upper levels. Authority/influence and enriching opportunities appear especially relevant to alienation. Older individuals also appear to be better adjusted psychologically, as do those who belong to longer hierarchies. As with most regression analyses, however, we cannot distinguish cause from effect.

Perceptions

It is our hypothesis that persons at different levels differ in their perceptions of organizational life. More specifically, persons at upper levels are likely to see their organization in a more favorable light than do persons at lower levels. Furthermore, upper-level persons are likely to see their organization working the way it *should* be working, while persons at the bottom are more likely to see a substantial gap between the way the organization is and the way it should be.

Table 4.19
ALIENATION[a]

Q.52. How true are the following statements?	Top Management	Middle Management	Rank and File
It is not possible to rely on others.	2.2	2.3	2.9
Today it is practically impossible to find real friends because everyone thinks only of himself.	2.0	2.1	2.9
Men like me cannot influence the course of events; only men in high position can have such influence.	2.0	2.3	3.4
I have never had the influence over others that I would have liked.	1.6	2.3	3.1
Public affairs are so complicated that one cannot help but be confused by them.	1.8	2.7	3.4
Despite the many advances science has made, life today is too complicated.	3.0	2.4	3.1
I can never do what I really like because circumstances require that I do otherwise.	2.2	2.7	3.4
Life is so routinized that I do not have a chance to use my true abilities.	1.7	2.2	2.9
Life seems to be moving on without rules or order.	1.9	2.2	2.6
Nowadays it is hard to know right from wrong.	1.3	1.8	2.4
Average	2.0	2.3	3.0

[a]High score means agreement with the item and, therefore, high alienation.

Table 4.20
THE RELATIVE IMPORTANCE OF THE
PREDICTORS OF PERSONAL ADJUSTMENT

Multiple R	Psychological Adjustment .49**		Alienation .53**	
Predictors	Beta	Rank	Beta	Rank
Enriching job qualities	.25**	1	−.19*	2
Authority/influence	.11	6	−.33**	1
Physical job qualities	.19**	2	−.05	5
Education	.01	9	−.05	7
Age	.13*	4	.00	9
Plant seniority	−.07	8	−.04	8
Length of chain	.15*	3	−.05	6
Level in hierarchy	−.12	5	.17	4
Salary	.07	7	−.17	3

*p ≤ .05.
**p ≤ .01.

Decision making. How do persons at the top differ from those at the bottom in their perception of decision making in the organization? Given the positive social connotations that are attached to participative decision making in contemporary Ireland, we would expect upper-level persons to see their organization, or at least to represent it, as more participative than do lower-level persons.

We rely for our measure of participation on the model proposed by Likert (1961), who defined four systems of organization that differed in participation from 1, "exploitative authoritative," through 2, "benevolent authoritative," and 3, "consultative," to 4, "group participative."

Some of the questions Likert devised to measure the participativeness of organizations are included in this study; these concern the extent to which workers are involved in making decisions about their work, or about the plants in which they work, and the extent to which workers are consulted when decisions affecting them are being made. Table 4.21 suggests that top and middle managers perceive their organization to be slightly more participative and consultative than do the rank and file; but perhaps more significantly, the gap between how decisions are made and how they should be made increases with hierarchical descent. According to persons at the top, decision making is pretty much the way it should be, but it is not so according to those at the bottom. Part of the explanation for the large gap at the bottom, of course, is the greater degree of participativeness for the organization that persons at the bottom want compared to what persons at the top want.

The average person at all levels sees the system of management as close to the "benevolent authoritative" variety; that is, workers are *sometimes* asked for their opinions and suggestions before decisions are made about their work or about the plants they work in, but they rarely, if ever, participate fully in making decisions about these matters. Rank-and-file and middle-management participants prefer a relatively "consultative" approach, where it would be the norm for workers to be consulted on such questions. Top-management participants, on the other hand, prefer only a slight modification of the prevailing "benevolent authoritative" type of system—although, like the middle managers and the rank and file, they agree that individuals should be consulted before decisions affecting them personally are made. It is clear from the top managers' answers that they think that the organization is already close to a consultative norm on this aspect of participation, whereas the rank and file report a more authoritative norm. It is on this subject that managers, both top and middle, differ most from the rank and file. Managers do "participate" more than workers do, of course, and, projecting from their own experience, they may therefore see the whole organization as relatively participative; or perhaps managers rationalize, seeing themselves as consulting with others when making decisions affecting these persons, since such consultation is the "proper" thing to do.

Distribution of control. As shown in Figure 4.2, the higher an individual's position in the hierarchy, the more influence or control he or she is seen to exercise. Figure 4.5 shows this distribution of control as perceived by persons at different hierarchical levels. All groups do, in fact, perceive a hierarchical distribution of control, and all agree that a hierarchical distribution should be maintained. The gap between how it is and how it should be, however, is greater at the bottom than at the top, in the view of groups at every level (Figure 4.5).

Rank-and-file and middle-management participants feel that workers as a group should exercise substantially more control, and middle management somewhat more control, than they currently exercise. On the other hand, middle managers more than the rank and file and even more than the top managers themselves think that top managers should have more influence in their plants than

Table 4.21

PERCEPTIONS AND PREFERENCES ABOUT THE PARTICIPATIVENESS
IN THE PLANTS, MEASURED IN TERMS OF LIKERT'S MODEL

	Perceptions by:[a]		
	Top Management	Middle Management	Rank and File
Q.34. Actual participation by workers in job decisions	2.1	2.2	2.0
Q.35. Preferred participation by workers in job decisions	2.4	2.9	3.0
Discrepancy Q.35 − Q.34	0.3	0.7	1.0
Q.36. Actual participation by workers in plant decisions	1.9	2.0	1.8
Q.37. Preferred participation by workers in plant decisions	2.1	2.7	2.7
Discrepancy Q.37 − Q.36	0.2	0.7	0.9
Q.39. Actual extent to which opinions are asked of those who are affected by decisions	2.8	2.5	2.0
Q.40. Preferred extent	3.0	3.4	3.4
Discrepancy Q.40 − Q.39	0.2	0.9	1.4

[a]The data presented in this table are averages for the respective groups on a four-point scale where 4 implies a high degree of participation.

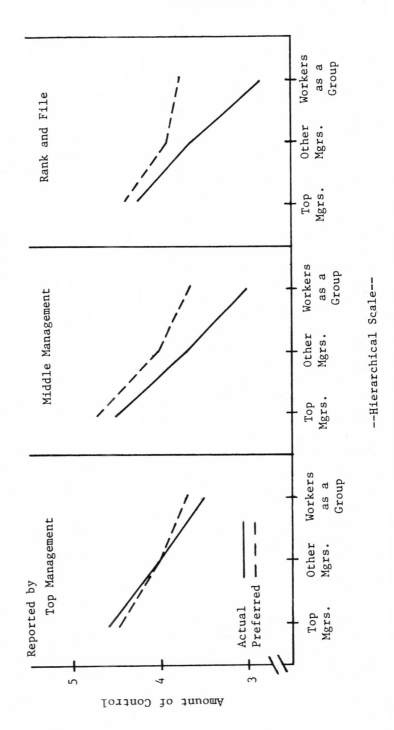

Figure 4.5

DISTRIBUTION OF CONTROL AS REPORTED BY PERSONS AT THREE HIERARCHICAL LEVELS

they already have. Top managers themselves do not wish for more control than they already have.

Rewards and sanctions. Table 4.22 presents the perceptions of top and middle managers and rank and file as to what the consequences are for particularly good work. Rank-and-file workers see fewer rewards of any kind being handed out than managers do. In fact, as can be seen from the bottom line of the table, a relatively high proportion of the rank and file (31 percent) feel that good work is not rewarded at all. There are other sharp differences between individuals at different points in the hierarchy. Most of the top managers and two-thirds of the middle managers think that an individual who has done an especially good job will have a better chance for promotion, and that the individual's superior will think highly of that individual and will praise him or her accordingly; but only about a third of the rank-and-file participants believe that. There are several possible explanations for these especially large differences, in addition to the fact that managers are normally the dispensers of rewards for good work and are therefore likely to give themselves credit for being effective in this area. Many managers, having themselves been promoted, might very well see promotion as a reward for good work. Table 4.6 showed that managers have more education than rank-and-file workers. In fact, unless persons have attained a certain educational level, they usually will not even be considered for promotion. Many workers may therefore come to understand that a worker who has only a basic education is not likely to be promoted, no matter how good his or her work is.

Managers who emphasize good work as a path to promotion might in fact be raising unrealistic expectations among the less educated workers, which may well lead to disappointment and frustration (Hurley, 1973). In motivating workers, it might be more constructive for managers to make clear the importance of education and to encourage company grants or state aid as a way of supporting the education of those workers who wish to advance.

The pyramidal structure of organizations limits opportunities for promotion; it is understandable, therefore, that promotion is not a frequent reward. The dispensing of praise for good work, on the other hand, need not be so constricted; yet rank-and-file members, unlike managers, are not likely to indicate that praise comes the way of the effective worker.

Table 4.23 shows that there is more agreement between individuals at the different levels about sanctions that might result from bad work than about rewards that might be dispensed for good work. Perhaps norms concerning sanctions are more clearly established than norms concerning rewards. Nonetheless, substantial

Table 4.22
REWARDS FOR GOOD WORK

Q.12. What happens if a member in this organization does an especially good job in his work?	Percentage of Respondents Checking the Response		
	Top Management	Middle Management	Rank and File
His superior will praise him.	70%	60%	36%
His co-workers will praise him.	20	21	21
His co-workers will criticize him.	10	18	5
He may be offered a better job at the same level.	20	21	14
He will be given a bonus or higher wage.	20	16	13
His co-workers will have a high opinion of him.	30	28	19
He will have a better opportunity for advancement.	90	60	30
His superior will have a high opinion of him.	80	66	32
Nothing will happen.	0	11	31

differences between ranks are apparent. Almost all of the top managers and a majority of the middle managers indicate that the inefficient worker will have fewer opportunities for advancement— an opinion shared by less than half of the rank and file. Again, a majority of the top managers think that superiors will have a low opinion of inefficient workers; less than half of the middle managers and rank-and-file persons think so. On the other hand, comparing Tables 4.22 and 4.23, the rank and file see their organization as somewhat more likely to penalize workers when they do poor work than to reward them when they do especially well. For example, 31 percent of the rank-and-file workers say that nothing will happen if a worker does a good job; only 9 percent say that nothing will happen as a result of bad work. Managers do not observe this imbalance between rewards and sanctions.

Table 4.23

SANCTIONS FOR BAD WORK

Q.14. What happens if a member in this organization does a very poor job?	Percentage of Respondents Checking the Response		
	Top Management	Middle Management	Rank and File
His superior will criticize him.	60%	73%	54%
His co-workers will criticize him.	20	21	18
His co-workers will support him against criticism	10	13	18
He will be given an inferior job.	0	12	13
His salary will be reduced.	0	2	2
His co-workers will have a low opinion of him.	20	20	14
He will have less good opportunities for advancement.	90	61	43
His superior will have a low opinion of him.	60	44	39
Nothing will happen.	10	4	9

Advantages of advancement. Participants in the survey were supplied with a list of advantages usually associated with high rank and asked to indicate the three most important ones. Responses were scored from 0 to 3, a high score implying that a particular advantage was considered to be an important outcome of promotion. Table 4.24 presents averaged responses of top managers, middle managers, and rank-and-file persons, as well as relative rankings of these advantages for the different hierarchical groupings. The hierarchical level of participants clearly has some effect on their perception of the advantages of high rank. Top managers see opportunities for making decisions and for enhancing personal prestige or esteem as the primary advantages of promotion. Middle managers and rank-and-file persons, on the other hand, see higher wages as the most important outcome. Middle managers also emphasize the opportunities of enlarging one's knowledge.

Table 4.24

PERCEIVED ADVANTAGES ASSOCIATED WITH HIGH POSITION

Q.55. What do you think are the main advantages of moving into a higher position in this plant?	Top Management		Middle Management		Rank and File	
	Score	Rank	Score	Rank	Score	Rank
Prestige or esteem	2.3	2	0.5	7	0.4	7
Variety of work	1.2	5.5	1.4	4	1.4	3.5
Independence	0.3	8	0.8	6	0.9	6
Social contacts	0.4	7	0.1	8.5	0.1	9
Opportunity to make decisions	2.4	1	1.8	3	1.3	5
Opportunity to enlarge skills	1.5	3.5	1.3	5	1.4	3.5
Opportunity to enlarge knowledge	1.5	3.5	2.3	2	1.6	2
Influence people outside plant	0.0	9	0.1	8.5	0.2	8
Higher wages	1.2	5.5	2.5	1	2.5	1

Criteria for advancement. Respondents rated the importance of certain criteria for promotion on a five-point scale. Table 4.25 shows the average response of each hierarchical group, along with the ranking of each criterion according to its average relative importance. The rankings of the criteria, unlike their average scores, do not differ very much among the hierarchical groups. Managers and rank-and-file workers, for example, are of the opinion that, compared to most of the other criteria, quality of work and dependability carry a lot of weight when a promotion is being considered. At all levels, quality of work ranks ahead of quantity. This is particularly noteworthy, bearing in mind that all plants in the study are production units in which output assuredly counts a great deal.

An examination of the average scores rather than rankings reveals interesting differences between hierarchical groups. Predictably, managers more than rank-and-file workers think their organization considers a number of "rational" and socially valued criteria important in determining the advancement of personnel: quality and quantity of work, dependability, creativeness, professional knowledge, initiative, and ability to work with people. Rank-and-file members, on the other hand, think advancement depends on having friends in higher management, recommendations of a political nature, or "elbowing" one's way to get ahead. The differences between groups may not be large for each item, but they clearly conform to a pattern: Upper-level persons see their organization in a more favorable light than do lower-level persons.

Conclusions

Our sample of Irish industrial organizations documents that the nearer persons are to the apex of a hierarchy, the more authority, influence, and control they exercise. Decision making essentially rests in the hands of management, but individuals at all levels, while not seeking radical changes, would like to have more involvement of the rank and file. The endorsement of such participation is stronger among workers than among top managers, but it exists at all levels, even if not very strongly. There is general agreement that workers should more frequently be consulted when decisions affecting them are contemplated. Actual movement toward worker participation in Ireland is limited: The Act referred to earlier that provides for the election of workers to the boards of state enterprises, for example, is confined to the state-owned sector of the manufacturing industry, which is a very small proportion. Evidently, worker participation in plant-level decisions is destined to develop at a slow rate.

Table 4.25
CRITERIA FOR ADVANCEMENT

Q.16. How important is each of the following factors for getting ahead in this company?	Top Management		Middle Management		Rank and File	
	Score	Rank	Score	Rank	Score	Rank
Quality of work done	4.4	1.5	4.0	2	3.6	2.5
Quantity of work done	3.7	8.5	3.7	6.5	3.4	6.5
Supervisor's opinion	4.2	5.5	3.8	5	3.7	1
Dependability	4.3	3	4.1	1	3.6	2.5
Creativeness, inventiveness	3.7	8.5	3.4	9	2.8	9
Seniority in the plant	3.0	10	2.9	10	2.7	10
Having friends in higher management	1.5	12	2.3	11	2.6	11
Having good professional knowledge	4.2	5.5	3.9	3.5	3.5	4.5
Taking initiative	4.2	5.5	3.7	6.5	3.1	8
Having outstanding ability to work with people	4.4	1.5	3.9	3.5	3.4	6.5
Loyalty to the company	4.2	5.5	3.6	8	3.5	4.5
Recommendations of political nature	1.0	13	1.4	13	1.6	13
Elbowing one's way to get ahead	2.0	11	2.0	12	2.3	12

The distinction between formal and informal systems of worker participation in decision making (Tannenbaum et al., 1974) is relevant to Irish industry. Although rank-and-file workers in the Irish study are not ordinarily involved formally in the making of decisions relating to their places of employment, informally they find their immediate superiors approachable in the matter of work problems and complaints, which is very similar to the situation found in the United States. This is also the case for middle managers, but with the difference that their superiors turn to them for opinions and suggestions, which are frequently acted upon. Perhaps it is because rank-and-file workers' views are less frequently canvassed and acted upon that the demand for formal participation in decision making is most evident among this group. Demand for worker participation is less pronounced among middle management and less still among people at the top.

Individuals near the top of a hierarchy reap more rewards than do rank-and-file persons. Some rewards, however—for instance, the enriching opportunities defined in this chapter—are fundamental to the well-being of the individual at any level; therefore, they should be available to persons at all levels. Furthermore, our regression analyses show that enriching opportunities may not only increase job satisfaction but also incline individuals to take initiative on the job and to feel a larger responsibility for the success of their enterprise.

Rank-and-file workers, like managers, clearly desire jobs that enable them to develop their potential, to contribute ideas, and to control the pace at which they work; these desires for enriching job qualities may be more relevant to their current needs than is participation in decision making at the departmental or plant level. Most rank-and-file contributions to such decisions would, in any event, be made by union representatives, which is much less satisfying than personal involvement. For most individuals, decision making is probably most meaningful in relation to the particular job in which they are engaged from day to day (see Figure 4.3).

It is clear that persons who have relatively more years of formal education are more predisposed than persons with fewer years of education to make their own decisions rather than to seek direction from others. The educational level of the work force is rising, which emphasizes the need for jobs that allow workers more enriching opportunities.

We noted that the rank and file are more inclined to think that bad work results in punishment than that good work results in reward. Managers see no such imbalance. If the perception of the rank and file is accurate, however, it is relevant to recall Skinner's

(1974) argument that control in organizations is indeed characterized by such imbalance, even though positive (e.g., rewarding) re-
inforcement is more likely to be effective than negative reinforce-
ment or punishment. If Skinner is right, management that is inclined toward coercive means is not as effective as it might be.
Thus, Skinner's thesis might help to explain the prevalence of the
apathy, and even resistance, found at the bottom of hierarchies.
Skinner's theory is not the only one that helps to explain these
maladjustments at the bottom of the hierarchy, however. The
"group dynamics" and "human relations" approaches to organizations (e.g., Coch & French, 1948; Likert, 1967) see participative
decision making as the means for reducing the divisiveness and
other dysfunctional effects of hierarchical structures. For all their
faults, such structures are necessary for the welfare of society.

Notes

[1]The data on which this report is based were collected by Noirin O'Broin
and John Hurley for the Economic and Social Research Institute (ESRI). Noirin
O'Broin was a research officer with the ESRI at the time of this study. John
Hurley is head of the School of Staff Development at the National Institute for
Higher Education, Dublin.

5

Mexico

Germán Otálora-Bay[1]

Introduction

Authority in Mexican Organizations

Organizational hierarchy is ultimately the legitimation of a differential distribution of power, a graded sharing of authority. This distribution in a given society results from historical processes having to do with the way land and other productive resources are allocated among the members of society, both initially and over time. In Mexican society we can identify two basic periods during which the cultural norms determining current modes of the hierarchical exercise of power were formed. First, the Spanish conquerors initiated a highly authoritarian pattern, although the roots of the pattern can be traced back to the Indian nations flourishing in Middle America before the Conquest. With large portions of the land given to them as *encomiendas* (trusteeships) by the king of Spain, the conquerors became feudal lords, owners of lives and destinies; but they were also responsible to the Church for the spiritual welfare of their workers. From this relationship arose a highly centralized, authoritarian yet benevolent, and paternalistic style of leadership. After 1900, with the advent of the Industrial Revolution, formal bureaucratic modes of authority, derived from both French and American managerial practices, were introduced, but without much real effect on the system of authority.

In Weberian terms, we could say that legal authority came to reinforce traditional authority; formal and written norms came to reinforce informal mores, preserving the same authoritarian tradition. The Roman Catholic Church and the military have reinforced the authoritarian tradition in Mexico—the Church, tinted with benevolence; the army, fully authoritarian. Conquerors, clergymen, landowners, and officers have constituted one class in Mexican society: those with power. Below them has been the powerless

105

mass of workers. The two have only recently been mediated by a weak middle class of bureaucrats and professionals.

This brief sketch of authority relations in Mexico, coupled with what we know from organization theory, should provide the framework for understanding our findings about how hierarchy is experienced in Mexican organizations. The core idea is that managers view themselves as authoritarian parents; this perception corresponds with filial expectations on the part of subordinates to be controlled, directed, and protected.

Characteristics of Plants Studied

We selected ten industrial plants, located in different cities in Mexico and owned by different corporations. The five industries represented were chosen to match those in the larger project of which this research is a part. In each industry, we selected one large and one small factory. Large plants have over 500 people; small, under 300. The industries include food canning, textiles, metal works, plastics, and chemicals. Data were collected from December 1972 to December 1973.

We drew a sample of 35 persons from each plant, trying to maximize the number of complete hierarchical chains from the top to the bottom of the organization and also to include an equal number of respondents at each level wherever possible. We are well aware that this procedure does not follow the rules of probability sampling. It did achieve the objective, however, of coupling each individual included in the sample with his or her immediate superior, so that the sample included uninterrupted lines of authority.

Data for the study were collected through a written questionnaire administered to the 35 people in each organization. This uniform set of questions was translated into Spanish and pretested in Mexico. The final version was retranslated into English by an independent translator and compared for equivalence with the original.

The plants of the study are located in several states of Mexico, although there was some overrepresentation of companies based in Monterrey, the industrial capital of the country. After having invited many firms to participate in the project, we ended up with the 10 plants whose characteristics are described in Table 5.1.

The large plastics plant, which is located in a large urban region, was founded in the early 1950s. It is part of a large industrial group with a minority share held by an international corporation. The home company has grown to be the largest one in the industry. Labor relations are fair to good. Production technology is

Table 5.1

CHARACTERISTICS OF PLANTS

Plant	Number of Employees	Percentage Female	Number of Hierarchical Levels	Percentage Union Members	Percentage Absenteeism Year Prior to Research[a]	Percentage Turnover Year Prior to Research[b]
Plastics						
Large	892	4%	7	62%	3%	1%
Small	215	7	5	59	4	1
Canning						
Large	740	8	9	77	3.5	2
Small	268	64	4	88	1.5	0
Textiles						
Large	580	4	7	0[c]	1	0
Small	150	0	3	90	1	0
Metal Works						
Large	1,962	10	7	88	2	1
Small	221	2	4	91	1	0
Chemicals						
Large	549	3	6	76	1.5	1
Small	61	0	3	67	0.5	0

[a] Absenteeism = percentage of days lost over number of working days.

[b] Turnover was computed as percentage of people leaving the company over total number of employees. Zero means that the percentage was smaller than 0.5. The figures are extremely low because (1) the year we collected our data, we had a small recession and unemployment went up sharply and (2) unions and the Mexican laws strongly protect job tenure.

[c] This plant is run by a cooperative ownership. By Mexican law, workers here cannot be unionized, since they are owners.

batch and mass production. The plant is in good economic standing.

The small plastics plant is in the same metropolitan area as the large one. It is 15 years old and owned by Mexican and American stockholders. Its technology is the same as in the large plant, but this plant belongs to a smaller industrial complex. It has been doing quite well as a minor participant in the market.

The large and small canning plants are located in different medium-sized cities. Both started long ago as family concerns, but they are currently owned by large holding corporations. Their labor relations have been somewhat less stable than relations in the other industries. Expanding markets offer excellent economic perspectives for the two factories.

The large textile plant is a very interesting one: It is 80 years old, and after a long strike in the 1930s it was given to the workers, who have run it since. (This type of ownership is not very common in Mexico.) With the advent of synthetic fibers, this company's future seemed somewhat uncertain. Recently, the worker-owners have started to convert some of their production lines to blending synthetic and natural fibers. This, they hope, will put them in a strong leadership position again for most of their products. The company has not grown much in the past 25 years. Top management positions are held simultaneously by a general manager, a representative of the cooperative, and the general comptroller; this speaks of a climate of distrust among members.

Both textile plants are located in the more traditional sector of the country. The small one, which is privately owned, is very old and is going through a process of renovation of machinery, equipment, and technology. For an industry and a region with serious labor problems, labor relations in this company are very good. The future looks stable for cotton textiles and for the company.

The large metal works plant is 20 years old. It is part of a larger family corporation. Relations between workers and management are excellent. Technology is typically unit and small batch production. Profits and sales have been growing steadily during the last decade.

The small metal works is also a family company, located in the same industrial city as the large one. Although it has gone through severe labor problems in the last two years, excellent management and new technology have put it ahead of others in its industry. Future prospects look excellent.

The large chemical plant has American technology, but its major stockholder is a big Mexican industrial group. It lies in an urban setting within a larger industrial complex. Labor relations have been excellent. The process technology is well updated. Business prospects are fairly good.

The small chemical plant is an example of industriousness and good management. It has developed its own process technology. Owned by one family, it has had excellent relations between management and workers. Prospects for this company are bright.

Correlates of Hierarchy

Economic and Demographic Characteristics

Middle managers in our study receive average wages of 7,000 pesos a month,[2] while rank-and-file employees receive only a monthly mean of 1,680 pesos. This confirms the hypothesized gradient. These figures, however, do not give an accurate idea of the real income distribution in Mexico. The mean salary for the top level nationally is 18,500 pesos, more than ten times the salary made by a blue-collar worker. The standard deviation around these figures, however, is high, and regional differences are pronounced.

The distribution of demographic variables by hierarchical levels may shed some additional light on the character of hierarchy. Rank-and-file workers have had an average of 6 to 8 years of schooling; managers an average of 10 to 12. This difference may not seem impressive, but it means that most rank-and-file workers have only finished elementary or grade school, while managers, on the average, have finished at least secondary and preparatory school. Few managers, however, have gone through college, and only a very few have been to graduate school. The gradient of education reinforces the image of unequal opportunities and rewards associated with hierarchy.

Age presents a puzzling picture. In general, middle managers are younger than rank-and-file workers by almost five years, with the same standard deviation in both groups. This may imply that well-trained young persons have more opportunity to advance in the hierarchy than the less-educated. Age and lack of education thus make hopeless the case for advancement for most rank-and-file workers. One indication of this is the higher interorganizational mobility among the rank-and-file group than among managers, which means that many workers seek better opportunities elsewhere. Job seniority, however, is the same for both groups.

Finally, extremely few women are found among upper levels, although women are not represented strongly among the rank and file in these plants either.

Role Characteristics

Authority and influence. Measures of authority and influence were combined into an index (Q.1g and Q.26d), which follows an ascending gradient from the bottom to the top of the organization, as can be seen in Figure 5.1. Furthermore, the distribution of the authority/influence that members prefer for themselves, also shown in the figure, has a negative slope, although it is somewhat flatter than that for the "actual" distribution. Preferred power is more evenly distributed than actual power. Thus, persons at the top are equally high on both indices: They have the power they want. Among lower managers and foremen, we find a 0.4 difference between actual and preferred authority; for the lowest ranks, the difference is 0.7. Persons in lower echelons not only have less power; they are also more likely to feel that what they have is not enough.

Enriching qualities of the job. A fuller exercise of authority implies better opportunities for control of the job and for personal growth. This results in better opportunities for using initiative and skills and for learning new things. Hierarchy thus provides more psychologically enriching opportunities in the job itself to high ranks than to low ones. This hypothesis is supported by the Mexican data.

Figure 5.2 shows hierarchical distributions for an index of the actual and preferred opportunities. Again, we find a negative slope in both cases, although the slope is slightly flatter for the "preferred" curve. And, as predicted, the gap between the two lines increases with hierarchical descent. This gap is different from the one found in the case of authority/influence, however. First, top managers would like to have more enriching opportunities in their jobs, even though they do not prefer to have more authority/influence. Second, the difference between actual and preferred opportunity is about equal for middle and bottom employees.

Physical qualities of the job. The technology of a job is different at different levels; therefore, physical conditions of work differ between levels. We asked a question concerning physical qualities of the job, such as the extent to which it is dirty or clean, heavy or light, dangerous or safe, and physical or mental. Table 5.2 shows how ranks differ on an index of such qualities coded in terms of their "favorableness"—for example, clean, light, safe, and mental. The gradient in the Mexican plants shown in Table 5.2 conforms to the expected pattern.

Reactions and Adjustments

Mexican organizations, as we will see, place strong emphasis on

Figure 5.1
HIERARCHICAL DISTRIBUTION OF AUTHORITY/INFLUENCE
BASED ON SELF-REPORTS

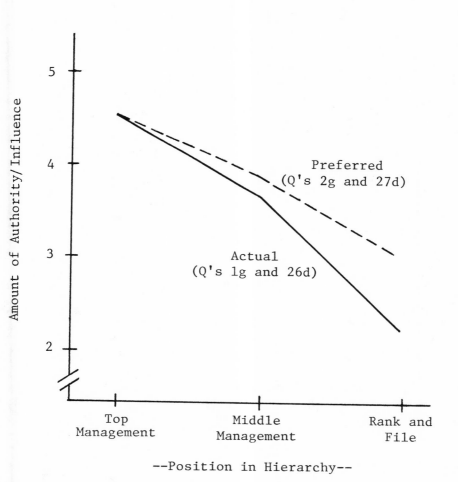

--Position in Hierarchy--

Figure 5.2
ENRICHING QUALITIES OF THE JOB BASED ON SELF-REPORTS

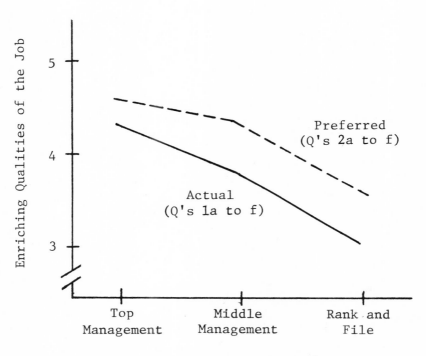

--Position in Hierarchy--

Table 5.2

PHYSICAL QUALITIES OF THE JOB

	Top Management (n = 13)	Middle Management (n = 170)	Rank and File (n = 165)
Tiring (1)			
− not tiring (7)	4.5	4.6	4.0
Unhealthful (1)			
− healthful (7)	6.2	5.6	4.9
Physical (1)			
− mental (7)	6.7	5.6	3.6
Dirty (1)			
− clean (7)	6.7	5.5	4.7
Heavy (1)			
− light (7)	4.4	4.6	3.4
Same tasks during the day (1) − different tasks during the day (7)	6.5	5.2	4.4
Dangerous (1)			
− safe (7)	6.2	5.2	4.8
Alone (1) − together with others (7)	5.8	5.6	4.9
Dependent on others (1) − independent of others (7)	5.8	3.9	3.1
Average (Q.3)	5.8	5.1	4.3

hierarchy and relatively little emphasis on participativeness. This could be interpreted as the expression of external cultural norms within formal micro-structures; authority in bureaucracies is patterned after the models offered by the society at large. Mexican organizations follow the pattern modelled in Mexican society, with a centralized form of decision making that is blended with paternalistic benevolence. In this way, monopoly of power is secured without facing interpersonal problems and without openly contravening the more modern, democratic values of the industrial/urban sector of

Mexico.

Reactions and adjustments to this situation illustrate ways of reducing the probability of conflict, either intra- or interpersonal, and reducing very aggressive and violent ways of coping with personal conflict that are learned and well established in the Mexican culture. In formal organizations, one has to minimize the likelihood of such behavior in order to avoid destructive confrontations. As a consequence, one may expect adaptive behavior tending to minimize both personal involvement and interpersonal conflict.

We therefore expect that accompanying the low morale of persons at lower levels will be psychological withdrawal from the organization, indicated by a low sense of responsibility and motivation and by alienation and generally poor psychological adjustment. Thus, people at the top should be more satisfied and motivated in the company and should experience better personal adjustment than those at the bottom.

Morale

Table 5.3 shows the average responses of persons at the three hierarchical levels concerning job satisfaction, satisfaction with pay, and attitude toward plant leadership. Some of these gradients are not very steep; nonetheless, all three demonstrate predictable hierarchical differentiation.

Table 5.3

MORALE

	Top Management (n = 13)	Middle Management (n = 170)	Rank and File (n = 163)
Job satisfaction (Q.8, 9, 10)	4.3	3.7	3.5
Satisfaction with pay (Q.59)	4.4	3.1	3.1
Attitude toward plant leadership (Q.24, 25, 28)	4.4	4.0	3.4

Motivation

Table 5.4 shows the results concerning the feeling of responsibility that members have as well as their motivation to improve performance and their initiative to find better ways of doing the work without depending on a superior. Again, the predicted hierarchical gradients are apparent, some of them being relatively steep.

Table 5.4

MOTIVATIONAL ASPECTS

	Top Management (n = 13)	Middle Management (n = 165)	Rank and File (n = 154)
Responsibility for the system[a] (Q.11a, b, c)	4.8	4.2	3.7
Motivation on the job (Q.6)	4.5	3.7	2.7
Initiative (Q.7)	4.1	4.0	3.1

[a]Index based on measures of responsibility for success of work group, department, and plant.

Personal Adjustment

Tables 5.5 and 5.6, which present the results concerning measures of personal adjustment and alienation, also show substantial gradients.

Mobility Aspirations

The strong emphasis on hierarchy in Mexican organizations defines hierarchy as a means for personal upward mobility and as a way to maintain isolated strata within the corporation that reflect cultural constraints. Advancing up the steps of the hierarchy, therefore, is expected to be highly valued by those who have strong mobility aspirations and are consequently willing to absorb the inconveniences that may be attached to the superior position.

This should hold true at least for persons in organizational positions where upward mobility is a real possibility. For rank-and-file (blue-collar) workers, such mobility is really not as feasible.

Table 5.5
PSYCHOLOGICAL ADJUSTMENT

Q.49. How true are the following statements?[a]	Top Management (n = 13)	Middle Management (n = 167)	Rank and File (n = 163)
I feel depressed.	4.5	3.9	3.7
Other people are always more lucky than I.	4.9	4.0	3.4
I often feel bored.	4.2	4.0	3.7
I seem not to get what is coming to me.	4.5	4.1	3.8
Usually everything I try seems to fail.	4.8	4.3	4.0
Things seem hopeless.	4.9	4.3	3.7
I feel resentful.	4.8	4.2	3.9
Almost every week I see someone I dislike.	4.9	4.3	3.8
I sometimes feel that my life is not very useful.	4.5	4.3	3.8
It seems to me that I am a failure.	4.8	4.6	4.3
Average	4.6	4.2	3.8

[a] A high score implies disagreement with the item and, therefore, "good" adjustment.

Therefore, we would expect fewer lower-level employees than managerial persons to aspire to advancement. Our data shown in Table 5.7 support this hypothesis.

Rank-and-file workers are less enthusiastic about moving up and taking the burdens that might be associated with status. It is noteworthy that respondents are less willing to advance if advancement entails interpersonal problems than if it entails some of the other costs indicated in the table. For example, the percentage of those desiring to move up is lowest if the cost is criticism or problem

Table 5.6

ALIENATION

Q.52. How true are the following statements?[a]	Top Management (n = 13)	Middle Management (n = 171)	Rank and File (n = 163)
It is not possible to rely on others.	1.8	2.5	2.9
Today it is practically impossible to find real friends because everyone thinks only of himself.	1.5	2.5	3.2
Men like me cannot influence the course of events; only men in high positions can have such influence.	1.5	2.1	3.0
I have never had the influence over others that I would have liked.	1.5	2.6	3.0*
Public affairs are so complicated that one cannot help but be confused by them.	2.2	2.7	3.3
Despite the many advances science has made, life today is too complicated.	2.8	2.9	3.3
I can never do what I really like because circumstances require that I do otherwise.	1.5	2.4	2.8
Life is so routinized that I do not have a chance to use my true abilities.	1.5	2.3	3.0
Life seems to be moving on without rules or order.	1.5	2.1	2.8
Nowadays it is hard to know right from wrong.	1.5	2.1	3.0
Average	1.7	2.4	3.0

[a]A high score means agreement with the item and, therefore, high alienation.

Table 5.7

UPWARD MOBILITY ASPIRATION

Q.48. Imagine you were offered the following possibilities within this plant. Would you accept them or not?	Percentage Who Would Accept a Higher Position Despite Difficulties	
	Middle Management (n = 172)	Rank and File (n = 162)
Move to a higher position involving:		
Additional obligations and responsibilities	90%	76%
Training requirements	85	74
Frequent criticism	65	40
"Problem" employees	68	39
More work worries	78	60

employees. It is greatest when the price of advancing is only increased obligations. It seems that Mexican industrial employees are less willing to tolerate interpersonal stress than other kinds of stress. This is consistent with the findings about the social character of the Mexican people (Fromm & Maccoby, 1970). Resistance to facing interpersonal stress and threats to esteem may be explained in terms of the high price put by traditional culture on status and friendships. Perhaps managers are less sensitive to these cultural norms because most of them belong to the modern sectors of Mexican society and because they have already tasted the rewards of success and care less about its costs.

In any case, many rank-and-file workers indicate a desire to move up the hierarchy, even though their aspirations may not be as strong as those expressed by middle managers. In this desire for advancement despite the inconvenience it may bring, we have an indication that members envision benefits of power and other rewards associated with high rank, some of which were illustrated in the earlier section.

Perceptions

Decision making. This section will consider differences in the way organizational decision making looks to persons at different levels. Likert has created an index, from which we adopted a number of questions, for measuring the participativeness of decision making. In Likert's model, system 1 refers to the authoritative system of organization and system 4 to the participative. Figure 5.3 indicates that the profile provided by managers in response to the Likert questions looks a little more like system 4 than that provided by workers, although the profiles overlap and the differences are not very great.

In addition to the questions about how decisions are made, we asked three parallel questions about how decisions should be made. Table 5.8 presents the discrepancies between the pairs of questions for the respective groups. Predictably, the discrepancy increases with hierarchical descent.

Distribution of control. Table 5.9 presents the perceptions of the three hierarchical groups of the distribution of control in the plant; it indicates that all three groups perceive the distribution to be hierarchical, although managers may attribute somewhat more control to the top group than rank-and-file workers do.

Answers to questions about the influence that *should* be exercised by the different groups reveal the preferences of Mexican members for distribution of power. Table 5.10 presents these data, which indicate a hierarchical distribution, although a somewhat flatter one than that which respondents perceive to exist already. All groups of respondents also seem to prefer that each group exercise more control than it is presently perceived to exercise; the preference for an increase tends to be greater among respondents in the bottom groups than among those at the top. Thus, all groups appear to prefer a greater total amount of control and a distribution that tends to be somewhat flatter than the "actual" distribution; these findings are consistent with the results in other countries where these questions have been asked (Tannenbaum & Cooke, 1979).

Rewards and sanctions. A better understanding of the perception of participativeness and control may be gained by considering the rewards and sanctions that are used to secure good work. Table 5.11 presents the perceptions of respondents at each level regarding what happens when a worker does an especially good job.

All of the groups see opportunity for advancement as the most likely of the listed consequences of good work, but that perception is much more prevalent at upper than at lower levels (92 percent com-

Figure 5.3
PERCEPTIONS ABOUT THE PARTICIPATIVENESS OF THE ORGANIZATION

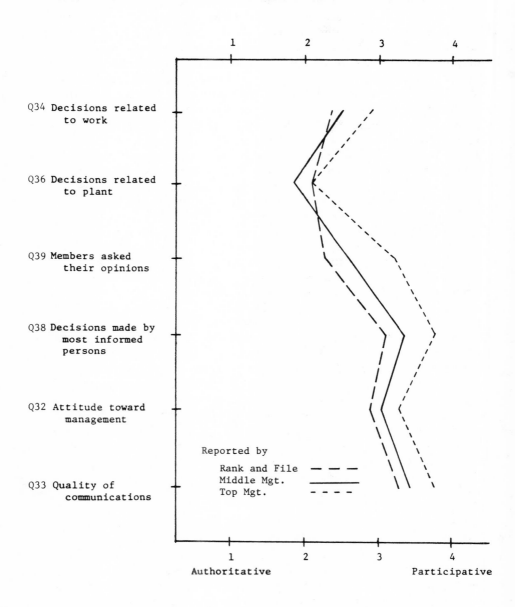

Table 5.8

PERCEPTIONS AND PREFERENCES ABOUT THE PARTICIPATIVENESS
IN THE PLANTS, MEASURED IN TERMS OF LIKERT'S MODEL

	Perceptions by:[a]		
	Top Management (n = 13)	Middle Management (n = 170)	Rank and File (n = 165)
Q.34. Actual participation by workers in job decisions	2.9	2.5	2.4
Q.35. Preferred participation by workers in job decisions	3.2	3.0	3.0
Discrepancy Q.35 − Q.34	0.3	0.5	0.6
Q.36. Actual participation by workers in plant decisions	2.1	1.9	2.1
Q.37. Preferred participation by workers in plant decisions	2.5	2.6	2.6
Discrepancy Q.37 − Q.36	0.4	0.7	0.5
Q.39. Actual extent to which opinions are asked of those who are affected by decisions	3.1	2.6	2.4
Q.40. Preferred extent	3.2	3.2	3.0
Discrepancy Q.40 − Q.39	0.1	0.6	0.6

[a]The responses presented in this table are averages for the respective groups on a four-point scale where 4 implies a high degree of participation.

Table 5.9

DISTRIBUTION OF CONTROL

Q.26. How much influence do the following groups or persons actually have on what happens in their plant?	Perceived by:		
	Top Management (n = 13)	Middle Management (n = 171)	Rank and File (n = 163)
Board and top manager	4.7	4.4	4.1
Other managers	3.8	3.9	3.8
Workers as a group	3.4	3.3	3.2

Table 5.10

PREFERRED CONTROL

Q.27. In your opinion, how much influence *should* the following groups or persons have on what happens in this plant?	Perceived by:		
	Top Management (n = 13)	Middle Management (n = 173)	Rank and File (n = 164)
Board and top manager	4.8	4.5	4.3
Other managers	4.2	4.2	3.9
Workers as a group	3.9	3.6	3.7

pared to 49 percent). In fact, all of the consequences, with the exception of criticism from co-workers, are seen as more likely by upper- than by lower-level persons. "Nothing" is checked a bit more often by persons at lower than at upper levels, but this is a *non*consequence of good work. Thus, managers more than workers see a good deal of material and psychological support for good work.

The consequences of poor work as perceived by members are shown in Table 5.12. These consequences are in some ways symmetrical to those for good work. For example, the most frequently checked consequence is "less good opportunities for advancement,"

Table 5.11
REWARDS FOR GOOD WORK

Q.12. What happens if a member in this organization does an especially good job in his work?	Percentage of Respondents Checking the Response		
	Top Management (n = 13)	Middle Management (n = 172)	Rank and File (n = 165)
His superior will praise him.	62%	34%	28%
His co-workers will praise him.	31	27	19
His co-workers will criticize him.	8	14	13
He may be offered a better job at the same level.	38	16	14
He will be given a bonus or higher wage.	46	20	13
His co-workers will have a high opinion of him.	62	20	25
He will have a better opportunity for advancement.	92	59	49
His superior will have a high opinion of him.	62	45	33
Nothing will happen.	0	10	14

and here again, managers are more likely than workers to see performance (bad as well as good) as having consequences. The difference between hierarchical groups, however, is not as sharp and consistent in this table as in the previous one. The finding that as many as 30 percent of the rank-and-file workers see criticism by co-workers as a consequence of bad work is surprising. This figure, combined with the percentage of those who believe a superior will have a low opinion of a poorly performing worker, is consistent with the emphasis put on productivity by the industrial sector of the country. The measurement may be somewhat optimistic; respondents may be inclined to give socially desirable answers. Nevertheless, it may be taken as an indication of a weakened class consciousness.

Table 5.12

SANCTIONS FOR BAD WORK

Q.14. What happens if a member in this organization does a very poor job?	Percentage of Respondents Checking the Response		
	Top Management (n = 13)	Middle Management (n = 172)	Rank and File (n = 165)
His superior will criticize him.	23%	47%	33%
His co-workers will criticize him.	8	33	30
His co-workers will support him against criticism	0	7	15
He will be given an inferior job.	0	13	16
His salary will be reduced.	8	5	3
His co-workers will have a low opinion of him.	31	22	19
He will have less good opportunities for advancement.	69	64	51
His superior will have a low opinion of him.	54	47	37
Nothing will happen.	0	5	7

Criteria for advancement. The data we have presented so far suggest that employees in these Mexican firms place a high value on advancing in the organization, despite the costs and investments advancement might entail. A clear differential of rewards compensates for the costs and makes high positions attractive.

A further understanding of organization members' reactions to advancement may be gained by considering the requirements, as members see them, for getting ahead in the company. Table 5.13 shows how such requirements are perceived by persons at the respective levels.

The general ranking of these requirements is very similar for the three groups, but the low importance attributed to interpersonal factors is surprising in a culture where having the right contact seems to be the most direct way to achievement. The industrial and urban sector of the country in which these plants are located, however, is the one that has suffered the most significant change in the direction of modern society; we may be seeing here some of the effects of modernization. In any case, lower-level persons are somewhat more likely than upper-level persons to see having friends in management as a requirement for advancement; they are also somewhat more likely to see political influence and "elbowing one's way to get ahead" as criteria. Managers, on the other hand, see a more "reasonable" set of criteria such as "quality of work done," "dependability," "creativeness," "initiative," and "outstanding ability to work with people." We thus see an indication of hierarchical gradients in the perceptions of members concerning what it takes to get ahead in the company. Managers, with some degree of predictability, see this important aspect of organizations differently than do workers.

Conclusions

Marx emphasized that alienation arises from the worker's position relative to the means of production. He defined alienation in objective terms, although he also referred to the subjective feeling of alienation. According to Seeman (1959), subjective alienation can be understood as a complex feeling of powerlessness, normlessness, social isolation, self-estrangement, and meaninglessness. Such a feeling of alienation is typical of the adjustment of many organization members, although high scores on alienation among older and less-educated employees, a large proportion of whom are located at the bottom of the hierarchy, could be expected not only as a consequence of hierarchy in the work organization but also as a result of the larger culture. Traditional societies emphasize the passivity and hopelessness of the individual in a world ruled by unknown forces, and poorly educated persons may be more subject to the effects of that emphasis (Hagen, 1962; Tannenbaum, 1980). Indeed, as

Table 5.13

CRITERIA FOR ADVANCEMENT

Q.16. How important is each of the following factors for getting ahead in this company?	Top Management		Middle Management		Rank and File	
	Score	Rank	Score	Rank	Score	Rank
Quality of work done	4.5	2	4.2	1	3.8	2
Quantity of work done	3.9	6.5	3.8	8	3.5	4
Supervisor's opinion	3.5	9	3.8	8	3.4	6
Dependability	4.1	5	4.0	4.5	3.4	6
Creativeness, inventiveness	3.9	6.5	3.8	8	3.0	10
Seniority in the plant	2.8	10	3.0	10	3.1	9
Having friends in higher management	1.3	12.5	2.5	11	2.7	11
Having good professional knowledge	3.8	8	4.0	4.5	3.3	8
Having outstanding ability to work with people	4.4	3	4.0	4.5	3.7	3
Loyalty to the company	4.6	1	4.1	2	3.9	1
Recommendations of political nature	1.3	12.5	1.8	13	2.2	12
Elbowing one's way to get ahead	1.5	11	1.9	12	2.0	13

regression analyses in the other chapters of this book indicate, education is inversely related to alienation. But the evidence of this chapter that demonstrates a hierarchical gradient of authority/ influence and of psychologically enriching and physically compatible job qualities provides a good basis for arguing that hierarchy in the organization itself is a source, if not the only one, of the relatively high alienation on the part of workers in these factories.

We conclude from our data that Mexican employees at lower levels adapt themselves to hierarchy with a feeling of alienation, with reduced emotional and intellectual investment, and with diminished satisfaction.

Notes

[1]The author would like to acknowledge the Monterrey Institute of Technology and Higher Education (ITESM) for providing faculty research grants and time that were instrumental in data collection and processing.

[2]One peso = 0.08 U.S. dollars (official rate of exchange when the data were collected).

6

Hungary

Tamás Rozgonyi and Antal Gyenes

Introduction

Hierarchical Structure in Hungarian Plants

Relations of subordination and superordination within industrial organizations are generally determined by the totality of social relations. Economic relations, the division of labor, and the political superstructure are of first importance in defining these social relations.

Before going on to the subject proper, we shall briefly discuss some principles of industrial democracy in Hungary that are important in determining the social conditions surrounding work. An understanding of these principles will facilitate an understanding of our data relating to subordination and superordination.

Even under socialist social conditions, a society requires division of labor. This means that society itself does not directly control social property, but rather that persons who play managerial and executive roles are assigned the responsibility for exercising this control. Their job is to make decisions concerning the operation of the means of production as well as to supervise the execution of these decisions.

Social and industrial democracy, through which workers are included in management, are aimed at reducing inequalities in the control of property. Two aspects of the legal regulation of industrial democracy can be differentiated: direct participation of workers in management and indirect participation through trade union representatives.

Law requires meetings at the shop floor level as an important form of direct participation by workers in management. Such meetings ensure that workers are kept properly informed on the decisions of the management. At these meetings, workers have the right to express opinions, to make suggestions, and even to make decisions regarding certain defined questions on the departmental or workshop level. The law also states that the management must respond to all opinions expressed and suggestions made on the occasion of such meetings.

The law defines the role of unions in questions affecting the living and working conditions of their members. The appropriate union must be asked for its views before managers are appointed, replaced, or evaluated. Unions participate in decisions relating to working conditions and even to some social conditions outside of the firm, such as library and kindergarten facilities for workers. The role of the unions in collective bargaining is important because the negotiation between the union and the management leads to a binding agreement between them. The law also specifies an important role for the direct participation of workers in certain phases of the negotiation process.

Subsequent to the negotiation, decisions relative to the interests of workers are made by the management in conjunction with the union, and the law prescribes that the union must take into account the opinions of the workers when the union participates in such decisions. Unions have the right to veto decisions that do not conform to regulations regarding working conditions.

The Hungarian Code of Labor[1] requires an agreement between the union and the management of each enterprise that specifies the rights and obligations of the management and workers of the enterprise. This agreement is signed by the director and the secretary of the trade union in the enterprise. The director of the enterprise is responsible for its implementation, and the trade union supervises the implementation. A number of labor-management committees are established during the preparation of the agreement to deal with questions of wages, length of working hours, rest periods, holidays, and other matters. Each committee collects controversial questions and suggestions from the workers and submits these, along with their own suggestions, to the enterprise management and to the trade union leadership. The draft of the committee's proposals must be published and circulated among the workers. Then it is discussed with the management of the enterprise by the trade union committee and subsequently by the union committee.

A discussion of industrial democracy in Hungary requires some attention to industrial cooperatives, which account for 6.3 percent of the industrial production here.[2] Members of a cooperative, unlike members of a state enterprise, directly own the property of the enterprise and have the right to dispose of it within the framework of a socialist society. They can, for example, sell the enterprise to another cooperative or to the state. The 1971 Cooperative Act decreed that all important issues of the cooperatives are ultimately decided by a meeting of its members, which occurs several times a year and which is the supreme authority of the cooperative. The general meeting may decide issues such as the rules of the cooperative, the election and suspension of officers, the remuneration of the top management, and the approval of the production and financial plans. The top executive is elected by the membership for a term of four years; only members of the cooperative are permitted to be candidates for the position. The top executive is responsible to the general meeting. Elected committees exercise ongoing functions of supervision and control over the activities of the executive.

Hungarian firms are typically large. Firms of over 1,000 persons had achieved a certain preponderance in Hungary by the beginning of the twentieth century. Following World War II and the nationalization of industry—and particularly early in the 1960s—new, large enterprises took form. They did not come into being through the growth of existing small plants, but rather through the amalgamation of smaller plants. As a result, the proportion of firms in Hungary that are large is greater than in many other industrialized countries. Tables 6.1 and 6.2 give a telling picture of the situation.

Economic analyses suggest that the creation of most large firms in Hungary did not occur rationally. A justification for growth is that the whole is greater than the sum of its parts. A large firm should utilize its plant and equipment more efficiently and the productivity per worker should be greater than that of a number of smaller plants that jointly equal the size of the larger one. This economy of scale depends, in part, upon the systematization that characterizes an organization. In a number of cases, however, large firms in Hungary were created simply by adding together smaller plants without integrating them functionally (C. N. Belá, 1971). In effect, one large plant is simply several smaller plants under one name. Administratively the new plant is a more complex organization, but technologically it is no more than the original unrelated and unintegrated plants. Table 6.2 illustrates this problem. The per capita value of equipment is not much different between the largest and smallest firms (although in the middle-size range, per capita value of equipment decreases somewhat with size of plant), but the value of per capita productivity declines as size increases.

While the economic consequences of large-scale industrial concentration in Hungary are known, the social and human consequences are not well understood. We suspect that size of organization influences attitudes, behavior, and opinions of those working within

Table 6.1

PERCENTAGE OF PLANTS EMPLOYING MORE
THAN A THOUSAND PERSONS

Country	Year	Percentage of Plants
Socialist		
Hungary	1971	73%
Czechoslovakia	1969	90
Rumania	1969	80
Poland	1968	60
Soviet Union	1968	59
Bulgaria	1969	47
German Democratic Republic	1969	43
Capitalist and Mixed Economy		
Netherlands	1968	41
Federal Republic of Germany	1970	39
Great Britain	1968	36
Sweden	1970	20
Japan	1969	19
Italy	1971	17

[a]The computations for socialist countries are based on the number of blue-collar and clerical workers; for other countries, on the total number of employees, including supervisory and managerial personnel. The comparison in this table between social and other countries is, therefore, a conservative statement of the difference between them in the size of their plants.

Source: Economic Research Institute of the Central Bureau of Statistics (1971).

organizations. The larger the organization and the more extended the division of labor within it, the more difficult it is for an individual to understand the links between his or her own work and the organization as a whole: Work increasingly becomes a matter of routine, and organization is more rigid.

This routinization that we believe characterizes large enterprises may offer certain protection to individuals, since activities tend to be governed by impersonal, bureaucratic regulations rather than by the more personalized commands that we believe are usual in small organizations.

Table 6.2
VALUE PER WORKER OF EQUIPMENT AND
PRODUCTION OF HUNGARIAN PLANTS

Size of Plant	Equipment per Worker (100,000 Forints)	Annual Production per Worker (100,000 Forints)
101–500	1.0	3.0
501–1,000	1.8	3.3
1,001–5,000	1.4	2.3
5,001–10,000	1.2	2.0
More than 10,000	1.1	1.7

Source: Szabó, B. (1972).

Characteristics of Plants Studied

The sample within each plant was designed to permit an analysis of the hierarchical chain from the top to the bottom. Therefore, each person at and immediately below the top in each plant was included. Selection in the next category, which includes senior department heads and department heads, was made on the basis of the importance of their departments within the enterprise. Thus heads of the production, sales, supplies, and financial departments were included with certainty. (The accounting, personnel, and statistics departments were excluded.) The remaining respondents below these levels were selected randomly, except that a person was included only if his or her immediate superior was also selected. As a result, two-thirds of the sample is made up of rank-and-file members and one-third of supervisory and managerial personnel. Thus, the sample in each plant includes persons who are connected hierarchically from the top of the organization to the bottom. The size of the sample in each plant varied from 30 in the smaller plants to 150 in the larger; 11 were top managers, 316 were middle managers, and 543 were rank and file workers.

The selection of plants was governed primarily by the desire to see various types of enterprises represented. The sample naturally does not represent Hungarian industry as a whole. The firms can be classified into three categories according to the nature of their supervising authority:

1. Firms controlled by ministries (central authority)

2. Firms controlled by councils (local authorities)
3. Industrial cooperatives.

Those under central control are the "large" enterprises in our research, and those under local control are the "small" enterprises. Industrial cooperatives, which are not generally under direct supervision by the state, are usually smaller than the plants that we have called "small" enterprises. Another important feature of a plant is the ratio of those not engaged directly in production (for example, administrators, including managers, secretaries, and statistical workers) to those who are engaged directly in production (for example, rank-and-file workers and their foremen). Bendix (1956) proposes this as an index of bureaucratization that, as Table 6.3 indicates, tends to be greater in the large organizations than in the small.

The two large plants are highly mechanized, because the production processes in them require a good deal of equipment. The labor in these plants is mainly semi-skilled. The textile mill employs about equal proportions of semi-skilled and skilled workers, while the communications equipment works employs two and one-half times as many semi-skilled as skilled workers.

The small plants produce a wide range of goods. Many phases of production are unmechanized; these plants typically entail handwork that is relatively skilled. The largest proportion of skilled workers is in two of the small plants in our study: In the furniture plant, 1.6 times as many skilled as semi-skilled workers are employed; in the appliance plant the ratio is 1.3:1. Only one of the cooperatives includes more skilled than unskilled workers. Small enterprises use relatively obsolete equipment, largely because these enterprises came into being as a result of the amalgamation of even smaller independent firms, some of them originally privately owned.

The product range of three of the four industrial cooperatives is relatively limited compared to that of other small plants in the study. These three are highly mechanized, unlike the others. For example, the plastics plant has considerable automated equipment that requires semi-skilled work. One person may watch a number of machines, stopping them only if something goes wrong. The fourth cooperative produces a wide range of goods. The degree of mechanization is low and the proportion of skilled workers is high.

Table 6.4 shows data concerning the productivity and profit of the firms in our sample. These data are consistent with the implications of Table 6.3 that per capita production and profit tend to be greater in the small than in the large plants, although there are exceptions to this tendency.

Our interest in this research is to examine the possible effects of

Table 6.3
SIZE, PERCENTAGE FEMALE, AND
BUREAUCRATIZATION OF THE PLANTS STUDIED

Type of Plants	Size (Number of Employees)	Sex (Percentage Female)	Bureaucratization (Number of Nonproduction Workers/Number of Production Workers)
Large			
Communication equipment	8,047	64%	.35
Textile	1,917[a]	75	.37
Small			
Plastics	1,031	66	.28
Furniture	916	39	.32
Machine tools	698	53	.33
Electrical appliances	286	28	.47[b]
Furniture	206	25	.34
Cooperatives			
Automobile parts	493	52	.15
Plastics	273	62	.26
Furniture	131	34	.32
Furniture	120	35	.21

[a]This plant is a production unit of an enterprise of 7,000 employees.

[b]This plant is unique in that it not only manufactures appliances but also services the appliances of its customers. Hence, there are a substantial number of "non-production workers" who are responsible for sales and record keeping, in addition to some who do actual repair work.

organizational hierarchy on the reactions and adjustments of organization members. The effects that we find in general appear in all of the organizations of our sample, regardless of size or type. In most of the following tables, therefore, we show the data for all plants combined, without distinguishing between them according to their size or type. We do, however, present differences between the types of plants when these differences appear especially important,

Table 6.4

SIZE, PRODUCTIVITY, AND PROFIT PER WORKER OF THE PLANTS

Type of Plant	Size (Number of Employees)	Production (100,000 Forints)	Profit (1,000 Forints)
Large			
Communication			
equipment	8,047	1.4	8.5
Textile	1,917	1.1	5.1
Small			
Plastics	1,031	2.2	17.2
Furniture	916	1.9	17.6
Machine tools	698	1.5	26.9
Electrical			
appliances	286	3.6	32.3
Furniture	206	3.9	68.1
Cooperatives			
Automobile parts	493	6.2	115.0
Plastics	273	2.1	50.3
Furniture	131	—	38.9
Furniture	120	2.4	44.1

and we discuss in the concluding section the implications of size and type of plant for the general effects of hierarchy that are illustrated in the main body of this chapter.[3]

Correlates of Hierarchy

Economic and Demographic Characteristics

How do salary and certain demographic factors correlate with the hierarchical structure of the plants? Table 6.5 provides an answer to this question.

Without exception, these characteristics show a close relationship with the hierarchical structure of the organization. Salary range is determined by law; therefore, the data of Table 6.5 illustrate certain norms of socialist society in Hungary. "Achievement" is accepted as an important criterion in determining the amount of remuneration a person will receive. But monetary

Table 6.5

ECONOMIC AND DEMOGRAPHIC CHARACTERISTICS OF MEMBERS

	Top Management	Middle Management	Rank and File
Salary[a] (average forints per month)	6,577	4,197	2,471
Education[b] (average years)	14.9	11.6	10.2
Age (average years)	50.1	45.3	36.2
Plant seniority[c] (average years)	14.2	13.4	8.4
Sex (percentage female)	9.0%	20.8%	46.0%

[a] Figures do not include profit shares, bonuses, or other financial perquisites.

[b] These data are in years of formal education rather than in terms of the six-point scale used in the research of the other countries.

[c] Plant seniority is measured on the following scale: 1 = under 6 months, 2 = 6 months to 1 year, 3 = 1 to 2 years, 4 = 2 to 3 years, 5 = 3 to 6 years, 6 = 6 to 10 years, 7 = 10 to 20 years, and 8 = 20 years or more.

reward must take into account the principle of equality, which is also an important value in this society. Therefore, the ratio of the salaries at the top to those at the bottom is relatively small—less than 3:1. We shall consider in a later section the possible implications of this ratio for the aspirations of members to advance in the hierarchy.

Job seniority is an important criterion for promotion. It has the advantage suggested by Weber of limiting arbitrary action by superiors in promoting subordinates, and it may also help to encourage loyalty to the enterprise. On the other hand, because seniority provides security to some individuals, it may limit their motivation, initiative, and innovativeness, which are especially important characteristics during times of rapid technological change. One might expect a certain rigidity, therefore, in organizations where seniority and promotion are closely linked.

Role Characteristics

Authority and influence. Authority and influence are among the most essential characteristics of hierarchy in organizations. Hierarchical differentials in authority and influence, therefore, convey basic information about a hierarchy. Each respondent was asked to report, on a five-point scale, the amount of authority (Q.1g) and influence (Q.26d) that he or she personally exercises. Responses to these questions were combined into an authority/influence index. Respondents were also asked about the amount of authority and influence they would prefer to exercise (Q.2g and Q.27d); these form the basis of an index of "preferred" authority/influence.

Figure 6.1 presents graphically the distribution of authority/influence based on the data from all plants combined. Tables 6.6 and 6.7 present the results separately for the several types of plants. The figure, along with the tables, illustrates some features of the distribution of authority/influence in the Hungarian plants.

The data show that persons at the top of the hierarchy have more authority/influence than do those at the bottom. In addition, we see that:

1. With the exception of top managers in the cooperatives, persons in all groups, on the average, prefer to have more authority/influence than they perceive themselves to have.
2. Groups with relatively low authority/influence usually prefer a greater increase in their authority/influence than do persons with relatively high authority/influence. Accordingly, compared to managers, workers experience a greater gap between their "actual" and "preferred" authority/influence.
3. The greater authority/influence exercised by managers in the cooperative and small plants compared to that exercised by managers in the large plants is not accompanied by a lesser influence exercised by workers in the former compared to the latter plants. This illustrates that the total amount of authority/influence may vary from plant to plant. We shall discuss this point further in the next section.

Distribution of control (control graph). The above data are based on self-reports by individuals at different hierarchical levels concerning their own authority and influence. A further view of the distribution of control or influence in an organization can be obtained by asking all respondents to report about the influence that is exercised (and that should be exercised) by each hierarchical group. Figure 6.2 presents data based on the responses to these questions by all respondents in all organizations combined; Tables 6.8 and 6.9 present the data separately for the different types of organizations.

Figure 6.1
HIERARCHICAL DISTRIBUTION OF AUTHORITY/INFLUENCE
BASED ON SELF-REPORTS

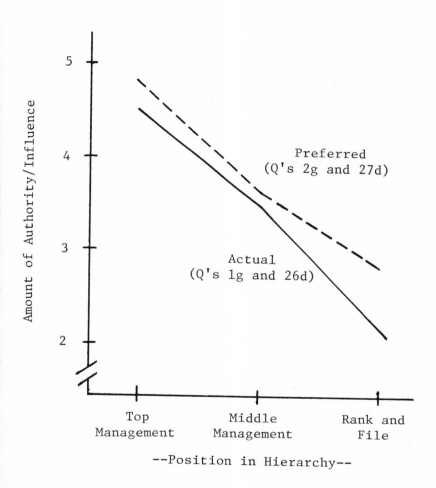

--Position in Hierarchy--

Table 6.6

ACTUAL AUTHORITY/INFLUENCE

Type of Plant	Top Management	Middle Management	Rank and File
Large	4.2	3.2	1.8
Small	4.8	3.5	2.0
Cooperative	4.8	3.7	2.1

Table 6.7

PREFERRED AUTHORITY/INFLUENCE

Type of Plant	Top Management	Middle Management	Rank and File
Large	4.7	3.4	2.7
Small	5.0	3.6	2.8
Cooperative	4.8	3.8	3.0

The results are very similar in their implications to those for authority/influence. According to all of the respondents combined, the distribution of control *is* and *should be* hierarchical. Members report that all groups should exercise more control than they do, but that the greatest increase should occur at the bottom of the hierarchy. This discrepancy between the actual and preferred distribution, however, is relatively small in the cooperatives (see Tables 6.8 and 6.9). Cooperatives also appear to be characterized by a somewhat higher amount of control throughout the hierarchy, while the large organizations are characterized by the lowest amount of control. Furthermore, as we have seen in Table 6.4, productivity and profit per worker tend, on the average, to be highest in the cooperatives and lowest in the large organizations. Thus, we see some support for the hypothesis that the total amount of control in an organization is associated with criteria of organizational effectiveness (Tannenbaum, 1968; Tannenbaum & Cooke, 1979).

This relationship between control and effectiveness was implied in interviews with a number of managers who indicated that deci-

Figure 6.2
DISTRIBUTION OF CONTROL AS REPORTED BY ALL MEMBERS

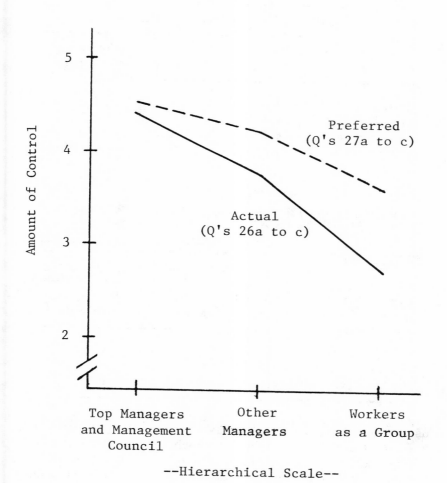

--Hierarchical Scale--

Table 6.8

ACTUAL DISTRIBUTION OF CONTROL AS REPORTED BY
ALL MEMBERS IN THREE TYPES OF PLANTS

	Control Exercised by:		
Type of Plant	Directorial Board	Other Managers	Workers as a Group
Large	4.3	3.6	2.4
Small	4.4	3.7	2.7
Cooperative	4.4	4.0	3.0

Table 6.9

PREFERRED DISTRIBUTION OF CONTROL AS REPORTED BY
ALL MEMBERS IN THREE TYPES OF PLANTS

	Control Exercised by:		
Type of Plant	Directorial Board	Other Managers	Workers as a Group
Large	4.6	4.1	3.4
Small	4.5	4.1	3.6
Cooperative	4.5	4.3	3.8

sions are not always made at levels where the information necessary for good decisions is available and where there is a concern for
optimizing decisions. Many decisions that are made at the top but
that must take into account local conditions at different places
within the organization, or that require information about sales and
supplies or the market, really require input from lower and middle
levels of management. The absence of such input and of the influence by lower and middle managers that such input implies leads
to decisions that further reduce the influence of all managers. Poor
decisions create "noise" and blockages in the system; they get in the
way of good decisions. Thus, the lack of influence on the part of
some members creates conditions that undercut and reduce the in-

fluence of others. The process is circular, and although the center of this circle may be located within management, its implications spread to the influence that might be exercised by the workers, since workers might exercise influence by influencing the decisions of their superiors. "Influencing" superiors who are themselves without influence cannot be counted as much influence, however. We do not know how widespread this problem may be, but it appears to occur in some of the organizations in this research. In any event, the covariation between control and performance among the organizations of this study suggests the operation of a dynamic that may apply to organizations in general.

Participativeness and supportiveness of superior. The relationship between superiors and subordinates cannot be entirely specified by organizational rules. Much of this relationship is spontaneous and informal, and its character would depend, in part, on the "style of leadership" of the superior. We are interested here in the leader's participativeness and supportiveness in relationships with subordinates as part of his or her style. Are such participativeness and supportiveness more typical of leaders at the top or near the bottom of the hierarchy?

Table 6.10 presents the results of an index based on questions asked of subordinates about their superior (Q.s 41 to 44 and 46). The questions are designed to measure such characteristics as the extent to which the superior asks and takes into account the opinions of his or her subordinates, is easily approachable when there are problems, and encourages subordinates to express their feelings or complaints to him or her. The data suggest that there may be more participativeness in the interpersonal relationship between superior and subordinate at upper than at lower levels.

Table 6.10

PARTICIPATIVENESS AND SUPPORTIVENESS OF SUPERIOR

	Middle Management	Rank and File
Average (Q.s 41 to 44 and 46)	4.3	3.8

Bases of superior's power. Max Weber (1964b) was the first bourgeois sociologist to study the bases of authority in detail. He distinguished between rational, traditional, and charismatic authority. We have employed a more recent set of categories that are designed to describe the reasons members of an organization obey the instructions of superiors (French & Raven, 1959). Weber pointed out that obedience need not depend on the personal subordination of the subordinate to the superior, and a number of authors since Weber have elaborated this point. For example, a sense of duty to the organization and a member's concern that the organization function effectively may be the bases for the member doing what his or her superior asks. Table 6.11 presents the questions that we employed, along with the results. Differences between hierarchical groups, however, are not very striking.

Table 6.11

BASES OF THE SUPERIOR'S POWER AS REPORTED BY SUBORDINATES

Q.47. When you do what your immediate superior requests you to do on the job, why do you do it?	Middle Management	Rank and File
I respect his competence and judgment.	3.9	3.7
He can give special help and benefits.	2.5	2.4
He's a nice guy.	3.0	3.0
He can penalize or otherwise disadvantage me.	1.9	2.2
It is my duty.	4.3	4.2
It is necessary if the organization is to function properly.	4.5	4.2

Enriching qualities of the job. Each respondent was asked (Q.1), "In your work, to what extent can you (a) learn new things, (b) use your own ideas, (c) do interesting work, (d) use your skills, knowledge, and abilities, (e) talk with other people during work time, and (f) decide your own pace of work?" As we see in Figure 6.3, which is based on an index that combines the responses to all of the above items and a parallel set of questions concerning preferred qualities (Q.2), persons at upper levels report greater opportunities to engage in activities that are "enriching" psychologically than do those at lower levels. Furthermore, persons at all levels prefer to have more of these opportunities than they perceive themselves to have, the greatest discrepancy between "actual" and "preferred" opportunities being at the bottom of the hierarchy.

Reactions and Adjustments

Morale

We examined several indices of morale. The first is job satisfaction. The satisfaction a member obtains through his or her job is important because it indicates the extent to which the job is personally rewarding and to which it provides a basis for the member to identify with what he or she is doing. We composed an index based on the responses of each respondent to questions concerning the extent to which the member is (a) satisfied with his or her work (Q.10), (b) satisfied with the company (Q.9), and (c) satisfied with his or her activities on the job compared to those outside of work (Q.8). The first line of Table 6.12 presents the results of this index. In fact, members at upper levels in the hierarchy are more satisfied with their jobs than are members at lower levels. For example, 44 percent of the top managers, compared to only 17 percent of members at the bottom, report that their jobs give them much more satisfaction than do their activities off the job. Members at the bottom are more likely to derive more satisfaction away from their place of employment.

We asked each respondent one question concerning his or her satisfaction with pay (Q.59). The second line of Table 6.12 shows the average responses to this question for the three hierarchical groups.

The satisfaction a member feels concerning his or her pay probably reflects more than satisfaction with what that pay will buy, since the pay a person receives is an indication to him or her of social appreciation or approval for the work he or she is doing. Income implicitly tells a person what place he or she occupies within the work community, if not in society itself. For example, highly trained, skilled workers express pride in their knowledge and skills, and they insist intensely on maintaining an advantaged position (compared to other workers) with respect to wages, even though the differentials between their earnings and those of other workers may be very small. The money differential itself does not appear to justify the effort expended to maintain it, except that the differential is an important symbol. In fact, the salary range within Hungarian

Figure 6.3
ENRICHING QUALITIES OF THE JOB BASED ON SELF-REPORTS

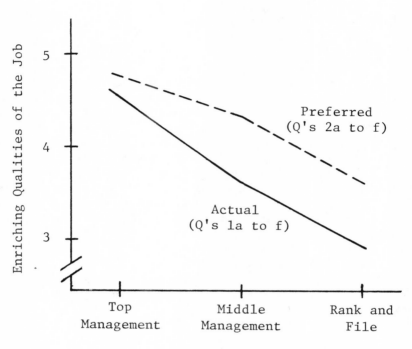

Table 6.12

MORALE

	Top Management	Middle Management	Rank and File
Job satisfaction (Q.8, 9, 10)	4.5	3.8	3.2
Satisfaction with pay (Q.59)	3.6	3.1	2.6
Attitude toward plant leadership (Q.24, 25, 28)	4.5	3.8	3.2

plants is small compared to that in many other societies; yet, as the second line of Table 6.12 shows, a clear gradient in satisfaction exists along the hierarchy.

The third line of Table 6.12 concerns the attitude of members toward plant management; the results are based on an index composed of the following questions:

Q.24. Do you think the responsible people here have a real interest in the welfare of those who work here?

Q.25. Do the responsible people in this plant improve working conditions only when forced to?

Q.28. When a worker in this plant makes a complaint about something, is it taken care of?

Again, it is clear that the more "positive" result occurs at the top of the organization rather than at the bottom.

Table 6.13 shows the results of a standardized regression analysis designed to examine possible determinants of the indices of morale we have studied. We do not include among the predictors in the regression of this chapter the measure of physical qualities of the job that is included in other chapters, because of a technical error in the questionnaire regarding this item.

Two of the determinants of job satisfaction that rank relatively high in importance—age and education—deserve special mention because in earlier studies in other countries they have been found to have an effect in much the same way they apparently do in these Hungarian plants (Tannenbaum et al., 1974). Older persons are more satisfied with their jobs, but relatively educated persons are less satisfied, other things being equal.

Table 6.13

THE RELATIVE IMPORTANCE OF THE PREDICTORS OF MORALE

Multiple R	Job Satisfaction .64		Satisfaction with Pay .44		Attitude toward Plant Leadership .58	
Predictors	Beta	Rank	Beta	Rank	Beta	Rank
Enriching job qualities	.14	4	−.06	6	.35	1
Authority/ influence	.05	7	.03	8	.17	4
Education	−.24	2.5	−.10	3	−.16	5
Age	.28	1	.27	1	−.18	3
Plant seniority	.04	8	−.19	2	−.03	8
Length of chain	.09	6	−.07	5	.05	7
Level in hierarchy	.24	2.5	−.04	7	.26	2
Salary	.13	5	.08	4	−.06	6

Motivation

Members may be formally assigned responsibility for achieving objectives within an organization, and sanctions may be applied to persons who do not meet their formal responsibility. Responsibility may not always be assigned in an explicit, formal manner, however, and members may feel a sense of responsibility whether or not it is formally assigned. We are concerned here with this subjective aspect of responsibility—the sense of responsibility that a person may feel for (a) his or her work group, (b) his or her department, and (c) the plant as a whole (Q.11). The first line of Table 6.14 presents the results of an index combining these aspects of responsibility. People at the top clearly feel more responsibility than do those at the bottom.

We used the label "motivation" to describe the results of a question (Q.6) concerning the extent to which the respondent feels that he or she as well as his or her superior should be concerned about the introduction of better and faster work methods. We employed the term "initiative" to describe the results of a question (Q.7) concerning the frequency with which the respondent tries to develop, on

Table 6.14

MOTIVATIONAL ASPECTS

	Top Management	Middle Management	Rank and File
Responsibility for the system (Q.11a, b, c)	4.8	4.3	3.5
Motivation on the job (Q.6)	–	3.7	2.6
Initiative (Q.7)	3.8	3.7	3.3
Mobility aspirations[a] (Q.48)	–	1.4	1.4

[a]Measured on a two-point scale. See text.

his or her own, better or faster ways of doing the work. This first question was not asked of top persons because it refers to the respondent's superior in the plant. The data on the second and third lines of Table 6.14 conform to the usual hierarchical pattern.

Mobility Aspirations

As a final aspect of motivation, we are concerned with the aspiration of members to climb the rungs of the hierarchy. The extent to which members want to advance is an indication of the degree to which high position is a mark of success in their eyes, and it provides important information about the place of hierarchy in the organization and in the lives of individual members. Each respondent was asked (Q.48) whether he or she would be willing to accept a higher position in the plant even if such advancement brought with it problems such as additional worries, criticism, problem employees, and sacrifices for additional training. The responses were either yes (2) or no (1); the fourth line of Table 6.14 provides the results of this index. Forty percent of the respondents would accept advancement in the face of the hypothetical problems posed; 60 percent would not. Managers do not differ from non-managerial members in this regard. Rejection of advancement might mean that the advantages of a higher position do not outweigh the hypothetical disadvantages or it might imply that members find their present positions satisfying enough. For example, some subordinates may receive more take-home pay than their immediate superior. As a result, well-trained, skilled workers often refuse promotion to the position of foreman. It even happens that experts with higher training would rather carry out the duties of skilled workers than be managers. Rejection of advancement by a member may also mean that his or her needs for additional satisfaction can be met elsewhere, outside the plant.

The regression analyses of Table 6.15 attempt to explain motivational aspects in terms of a number of predictors. We are surprised to find, however, that none of the motivational aspects are at all explained by the authority/influence that persons feel they exercise. Substantial arguments have been mustered in support of the effect of authority and influence on the responsibility felt by organization members. Earlier studies (Tannenbaum et al., 1974), as well as those reported in other chapters of this book, offer empirical support for this relationship in a number of countries. We do not know why this relationship does not exist in the plants we have studied.

Personal Adjustment

We have seen that persons at higher levels of the hierarchy are more satisfied with their work than are those at lower levels. The character of work, however, may have important psychological consequences that go beyond the satisfaction a person feels with his or her job. A job may affect a person's self-evaluation: This evaluation will be low where personal failure and frustration are frequent and self-realization is impossible. Self-evaluation is affected not only by the work itself but also by the recognition and respect that might be accorded by others. Such recognition is likely to be greater for persons at upper levels than for those at lower levels.

We employed an index of psychological adjustment based on nine items designed to measure the extent to which a person feels depressed or resentful or has low self-esteem—which we take as criteria of (poor) adjustment (Q.49). The data in the first line of Table 6.16 show the predictable hierarchical gradient. (A high score in this table means "good" adjustment.)

A second aspect of adjustment that we consider here concerns the notion of alienation. Alienation has been discussed in the literature from two standpoints—subjective and objective. At the societal level, alienation in Marxist terms must be defined at a very abstract level of objective social relations. We do not have measures of this objective and ultimate conception of alienation. We do have a measure of subjective feelings of powerlessness, normlessness, meaninglessness, social isolation, and self-estrangement (Dean,

Table 6.15

THE RELATIVE IMPORTANCE OF THE PREDICTORS OF MOTIVATIONAL ASPECTS

Predictors	Responsibility for System .53		Motivation .69		Initiative .29		Mobility Aspirations .21	
Multiple R	Beta	Rank	Beta	Rank	Beta	Rank	Beta	Rank
Enriching job qualities	.18	3	.14	3	-.17	2.5	-.03	7
Authority/influence	.07	6	-.01	7.5	.03	8	.03	6
Education	-.04	8	.32	1	-.13	5	.15	1
Age	.29	2	-.23	2	.15	4	.02	8
Plant seniority	-.06	7	.09	5	.08	7	.13	2.5
Length of chain	.17	4	-.01	7.5	-.17	2.5	.07	5
Level in hierarchy	.34	1	.02	6	-.18	1	.10	4
Salary	.10	5	-.12	4	-.10	6	.13	2.5

Table 6.16
PSYCHOLOGICAL ADJUSTMENT

	Top Management	Middle Management	Rank and File
Psychological adjustment (Q.49)	4.5	4.1	3.6
"Alienation" (Q.52)	2.0	2.4	3.1

1961; Seeman, 1959) (Q.52), which have been referred to in the literature as the subjective or psychological aspects of alienation. We accept this conception for present purposes, even though it is an inadequate representation of the true Marxist conception.

The second line of Table 6.16 shows the results of this subjective measure. A high score implies relatively high feelings of powerlessness, normlessness, and the other subjective aspects we have measured. As the table indicates, these are higher at the bottom than at the top of the hierarchy.

Table 6.17 presents regression analyses concerning the determinants of the measures of adjustment. It is interesting to see the importance of age as a predictor of adjustment—it is associated with "poor" psychological adjustment in the case of both measures—and to note that increasing education appears to be associated with decreasing psychological alienation. We saw earlier (Table 6.13) that age appeared to have positive—and education negative— implications for job satisfaction. This mixed effect of age and education on the two psychological outcomes (job satisfaction and alienation) is precisely what was found in an earlier study in other countries (Tannenbaum et al., 1974); it illustrates how psychological alienation differs from job (dis)satisfaction. Being dissatisfied is not the same as being alienated. Relatively speaking, older and less educated members are satisfied with their jobs, but they are nonetheless psychologically alienated; younger and more educated members are dissatisfied with their jobs, but they are not alienated psychologically—other things being equal. Nonetheless, even though these variables relate to one another in these seemingly contrary ways, the hierarchical effect is clear—people at the top are both older and more educated; they are also more satisfied with their jobs and feel less alienated psychologically than those at the bottom (Table 6.17).

Table 6.17
THE RELATIVE IMPORTANCE OF THE PREDICTORS
OF PERSONAL ADJUSTMENT

Multiple R	Psychological Adjustment .67		Alienation .66	
Predictors	Beta	Rank	Beta	Rank
Enriching job qualities	.24	2	−.19	3
Authority/influence	.09	5	−.13	5
Education	.10	4	−.20	2
Age	−.34	1	.29	1
Plant seniority	.05	7	−.05	8
Length of chain	.03	8	−.10	7
Level in hierarchy	.08	6	−.17	4
Salary	−.15	3	.10	6

Perceptions

We are concerned in this section with the possible differences between members of different rank in how they view the same facts in their organization. Do those at the bottom see their plants to be as participative as do persons at the top? Do members at different levels share a common perception of the distribution of control and of the system of rewards and sanctions in their plant?

Decision making. Table 6.18 presents responses of members at different levels to several questions designed to measure how participative the decision making is in a plant and how participative it *should* be. The table shows clearly that persons at the top see (or at least report that they see) their plant to be more participative than do those at the bottom. These members do not differ from one another with respect to their judgment about how participative decision making in their plant should be, but the discrepancy between the amount of participation members perceive in the organization and the amount they would prefer to see clearly decreases with hierarchical ascent. The organization works the way it should in the eyes of those at the top more than in the eyes of those at the bottom. This, of course, fits the hypothesis we are exploring in this research.

Table 6.18

PERCEPTIONS AND PREFERENCES ABOUT THE PARTICIPATIVENESS
IN THE PLANTS, MEASURED IN TERMS OF LIKERT'S MODEL

	Perceptions by:[a]		
	Top Management	Middle Management	Rank and File
Q.34. Actual participation by workers in job decisions	3.0	2.6	2.4
Q.35. Preferred participation by workers in job decisions	3.4	3.2	3.4
Discrepancy Q.35 − Q.34	0.4	0.6	1.0
Q.36. Actual participation by workers in plant decisions	3.0	2.6	2.3
Q.37. Preferred participation by workers in plant decisions	3.2	3.2	3.2
Discrepancy Q.37 − Q.36	0.2	0.6	0.9
Q.39. Actual extent to which opinions are asked of those who are affected by decisions	3.4	3.0	2.6
Q.40. Preferred extent	3.6	3.6	3.5
Discrepancy Q.40 − Q.39	0.2	0.6	0.9

[a]The data presented in this table are averages for the respective groups on a four-point scale where 4 implies a high degree of participation.

Distribution of control. Figure 6.2, based on a simple average of the reports of all respondents, showed the distribution of control in the Hungarian plants. Figure 6.4 presents data about the distribution of control as reported separately by respondents at different levels. It is apparent that individuals at these levels differ somewhat from one another in the pictures they provide. All groups report the distribution of control to be hierarchical, but the distribution is flatter as perceived from the top of the organization than as perceived from the bottom. The difference between the views of the respective groups is most apparent with respect to the amount of influence or control exercised by the workers. Managers see workers as exercising more control than the workers see themselves as exercising.

Figure 6.5 presents the preferred distribution of control as reported by the respective groups, and Figure 6.6 presents the discrepancies between the actual and preferred distribution of control as reported by the respective groups.

The groups do not differ very much from one another in the distribution of control that they prefer, although all groups report that they prefer a distribution of control that is somewhat higher and flatter than that which they perceive to exist. However, as Figure 6.6 demonstrates, managers prefer more increase for managerial groups than do the workers, while the workers prefer a greater increase in the control exercised by the workers than do the managers—demonstrating, again, a distinct hierarchical effect.

Rewards and sanctions. Do members at different levels share a common perception of the rewards and penalties that are likely to be dispensed to members of the organization for good work and bad work? Tables 6.19 and 6.20 indicate that the system of rewards and penalties may be perceived differently by persons at different levels. Compared to persons at lower levels, those at upper levels in general see a more substantial set of consequences following from unusually high or low performance by organization members. For example, as Table 6.19 shows, upper levels more than lower levels see bonuses or pay raises and opportunities for promotion as well as psychological support, such as praise by superiors, to be consequences of unusually good work by a member. A small percentage (12 percent) of the rank-and-file workers report that "nothing will happen" as a consequence of good work, but none of the top managers report this. Similarly, upper-level more than lower-level members see criticism by superiors and fewer opportunities for promotion as consequences of poor work (Table 6.20). Again, a small percentage (9 percent) of the rank-and-file workers say that nothing at all will happen in the case of unusually poor work by members of the or-

Figure 6.4

DISTRIBUTION OF CONTROL AS REPORTED BY
PERSONS AT THREE HIERARCHICAL LEVELS

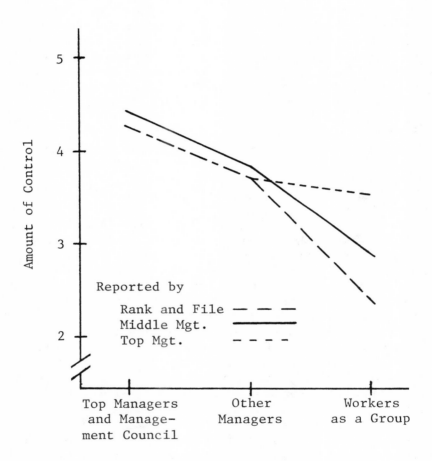

--Hierarchical Scale--

Figure 6.5
PREFERRED DISTRIBUTION OF CONTROL AS REPORTED
BY PERSONS AT THREE HIERARCHICAL LEVELS

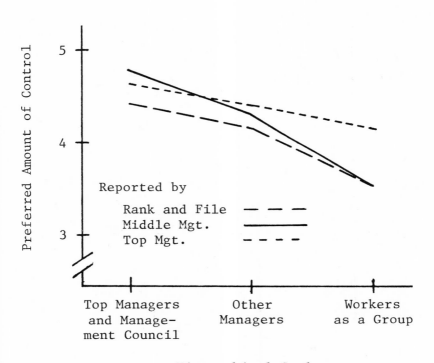

--Hierarchical Scale--

Figure 6.6
DISTRIBUTION OF DISCREPANCY BETWEEN
PREFERRED AND ACTUAL CONTROL AS REPORTED
BY PERSONS AT THREE HIERARCHICAL LEVELS

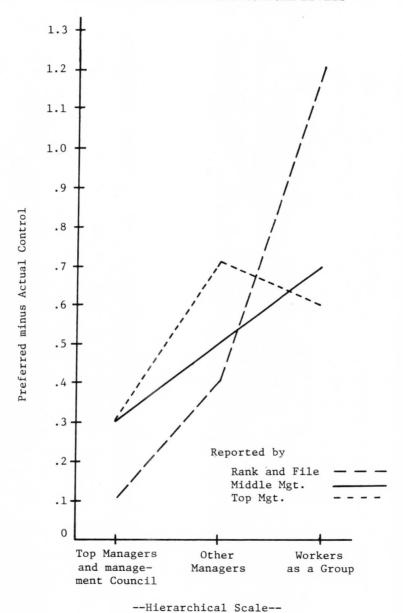

ganization, but none of the top managers indicate this consequence of poor work.

Table 6.19
REWARDS FOR GOOD WORK

Q.12. What happens if a member in this organization does an especially good job in his work?	Percentage of Respondents Checking the Response		
	Top Management	Middle Management	Rank and File
His superior will praise him.	75%.	61%	51%
His co-workers will praise him.	19	10	15
His co-workers will criticize him.	6	8	9
He may be offered a better job at the same level.	19	13	8
He will be given a bonus or higher wage.	81	65	54
His co-workers will have a high opinion of him.	31	26	22
He will have a better opportunity for advancement.	38	24	11
His superior will have a high opinion of him.	50	45	42
Nothing will happen.	0	7	12

Advantages of advancement. Table 6.21 shows a list of possible benefits associated with high rank. Respondents were asked to select and rank in order of their relative priority the three most important benefits. We assigned a score of 3 to the benefit given the highest priority, 2 to the next most important benefit, and 1 to the

Table 6.20

SANCTIONS FOR BAD WORK

Q.14. What happens if a member in this organization does a very poor job?	Percentage of Respondents Checking the Response		
	Top Management	Middle Management	Rank and File
His superior will criticize him.	81%	76%	67%
His co-workers will criticize him.	38	28	28
His co-workers will support him against criticism	6	4	6
He will be given an inferior job.	13	15	10
His salary will be reduced.	13	17	15
His co-workers will have a low opinion of him.	38	23	20
He will have less good opportunities for advancement.	63	33	25
His superior will have a low opinion of him.	50	41	37
Nothing will happen.	0	9	9

third most important benefit. The remaining items were scored 0. The numbers under Rank in Table 6.21 indicate the relative importance of the items for each hierarchical group in terms of the ranking of the average scores for the items in the group. Differences between levels in their perceptions of these benefits are not very striking. All groups see high wages as a major benefit of high rank, but managers somewhat more than rank-and-file workers may also see the opportunity to make decisions as a benefit of high rank.

Table 6.21

PERCEIVED ADVANTAGES ASSOCIATED WITH HIGH POSITION

Q.55. What do you think are the main advantages of moving into a higher position in this plant?[a]	Top Management		Middle Management		Rank and File	
	Score	Rank	Score	Rank	Score	Rank
Prestige or esteem	0.9	7	0.6	7	0.9	5.5
Variety of work	1.8	4.5	1.5	3	1.7	2
Independence	2.0	3	0.8	4.5	0.9	5.5
Social contacts	0.1	9	0.0	9	0.3	8
Opportunity to make decisions	2.2	1.5	1.8	2	1.2	3.5
Opportunity to enlarge skills	1.8	4.5	0.8	4.5	1.2	3.5
Opportunity to enlarge knowledge	1.2	6	0.7	6	0.8	7
Influence people outside the plant	0.4	8	0.1	8	0.1	9
Higher wages	2.2	1.5	2.6	1	2.4	1

Criteria for advancement. Table 6.22 illustrates some differences in how members at different levels perceive what it takes to advance in the hierarchy. Again, these perceptions do not differ markedly, although upper-level persons are more likely than lower-level persons to see quality of work, initiative, creativeness, and outstanding ability to work with people as important criteria for advancement, while lower-level persons more than upper-level persons may see having friends in higher management or "elbowing one's way to get ahead" as important criteria, even though these latter items rank relatively low in all groups.

Table 6.22

Q.16. How important is each of the following factors for getting ahead in this company?	Top Management		Middle Management		Rank and File	
	Score	Rank	Score	Rank	Score	Rank
Quality of work done	3.9	2	3.5	4.5	3.0	7.5
Quantity of work done	3.7	5.5	3.4	7	3.2	4
Supervisor's opinion	3.5	7.5	4.1	1	3.7	1
Dependability	3.8	3.5	3.8	3	3.5	2.5
Creativeness, inventiveness	3.7	5.5	3.1	11	2.6	11.5
Seniority in the plant	3.2	10.5	3.3	9.5	3.1	5.5
Having friends in higher management	2.1	12	2.5	12	2.9	9
Having good professional knowledge	4.1	1	4.0	2	3.5	2.5
Taking initiative	3.8	3.5	3.4	7	2.8	10
Having outstanding ability to work with people	3.5	7.5	3.3	9.5	2.6	11.5
Loyalty to the company	3.4	9	3.5	4.5	3.0	7.5
Recommendations of political nature	3.2	10.5	3.4	7	3.1	5.5
Elbowing one's way to get ahead	1.8	13	2.0	13	2.5	13

Conclusions

We have found that hierarchical level is correlated substantially with the reactions and adjustments of organization members and that a gradient of reaction and adjustment accompanies hierarchy. We assume that the hierarchical distribution of authority and reward helps to explain this hierarchical gradient of reaction and adjustment. Members at upper levels exercise more control, receive higher pay, and have greater opportunities to do work that is personally fulfilling than do members at the bottom. Consequently, those members at upper levels compared to those below are more satisfied with their job and their pay, have more positive attitudes toward their plant leadership, feel a greater sense of responsibility and work motivation, and tend to see the organization in a more favorable light—for example, as being more participative and as providing appropriate rewards for those who perform well.

All groups within the plants indicate that the level of participation in the plant, and in particular the control exercised by the workers, should be greater than it is. The discrepancy between the actual and preferred levels of control and participation, however, is greater as reported by persons at lower levels than at upper levels. The organization functions more as it should in the view of managers than in the view of workers. In any event, the general support within these plants for increasing the plants' participativeness is consistent with the attempt in Hungarian society to achieve the socialist ideal of industrial democracy.

We have also found substantial correlations between hierarchical position and a number of demographic characteristics. Persons at upper levels compared to those below are older, more educated, more likely to be male, and more likely to have greater seniority in the plant. Age and seniority as correlates of hierarchy pose an interesting problem for the development of Hungarian plants, because the managerial and technological skills that are needed in a modern plant are more likely to be found among relatively young, recent graduates of universities or training establishments. The emphasis on seniority in promotion impedes the placement of these young people in positions of responsibility where their skills are needed. Furthermore, older and senior members acquire a sense of security that may reduce their motivation and innovativeness; hence, seniority as a criterion of promotion may be an impediment to the development of modern, flexible, and effective organizations.

For each of the variables of this chapter, we examined (but did not present data regarding) differences between the large and small plants and between the cooperatives and the others. Insofar as the effects of hierarchy are concerned, the similarities between these plants are more apparent than are the differences. All plants show predictable hierarchical effects, and we are not able to see any persistent differences between these plants in the magnitude of these effects. There is some indication, however, that small plants, and particularly the cooperatives, may be somewhat more participative (according to reports of members) than the others and that the total amount of control may be higher than in other plants. Similarly, the data from the small plants and the cooperatives show small but consistent superiority with respect to morale, job opportunities, sense of responsibility felt by members, and the satisfaction with pay felt by managers.

We are not able to argue with certainty about the superiority of the small plants and the cooperatives with respect to the above variables, since the differences that we find are small and we do not have the basis for a carefully controlled comparison. Nor do we know how much of the seeming superiority of the cooperatives is attributable to their size and how much to the cooperative system itself. We take these results, nonetheless, as suggestive of hypotheses that deserve further exploration.

Notes

[1] Code of Labor, Munkatörvénykönyv, Budapest, 1967.

[2] Közpon   ti Statisztikai Hivatal, Ipari adatok, 1977.

[3] For further details of this and other aspects of this research project, see Gyenes & Rozgonyi (1974).

7

Bulgaria

Zahari Staikov, Sasha Todorova, and Krastu Petkov

Introduction

The building of a highly developed socialist society depends not only on the development and improvement of its material bases but also on the development and improvement of socialist relations of production, which are the bases of social progress. Socialist relations of production imply three primary conditions: (1) the means of production are owned by the working people of a society; (2) the goods of organizations are distributed to persons according to their contribution to the production of goods and also, partly, according to their needs; and (3) all persons in society participate in the management of the production process as well as in other aspects of social life.

The work collective (or work organization), such as a factory, is a basic unit in the functioning of socialist relations of production. The work collective also plays an important role in the development of the member as a person, since members spend a large part of their active lives in the work collective. The impact of the work collective on the member is complex and substantial because the work collective enters into many aspects of social life.

One of the basic characteristics of socialist hierarchical relations is the participation of work group members in the management of production and in solving the social problems associated with production. The participation of workers in the management of production as well as in solving its social problems is a direct manifestation of socialist democracy. This participation is broadened through the creation of management bodies such as economic councils and committees and general meetings of all workers. These bodies include representatives of the state, persons from the plant who represent the workers in the plant, and those who are responsible for representing the interest of the general public.

A major domain of participation by workers concerns their formulation of the plan for social and economic development of their
collective and the formulation of the "counterplan." Counterplans
are a recently introduced and more advanced form of socioeconomic
planning in Bulgaria. The notion of the counterplan appeared
several years ago as an outcome of the popular movement in our
country concerning the levels at which the state social and economic
goals should be set. The counterplan is a response to the state plan.
It changes the centrally defined targets of the state plan on the
basis of the existing capacities and possibilities of each work collective. In this way, the inner reserves and possibilities of the socialist
enterprise and its working groups are discovered. The drafting and
approval of counterplans introduce perspective and a dialectic into
planning. Counterplans include the targets for both the production
and social spheres of life. These targets are evaluated by the state
economic organization. If they are found to be realistic, they are
"confirmed," and the plan is adopted officially.

The participation of workers in the management of the plant is
facilitated by several social and political organizations. These include the Communist Party, the Trade Union, the Young Communist League (Komsomol), scientific and technological societies,
and voluntary groups within the plant that assume responsibility
for social control.

Characteristics of Plants Studied

The research described here was carried out from August to
December of 1970 by a scientific team of the Labor Research Institute under the scientific guidance of Professor Zahari Staikov.
The study is based on a total of 499 questionnaires administered to
persons in one small and one large plant in each of five industries.
The industries and the number of persons in our sample from each
plant are: plastics, 74; machine building, 167; canning, 101; non-
ferrous foundry, 91; and furniture, 66 (see Table 7.1). All the
plants studied are independent of one another, and each is a sub-
division of a corresponding state economic organization. The smallest plants contain some 300 members, while some of the large
plants include more than 5,000.

Two plants are located in Sofia; six are in well-developed
economic regions; one is in a developing economic center; and one is
in a rural region. All of the plants have been built during the years
of people's power (established on September 9, 1944), and they are
public property.

We have made the following assumptions in the analysis of our

Table 7.1

CHARACTERISTICS OF PLANTS AND SAMPLE

	Number of Levels	Sample (Number of Respondents)			
		Top Management	Middle Management	Rank and File	Total
Plastics					
Large	6	1	29	9	39
Small	5	1	22	12	35
Machine building					
Large	6	1	57	28	86
Small	6	1	62	18	81
Canning					
Large	8	1	51	11	63
Small	5	1	25	12	38
Foundry					
Large	5	1	38	19	58
Small	5	1	20	12	33
Furniture					
Large	5	1	19	13	33
Small	5	1	26	6	33
Total		10	349	140	499

data:

a. What happens within a work organization cannot be entirely understood without taking into account the larger social system within which the work organization functions. We therefore will consider the implications of the larger system in interpreting data concerning such phenomena as alienation, mobility aspirations, and participation, although speculation concerning these implications cannot be verified through the empirical data of this study.

b. Within each work organization there are units of the party and of the trade union organization that parallel major units of the work organization, such as the work group, the department, and the work organization as a whole. These organizations perform control and managing functions with respect to the fulfillment of the production and the social plans, personnel policy, labor discipline, socialist competition, and the participation by workers in management. This parallel structure helps to explain the behavior of the members of the work organization.

c. There is a need to supplement the subjective measures employed in this research with more objective measures. We have therefore employed a method that we refer to as the method of time budget. The idea of the time budget as an approach to investigating hierarchical relations, and workers' participation in particular, springs from the Marxist-Leninist notion of time as basic to the definition of matter. We have in mind Karl Marx's thought that time is an essence and therefore provides a basis for measuring human activities (see Staikov, 1973, p. 34). Time lends itself well to both quantitative and qualitative analyses. For example, the amount of time people devote to an activity provides an important indicator of the significance of that activity. The concepts of time and space also play a fundamental role in systems theory analyses. The notion of space must include the notion of time; the total amount of time at the disposal of an organization is a dimension of the space it occupies. By measuring time, it is possible to determine and to measure objectively important characteristics of any organization. For example, comparisons of the amount of time spent by workers in participative activities, whether inside the plant or out, are more objective than comparisons based on members' purely subjective estimates of the degree of participation of workers.

Correlates of Hierarchy

Economic and Demographic Characteristics

Salary. A characteristic feature of the hierarchical structure of salary in our country is the narrow range between the highest and the lowest level. This relatively high degree of equality is found in both small and large plants. The fact that the ratio of the salaries of workers to plant managers is 1:2 and of workers to middle managers 1:1.3 shows that the distribution of income depends not only on the degree of responsibility and complexity of the job but on other social and economic considerations as well (see Table 7.2).

On the basis of these peculiarities, we conclude that large salary differentials are not an inherent characteristic of organizational hierarchy, although they may be an incidental indicator that helps

Table 7.2

ECONOMIC AND DEMOGRAPHIC CHARACTERISTICS OF MEMBERS

	Top Management	Middle Management	Rank and File
Salary (average leva per month)	253.0	162.9	122.1
Education[a]	5.8	5.2	3.7
Age (average years)	46.3	37.6	36.1
Plant seniority[b]	5.9	6.1	5.1
Sex (percentage female)	0.0	14.5	37.1

[a]Education is measured on a scale where 1 = less than 4 years, 2 = 4 to 6 years, 3 = 6 to 8 years, 4 = 8 to 10 years, 5 = 10 to 12 years, and 6 = more than 12 years of education.

[b]Plant seniority is measured on the following scale: 1 = under 6 months, 2 = 6 months to 1 year, 3 = 1 to 2 years, 4 = 2 to 3 years, 5 = 3 to 6 years, 6 = 6 to 10 years, 7 = 10 to 20 years, and 8 = 20 years or more.

to describe the character of hierarchy in an organization. The relatively high degree of equality in distribution of salary in Bulgaria illustrates the effect of the larger social system on the work organization.

Education. One feature of the hierarchical distribution of education in the plants studied is the small difference between top and middle managers in their level of education. Calculated in terms of a six-point scale, on which 1 means less than four years of school and 6 means more than twelve years, the average level of education is 5.8 for the top managers and 5.2 for middle managers. In large plants where the specialists are usually highly qualified, the level of education is above average—6.0 and 5.2 for the top and middle levels, respectively. Top managers have university degrees in four out of five of both the small and the large plants studied. The requirements of high educational qualification have become a rule in Bulgaria. It is now typical of our industrial system that specialists with a university education enter positions that were traditionally occupied by specialists with only a high school education or less. This can be seen as a positive trend if we consider the growing requirements of modern technology for the training of highly qualified specialists.

Education is one of the most important requirements for advancement in the hierarchy. In the absence of other social barriers, workers' efforts to achieve more education are likely to lead to upward social and professional mobility.

Age. The average age of the personnel in the plants studied is 37.3 years. With the exception of top managers (who are older in the large plants than in the small ones), no significant difference exists in the average age of those employed in large and in small plants. Middle managers are surprisingly young in view of the extra years most of them take for a university education.

Seniority in the plant. Compared to the other demographic characteristics, hierarchical differences in seniority are the smallest. In the large plants, however, the highest seniority is observed at the top and the middle of the hierarchy.

Sex. The proportion of women in both large and small plants diminishes with hierarchical ascent. Women's share in middle management, however, is higher in the large plants than in the small ones—17.1 percent compared to 10.8 percent. The relatively high percentage of female workers in the total sample can be attributed mainly to the canning plants and, to some extent, the engineering plants (where most of the jobs occupied by women require high qualifications). On the other hand, the number of women in the foundries is practically zero, due to the difficult working conditions in these plants.

Role Characteristics

Authority and influence. The exercise of influence by all members of a plant is a realization of their status as co-owners of the means of production under socialism. Increasing the influence exercised by members should therefore be looked upon as a means of increasing democracy. Socialist society in Bulgaria has therefore created the necessary conditions and social structures for members to exercise effective influence as a way of contributing to the solution of the social, economic, and other problems of the work organization.

The degree of authority and influence of plant members at different levels is different as reported by persons at those respective levels. Figure 7.1 shows these data.

Persons at the top have the highest influence; rank-and-file workers, the lowest. The relatively low level of influence that each worker ascribes to himself or herself, however, does not imply necessarily a correspondingly low level of influence of the workers as a group. Through appropriate organization, workers, each of

Figure 7.1
HIERARCHICAL DISTRIBUTION OF AUTHORITY/INFLUENCE
BASED ON SELF-REPORTS

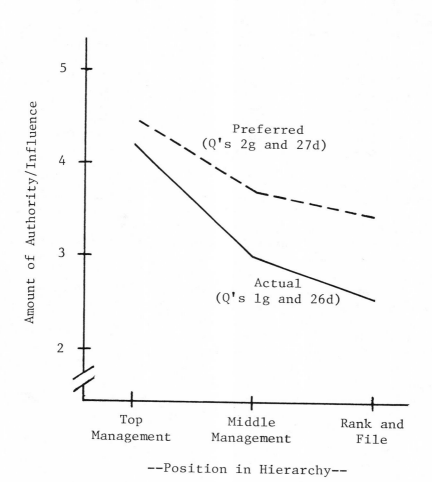

whom has only modest influence, may together exercise substantial influence. Nonetheless, individual workers do have less influence than individual managers.

The influence of individual workers may be lower than it should be according to the socialist ideal. This may be explained by several circumstances in Bulgaria. First, the level of education of the work force is relatively low. Effective participation requires certain technical knowledge and intellectual skill, and this knowledge and skill on the part of the worker will increase as workers become more educated. Second, participation by workers in management was introduced in Bulgaria only 30 years prior to this study. Traditionally, Bulgarian plants, like plants in most societies, had been authoritarian. The changing structure of Bulgarian society, which is becoming more participative, will help to create the habits and attitudes on the part of the workers that are appropriate to their participation in management.

Participativeness and supportiveness of superior. The relationship between subordinates and their immediate superior is one of the most important aspects of the work organization. We attempted to gauge this relationship through responses to the questions indicated in Table 7.3. In Bulgaria, middle managers assign high scores to their immediate superior, especially with respect to their superior asking their opinion when a problem related to their work comes up. Furthermore, the style of management of top managers is such that it wins the trust of their subordinates. The fact that "trust in the immediate superior" comes second in the evaluations given by the middle managers is important, since it shows subordinates' acceptance of the manager and his or her style of work. On the whole, the workers' estimate of their immediate superior's participativeness is slightly lower than the estimate given by middle managers, although workers do express a high degree of trust in their superiors. The lowest score in Table 7.3 has to do with workers' evaluations of whether superiors take into account the opinions of the subordinates.

Bases of superior's power. Superiors must have a basis of power if they are to function effectively in their role. Accordingly, we asked respondents about their reasons for doing what their immediate superior asks of them. The results in response to this question are presented in Table 7.4. Members attach very great importance to the need for the organization to function properly, and this need is cited as a primary reason for doing what their superior asks of them. Members also cite their sense of duty. These bases of the superior's power reflect the absence of conflicting group and personal interests in the plant and contribute to obedience by subor-

Table 7.3

PARTICIPATIVENESS AND SUPPORTIVENESS OF SUPERIOR

	Middle Management	Rank and File
Q.41. Does your immediate superior ask your opinion when a problem comes up that involves your work?	4.4	3.9
Q.42. Is your immediate superior inclined to take into account your opinions and suggestions?	3.8	3.4
Q.43. Is your immediate superior friendly and easily approached if there are problems?	3.6	3.5
Q.44. Does your immediate superior make people under him feel free to take their complaints to him?	3.7	3.7
Q.46. Do you have trust in your immediate superior?	4.1	4.2

dinates to their superiors' requests or instructions.

Workers and middle managers differ from one another in citing their superior's attractiveness as a person and ability to penalize them as reasons for their doing what he or she asks. The workers attach more importance to personal attractiveness, while middle managers stress somewhat more the superior's ability to penalize, although this reason comes last for both groups.

Enriching qualities of the job. Persons at upper levels compared to those at lower levels report greater opportunities, such as the opportunity to use one's skills, to learn new things, to do interesting work, and to set one's own work pace. Figure 7.2 presents the distribution of an index based on an average of these enriching qualities of a job as reported by organization members. All groups indicate that they would like to have more of these opportunities

Table 7.4

BASES OF THE SUPERIOR'S POWER AS REPORTED BY SUBORDINATES

Q.47. When you do what your immediate superior requests you to do on the job, why do you do it?	Middle Management	Rank and File
I respect his competence and judgment.	3.7	3.9
He can give special help and benefits.	3.6	3.7
He's a nice guy.	3.3	3.8
He can penalize or otherwise disadvantage me.	3.0	2.6
It is my duty.	4.3	4.0
It is necessary if the organization is to function properly.	4.2	4.2

than they actually do have, but the discrepancy between actual and desired opportunities appears to be greater at the bottom than at the other levels of the hierarchy.

Physical qualities of the job. Physical qualities of the job, measured on a five-point scale, also vary as a function of hierarchical position, as can be seen in Table 7.5. For example, jobs at the bottom compared to those at the top are reported to be physical, dirtier, heavier, and more dangerous.

Reactions and Adjustments

Morale

Table 7.6 presents data concerning three indicators of morale. The first, job satisfaction, is based on an index consisting of measures of satisfaction at work compared with satisfaction outside of work (Q.8), satisfaction with company (Q.9), and satisfaction with job (Q.10). The second indicator, satisfaction with pay, is based on a single question (Q.59). The third is attitude toward company leadership, measured by an index consisting of three questions

Figure 7.2
ENRICHING QUALITIES OF THE JOB BASED ON SELF-REPORTS

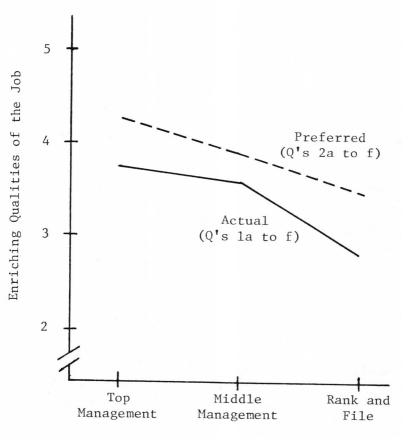

--Position in Hierarchy--

Table 7.5

PHYSICAL QUALITIES OF THE JOB

	Top Management (n = 9)	Middle Management (n = 170)	Rank and File (n = 165)
Unhealthful (1) – healthful (5)	3.3	2.3	2.1
Physical (1) – mental (5)	4.2	3.2	1.8
Dirty (1) – clean (5)	4.1	2.8	1.9
Heavy (1) – light (5)	3.2	2.4	2.2
Same tasks during the day (1) – different tasks during the day (5)	3.6	3.2	2.5
Dangerous (1) – safe (5)	4.1	2.7	2.4
Average (Q.3)	3.8	2.8	2.2

Table 7.6

MORALE

	Top Management	Middle Management	Rank and File
Job satisfaction (Q.8, 9, 10)	4.2	3.7	3.4
Satisfaction with pay (Q.59)	3.7	3.2	3.1
Attitude toward plant leadership (Q.24, 25, 28)	3.0	3.1	3.0

(Q.24, Q.25, and Q.28).

Job satisfaction and satisfaction with pay both increase with hierarchical rank, indicating that morale may be higher at the top of the organization than at the bottom, although the attitude of members toward plant leadership does not appear to be different for persons of different rank.

Table 7.7 presents regression analyses designed to predict each of the above measures of morale. The most important determinants of job satisfaction in this regression are the physical qualities of the job and the enriching opportunities it provides. Authority/influence ranks third in importance. The negative relationship of education to morale corresponds to findings in earlier work in a number of countries (Tannenbaum et al., 1974), including some in the other chapters of this book, indicating that education may have negative effects on a person's satisfaction with his or her job when rank and the other conditions defined by the regression analysis are controlled.

Table 7.7

THE RELATIVE IMPORTANCE OF THE PREDICTORS OF MORALE

Multiple R Predictors	Job Satisfaction .51		Satisfaction with Pay .59		Attitude toward Plant Leadership .50	
	Beta	Rank	Beta	Rank	Beta	Rank
Enriching job qualities	.43	1	.37	4	.16	5
Authority/ influence	.29	3	.16	6	.50	1
Physical job qualities	.32	2	.68	1	.41	2
Education	−.19	6	.02	8	−.05	9
Age	.18	7	.17	5	.13	6
Plant seniority	.26	5	.00	9	−.18	4
Length of chain	−.08	9	.03	7	−.08	7
Level in hierarchy	.27	4	.62	2	−.07	8
Salary	−.10	8	.54	3	.21	3

Salary presumably is an important aspect of a person's job, and one might expect it to be an important and positive determinant of one's satisfaction with one's job. But this does not prove to be the case. In fact, salary may be of little importance, for a couple of reasons. First, the range of salary is rather narrow in Bulgaria, and variation within this range may not make very much difference to organization members. Second, there is in Bulgaria a high degree of economic security for all organization members; therefore, salary does not have the important implications that it might have in the absence of economic security (see Yadov & Zdravomislov, 1967). On the other hand, a person's salary does have positive implications for his or her satisfaction with pay, although the qualities of the job and a person's rank may be even more important than salary as a determinant of a person's satisfaction with his or her pay.

The authority/influence that a person perceives himself or herself to have appears to be the single most important predictor in the regression analysis of a member's attitude toward plant management. Comparatively high beta values have also been obtained for salary and physical qualities of the job as predictors of attitude toward plant management. Presumably, the attitude of members toward plant leadership should depend on the members' hierarchical level, but the results of the regression analysis indicate very little importance for this factor. Thus, the lack of relationship between rank and attitude toward management indicated earlier in Table 7.5 is repeated under the controlled conditions of the regression analysis.

Motivation

Table 7.8 presents several indicators of motivation, including measures concerning (a) the feeling of responsibility that members feel for the success of their work group, department, and plant as a whole (Q.11); (b) their "motivation" or their (lack of) dependence on the supervisor for improving performance (Q.6); and (c) their initiative in developing new and better ways of doing the work (Q.7). Table 7.8 suggests that these indicators of motivation are higher among managers than among workers, although the differences between levels do not appear to be large. Nonetheless, as the regression analyses of Table 7.9 suggest, hierarchical position is the single most important predictor of work motivation and the responsibility that individuals feel in the organization. The managers' feeling of responsibility in the organization undoubtedly reflects the objective, formal responsibility that is assigned to them. If, however, we look

at the sense of responsibility for *one's own work group*, which is a
component of the larger index of responsibility, we find that
authority/influence, enriching qualities of the job, and physical
qualities of the job rank high as predictors, although the multiple
correlation in this regression is low.

Table 7.8

MOTIVATIONAL ASPECTS

	Top Management	Middle Management	Rank and File
Responsibility for the system (Q.11a, b, c)	4.3	4.2	3.9
Motivation on the job (Q.6)	3.1	3.5	2.7
Initiative (Q.7)	4.4	3.8	3.4

In general, the multiple regressions of Table 7.9 provide only a
very partial explanation of these measures of members' motivation.
Some of these measures might be better explained by other conditions, both internal and external to the plant, that we have not included in the regression analysis. For example, ownership of the
means of production itself—which is a condition defined by the
larger society—represents, we believe, an important determinant of
the sense of responsibility that members will feel in an organization.
Because this condition does not enter as a variable in our regression
analysis, the predictive value of the model is not as high as it might
be.

Mobility Aspirations

The aspirations of members to advance in the hierarchy
represent a further indicator of the motivation of members in the
organization. We measured such aspirations through a question
that asked whether respondents would or would not accept a higher
position in the organization despite difficulties that such a position
would create for them. Table 7.10 lists these difficulties. Managers
do not appear to differ very much from workers in their response to
these questions. For both groups, frequent criticism is the difficulty
they would be most reluctant to accept. Sacrifice associated with

Table 7.9

THE RELATIVE IMPORTANCE OF THE PREDICTORS OF MOTIVATIONAL ASPECTS

Predictors	Responsibility for System .56		Responsibility for Own Work .35		Motivation .41		Initiative .40	
Multiple R	Beta	Rank	Beta	Rank	Beta	Rank	Beta	Rank
Enriching job qualities	−.02	9	.46	2	−.15	5	.75	1
Authority/influence	.17	4	.51	1	.12	6	.25	3
Physical job qualities	−.07	6	.23	3	−.11	7	−.14	4
Education	−.04	8	−.10	7.5	−.24	3	−.04	6
Age	−.05	7	−.11	6	−.10	8	−.03	7
Plant seniority	.11	5	.10	7.5	−.17	4	.37	2
Length of chain	−.23	2.5	.05	9	−.09	9	−.02	8
Level in hierarchy	.98	1	−.13	5	.47	1	−.10	5
Salary	−.23	2.5	.19	4	−.41	2	−.01	9

acquiring skills is the most acceptable difficulty.

Table 7.10
UPWARD MOBILITY ASPIRATION

Q.48. Imagine you were offered the following possibilities within this plant. Would you accept them or not?	Percentage Who Would Accept a Higher Position Despite Difficulties	
	Middle Management	Rank and File
Move to a higher position involving:		
Additional obligations and responsibilities	56%	55%
Training requirements	59	55
Frequent criticism	43	40
"Problem" employees	45	47
More work worries	51	51
Average	51	50

Personal Adjustment

Table 7.11 presents data based on a question designed to measure the psychological adjustment of respondents. On the five-point scale that was employed, a high score—which implies disagreement with each of a number of statements—implies favorable adjustment. Two items in the original questionnaire, used in the other countries reported in this book, were dropped because of translation difficulties. In general, the data based on the six items that are shown in Table 7.11 are not different for members at different ranks.

We measured alienation as a further aspect of the adjustment of organization members. For Marx, man's relationship to his work is the basis for understanding alienation, and ownership of the means of production is the basis for defining the relationship of man to his work. Alienation derives from a lack of ownership; people are

Table 7.11

PSYCHOLOGICAL ADJUSTMENT[a]

Q.49. How true are the following statements?	Top Management	Middle Management	Rank and File
I feel depressed.	3.3	3.6	3.7
Other people are always more lucky than I.	3.2	3.1	3.4
Usually everything I try seems to fail.	4.3	4.2	4.0
Things seem hopeless.	3.9	4.1	4.2
I feel resentful.	3.8	4.0	4.3
I sometimes feel that my life is not very useful.	3.9	4.3	4.4
Average	3.7	3.9	4.0

[a]The data in the table are averages for the respective groups on a five-point scale in which 5 represents disagreement with the statement.

alienated if they do not own the means of production. Their behavior at work is determined strongly by the owner of the means of production, to whom they sell their work effort. Because they do not own the means of production, they do not own the product or the profit of production; they are thus alienated from their work. The subject of investigation, however, is not this social aspect of alienation, which originates in a society where private ownership dominates.

We have measured certain general, subjective aspects of alienation, general feelings of powerlessness, normlessness, and psychological isolation. Table 7.12 presents the data. These subjective aspects of alienation appear to be somewhat higher for workers than for managers.

Table 7.13 presents a regression analysis designed to explain the subjective feelings of alienation. Enriching qualities of the job along with the job's physical qualities appear to be relatively important for both psychological adjustment and alienation. On the other hand, some characteristics that are closely associated with hierar-

Table 7.12
ALIENATION[a]

Q.52. How true are the following statements?	Top Management	Middle Management	Rank and File
It is not possible to rely on others.	2.7	2.7	3.2
Today it is practically impossible to find real friends because everyone thinks only of himself.	1.8	2.6	3.1
Men like me cannot influence the course of events; only men in high position can have such influence.	2.2	3.5	3.8
I have never had the influence over others that I would have liked.	1.9	3.1	2.9
Public affairs are so complicated that one cannot help but be confused by them.	2.5	2.7	2.9
Despite the many advances science has made, life today is too complicated.	3.4	3.7	3.7
I can never do what I really like because circumstances require that I do otherwise.	3.4	2.8	3.3
Life is so routinized that I do not have a chance to use my true abilities.	2.3	2.6	3.0
Life seems to be moving on without rules or order.	1.8	2.1	2.4
Nowadays it is hard to know right from wrong.	1.5	2.3	2.8
Average	2.3	2.9	3.1

[a]The data in the table are averages for the respective groups on a five-point scale in which 5 represents agreement with the statement.

chy, such as level, authority/influence, and length of chain, are apparently less important.

Table 7.13

THE RELATIVE IMPORTANCE OF THE
PREDICTORS OF PERSONAL ADJUSTMENT

Multiple R	Psychological Adjustment .49		Alienation .53	
Predictors	Beta	Rank	Beta	Rank
Enriching job qualities	.61	1	−.45	2
Authority/influence	−.07	6	−.27	4
Physical job qualities	.54	2	−.38	3
Education	−.02	9	.21	5
Age	.16	4	.03	9
Plant seniority	−.06	7	.17	6
Length of chain	−.17	3	.08	8
Level in hierarchy	.03	8	−.09	7
Salary	.14	5	−.51	1

Perceptions

Decision making. Table 7.14 presents data to examine the extent to which hierarchical groups differ in their perception of the participativeness of their plants. Several facts are suggested by this table. First, managers see their plants as more participative than do workers. Second, all groups indicate that the plant should be more participative than they believe it is. Third, the discrepancy between members' perception of participativeness in the plant and the level of participativeness they prefer for the plant decreases with hierarchical ascent: Managers' perceptions of the plant fit their preference more than workers' perceptions fit theirs.

Rewards and penalties. Many activities in organizations can be viewed as learning processes that entail the possibility of mistakes and that, in turn, lead some workers to lag behind others or to fall short of requirements. Criticism is a means of expressing an attitude toward collective life and is a tool for eliminating defects. A critical attitude on the part of managers indicates a commitment to

Table 7.14

PERCEPTIONS AND PREFERENCES ABOUT THE PARTICIPATIVENESS
IN THE PLANTS, MEASURED IN TERMS OF LIKERT'S MODEL

	Perceptions by:[a]		
	Top Management	Middle Management	Rank and File
Q.34. Actual participation by workers in job decisions	3.1	2.8	2.3
Q.35. Preferred participation by workers in job decisions	3.4	3.4	3.3
Discrepancy Q.35 − Q.34	0.3	0.6	1.0
Q.36. Actual participation by workers in plant decisions	2.9	2.6	2.0
Q.37. Preferred participation by workers in plant decisions	3.3	3.1	3.0
Discrepancy Q.37 − Q.36	0.4	0.5	1.0
Q.39. Actual extent to which opinions are asked of those who are affected by decisions	2.8	2.8	2.4
Q.40. Preferred extent	3.2	3.3	3.2
Discrepancy Q.40 − Q.39	0.4	0.5	0.8

[a]The data presented in this table are averages for the respective groups on a four-point scale where 4 implies a high degree of participation.

high standards and helps to maintain a well-developed social system.

Control is closely connected with the established norms of life, including the norm of responsibility. Control by superiors and colleagues helps to define the mode of life in the working group. Table 7.15 illustrates some of the norms that apply to the regulation of work as perceived by persons at different hierarchical levels. The data of this table are based on a question designed to ascertain the consequences to members of their doing an especially good job. Table 7.16 shows data concerning the consequences of poor work. Top managers, more than middle managers and workers, indicate that praise by superiors and possibilities for advancement are the more common consequences of good work performed by an organization member, although relatively large proportions of middle managers and workers also report these consequences of good work. Some middle managers and workers also indicate that nothing will happen as a consequence of good work, but none of the top managers report this consequence.

Table 7.16 shows that relatively large percentages of all groups see criticism by the superior as a likely consequence of bad work, but a somewhat larger proportion of top managers than of middle managers and workers perceive worse opportunities for advancement or being given an inferior job as consequences of bad work. On the other hand, some middle managers and workers (but none of the top managers) indicate that nothing will happen or that co-workers will support the poor performer against criticism—although the percentage of respondents who report these consequences is small.

Advantages of advancement. An important objective of the hierarchical structure of the plant is to provide opportunities for the development of the individual. Tables 7.17 and 7.18 provide some indication of the values that organization members perceive to be associated with advancement in the hierarchy.

Table 7.17 indicates that high wages, prestige or esteem, and independence are considered by all groups to be relatively important benefits of advancement, although top managers attach somewhat more importance to independence while workers and middle managers give higher priority to wages and prestige or esteem. Workers and middle managers also attach importance to the possibilities that are provided through advancement to enlarge one's knowledge, but top managers do not rank this benefit high; nor do they consider influence outside the plant as a benefit of advancement.

The relatively high value attached to salary and to prestige

Table 7.15

REWARDS FOR GOOD WORK

Q.12. What happens if a member in this organization does an especially good job in his work?	Percentage of Respondents Checking the Response[a]		
	Top Management	Middle Management	Rank and File
His superior will praise him.	33.3%	24.0%	25.0%
His co-workers will praise him.	11.1	7.5	12.5
His co-workers will criticize him.	0.0	1.4	0.0
He may be offered a better job at the same level.	0.0	3.5	3.1
He will be given a bonus or higher wage.	11.1	11.9	19.4
His co-workers will have a high opinion of him.	11.1	10.1	5.0
He will have a better opportunity for advancement.	33.4	18.2	11.9
His superior will have a high opinion of him.	0.0	5.2	8.1
Nothing will happen.	0.0	18.2	15.0
Total	100.0	100.0	100.0

[a]Each person checked one response. In other countries, where respondents could check more than one response, the picture looks different.

helps to explain a conflict experienced by some organization members. Because salary differentials between ranks are not very great, some middle managers are paid less than some workers. These middle managers have more prestige than workers; nonetheless, they may prefer the larger salary of the workers. Some, in

Table 7.16

SANCTIONS FOR BAD WORK

Q.14. What happens if a member in this organization does a very poor job?	Percentage of Respondents Checking the Response[a]		
	Top Management	Middle Management	Rank and File
His superior will criticize him.	30.0%	39.2%	26.0%
His co-workers will criticize him.	10.0	13.0	17.5
His co-workers will support him against criticism.	0.0	2.3	10.4
He will be given an inferior job.	20.0	7.2	11.0
His salary will be reduced.	0.0	6.6	8.4
His co-workers will have a low opinion of him.	0.0	4.6	5.2
He will have a less good opportunity for advancement.	30.0	15.6	9.1
His superior will have a low opinion of him.	10.0	3.7	5.2
Nothing will happen.	0.0	7.8	7.2
Total	100.0	100.0	100.0

[a]In Bulgaria each person was asked to check one response rather than several, as in other countries.

fact, choose to become workers, giving up the prestige of their management position in order to have the somewhat higher salary. This issue deserves further study.

Criteria for advancement. Advancement not only provides benefits; it also implies requirements. Table 7.18 presents data concerning a list of criteria that respondents indicated are possible bases for advancement in their plant. All groups indicate quality of

Table 7.17

PERCEIVED ADVANTAGES ASSOCIATED WITH HIGH POSITION

Q.55. What do you think are the main advantages of moving into a higher position in this plant?	Top Management		Middle Management		Rank and File	
	Score[a]	Rank[b]	Score	Rank	Score	Rank
Prestige or esteem	0.9	3	1.6	2	1.9	2
Variety of work	0.8	4	1.3	3	0.7	6
Independence	1.4	1	1.2	4	1.0	4.5
Social contacts	0.4	6	0.8	5	1.0	4.5
Opportunity to make decisions	0.7	5	1.2	4	0.6	6
Opportunity to enlarge knowledge	0.3	7	1.6	2	1.1	3
Influence people outside plant	0.0	8	0.4	6	0.7	6
Higher wages	1.2	2	2.5	1	2.5	1

[a]Respondents were asked to select the three most important items and to rank them from 1 to 3 in the order of their importance. We assigned a score of 0 if the item was not ranked at all, 1 if the item was ranked third, 2 if the item was ranked second, and 3 if the item was ranked first. High scores imply high importance.

[b]Items are ranked according to their relative importance, based on the responses of all respondents.

work, loyalty to plant, and dependability to be relatively important criteria for advancement. Workers do appear to differ from top managers, however, in that they are less likely to see professional knowledge, initiative, and creativeness as important requirements. None of the groups indicate that having friends in higher management is an important requirement for advancement.

Table 7.18
CRITERIA FOR ADVANCEMENT

Q.16. How important is each of the following factors for getting ahead in this company?[a]	Top Management		Middle Management		Rank and File	
	Score	Rank	Score	Rank	Score	Rank
Quality of work	4.2	2	3.9	1	3.9	1
Quantity of work	3.2	7	3.7	3	3.6	3
Supervisor's opinion	3.9	4	3.8	2	3.6	3
Dependability	4.0	3	3.9	1	3.7	2
Creativeness, inventiveness	3.6	5	3.5	5	2.8	9
Seniority in the plant	3.5	6	3.4	6	3.4	5
Having friends in higher management	3.0	8	3.3	7	2.8	9
Having good professional knowledge	4.3	1	3.8	2	3.5	4
Taking initiative	4.3	1	3.7	3	3.3	6
Having outstanding ability to work with people	4.2	2	3.8	2	3.4	5
Loyalty to the company	4.3	1	3.8	2	3.7	2
Recommendations of political and social organizations	3.6	5	3.6	4	3.1	7
Personal drive[b]	3.6	5	3.4	6	3.0	8

[a]Worker respondents were asked to think in terms of advancement in their department.

[b]The idea of "personal drive," which has positive connotations in Bulgaria, was substituted in the questionnaire for "elbowing one's way to get ahead," which was an item included in the questionnaires of other countries.

Studying "Actual" and "Preferred" Participation Using the Time Budget Technique

The objective of this part of the investigation is to test the hypothesis that one can measure the basic parameters of an organization by means of time budgets.

Time is limited; therefore, the time that should be allocated to various activities might be studied as an optimization problem. The actual time spent in various activities might then be compared to the optimum time, and this comparison might provide a basis for evaluating the organization. We have approached this task by compiling a time budget for organization members. We asked each respondent, through an interview, to report how he or she allocated his or her time during a 24-hour period. On this basis we were able to calculate, among other things, the amount of time spent in participation in management. In addition, we administered a questionnaire designed to obtain estimates from respondents concerning their "actual" and "preferred" influence with respect to the 30 areas listed below. These estimates were made on a five-point scale. We also asked respondents to report the amount of time they spent and would like to spend on these activities. We defined the activities in terms of their relevance to participation rather than in terms of their form (such as whether or not the activities were council meetings or work group meetings). We are concerned here with participation in the plant, not with participation more generally. The 30 issues were divided into the four groups shown below:

1. Production planning and fulfillment of production plan and the counterplan:

   Amount of production
   Productivity of labor
   Variety of goods
   New construction
   Materials supply
   Supply of tools
   Counterplan

2. Industrial engineering and remuneration:

   Fixing rates
   Fixing bonuses
   Fixing rewards
   Fixing remuneration
   Improving discipline
   Organizing socialist emulation (competition)

3. Scheduling of work time and recreation:

   Food in canteens
   Rest during the working day
   Accident and disease prevention
   Days off and work shift routine
   Beginning and end of working hours

4. Selection and promotion of personnel:

   Recruitment
   Dismissal
   Punishment
   Promotion
   Recommendations for appointment of direct superior
   Selection of direct superior

The degree of impact a person has on specific events is, in fact, a manifestation of the amount of control the person exercises. Estimates on a five-point scale of influence are subjective indicators of such control. The amount of time spent by an individual in "influencing" events represents the "price" of control in terms of the effort made to exercise control.

The distribution of the time spent by a group in influencing various activities indicates where the main efforts of the group are directed and what issues the group is concerned about.

Several facts are suggested by our time budget data. In both large and small enterprises, more than 40 percent of the time devoted to participation in management is directed toward issues of production planning. However, the time that individuals prefer to spend on participation in production planning is greater than the amount they actually spend in only two of the ten enterprises, and those are large ones.

The issues of industrial engineering and labor remuneration are second in importance. They occupy about 30 percent of the time devoted to participation in management, and there is no significant difference between actual and preferred participation with respect to these activities.

Problems connected with the scheduling of work time and recreation routines occupy third place. On the average, these problems take up 15 to 18 percent of the time for participation in management, and no significant difference between ideal and real participation was observed.

Personnel issues are in fourth place; about 12 percent of the participation time is devoted to these issues. On the whole, there is no difference between small and large enterprises in the average amount of time for participation in decision making on personnel issues, but in large enterprises the *wish* is to reduce this type of time expenditure, while the reverse is true in small enterprises.

We have discussed above the relative share of time spent for various kinds of activities related to control, which we take as a way of describing an aspect of the structure of control in an organization. The total amount of time devoted to control, however, is also an important aspect of control in an organization. The sum of the time for control may be taken as an indication of the total amount of control, and this amount need not be constant in an organization. For example, if a greater right to exercise control is given to lower hierarchical units and greater time is therefore spent in participative activities, this need not curtail the time spent nor the amount of control exercised by higher units. Under socialism, an increase of control on the part of all people is possible for everyone's benefit, through general improvement of the efficiency of organization and the expansion of man's control over nature.

What is the total amount of time spent in enterprises for participation in management? Our investigation in the ten enterprises shows that 153 hours, on the average, are spent annually per person (for exercising influence concerning the 30 issues), while the preferred level of participation requires 143 hours. In other words, people wish to spend less time on participation in management than they are spending now. The subjective estimate by respondents of the influence they exercise is 2.1 on a five-point scale, and they would prefer 2.4. Apparently, members would like to increase their influence while decreasing the time spent in exercising it. This implies cutting the "price" of influence—which might, in principle, occur if participation were made more efficient.

The distribution of control (measured by the distribution of time spent in participation) is almost the same in large and small enterprises, but the amount of control (measured by the total amount of time) reveals significant differences between these two groups of enterprises. The annual expenditure per person is 165 hours in large enterprises and 132 hours in small ones. At the same time, participation in management, as estimated by members in terms of a five-point scale, is slightly greater in small enterprises than in large ones.

Thus, in the small enterprises, members spend less time participating in management, but their estimate of their influence is higher. Therefore, we may speak of greater efficiency of management in small enterprises. Efficiency can be measured by the "price" in hours per unit of influence.

One scale point of influence is achieved by the expenditure of 83 hours per person annually in large enterprises and 63 hours in small enterprises. The preferred price of participation is considerably lower than the real price. The real price in the ten enterprises is 73 hours, while the preferred price is 60 hours. Workers want to participate more actively in management—to have greater influence in making decisions on various issues—but at a lower price. Indices of price can be useful descriptors of organizational functioning. For example, what is the price of participation to various personnel categories and to different hierarchical levels? What are the trends over time in the price? Is the price going up or down?

We would like to discuss these question bearing in mind (1) that the price of participation in management is higher in large enterprises than in small, and the tendency in Bulgaria is toward larger enterprises; and (2) that the tendency in Bulgaria is also toward an increase in the number of hierarchical levels; and, as we shall see below, the price for participation increases with the number of hierarchical levels and is higher at upper levels than at lower levels.

While the average person in our sample wants to spend less time on influence, the workers themselves, as we shall see, are willing to devote more time to participation and to pay a higher price for it. (It is possible to state that the general tendency in Bulgaria is toward a rise in both the amount and the price of participation.)

Differences in the price of participation for different groups are very large. To a worker, the price of one point on our scale is 16 hours annually; to middle management, 80 hours; to directors, 203 hours. Directors, however, want to spend only 177 hours and middle management not more than 63 hours, while workers wish to spend 21 hours annually. (In small enterprises the figure is 25 hours; in large enterprises it is 18 hours.)

While managers do not want to spend more time for participation than they are spending at present, they do want to have greater influence. Thus, they will have to be more efficient in their exercise of influence if they are to achieve their intent. Workers, on the other hand, prefer to spend more time for participation and to have greater influence, and they are willing to pay a higher price for their increased influence. (For example, they propose an increase from 16 to 21 hours per unit of influence in large enterprises and from 17 to 25 hours in small ones.)

Conclusions Concerning Time Budgets

The ratio of efficiency that we have discussed assumes that the measures have equal intervals. This assumption may not be entirely valid; further work may be needed to improve these measures. We believe, nonetheless, that we are illustrating a method that has great potential. This method deserves further development because of the importance of the issues to which it can be applied and because of the possibilities that we have demonstrated in this exploratory study.

There is a need to compute time budgets in terms of the total amount of time in hours per year that persons in different groups spend with respect to a variety of issues (such as those shown earlier). Furthermore, there is a need to map out the time that individuals devote to participation throughout their working lives. It is desirable to obtain time budgets for extended periods of time, since participation in management, like many natural phenomena, has a cyclical character. Thus, important comparisons between industries, regions, and even nations might be made.

This aspect of the study was designed to explore the notion of time budgets as a way of describing important aspects of organizational behavior. A number of questions, however, that are relevant to the issues of this research and amenable to study in conjunction with time budgets have not been considered. It would be useful in further research, for example, to investigate the extent to which the range of activities involving control is acceptable in all countries and the extent to which people in various countries participate in decisions concerning the distribution of profits. Time budgets for participation provide a means for examining questions such as:

What is the level of efficiency of the management in the organization?

Are functions (control) properly distributed?

Do people fully utilize the right of control given to them?

The answers can be found by evaluating the time expenditures along with the subjective evaluations of groups of workers, hierarchical groups, or other task groups concerning participation.

Actions have already been taken in our country to expand the rights of the trade unions and to increase workers' participation in solving the fundamental production, communal, and social problems of any labor team. Methods that serve to measure and thus help to improve the efficiency of the time spent in participation in management, and the proper distribution and utilization of that time, can therefore be useful.

All of these complex problems will find their best solution in the expansion of international cooperation, especially between the socialist states.

Conclusions

The results of the investigation carried out in ten industrial enterprises suggest the following conclusions:

1. There is a close relationship between hierarchy and the sociodemographic characteristics of organization members. This applies mainly to education and only weakly to salary, seniority, age, and sex.

2. Hierarchical structure (together with the other socioeconomic factors) is an important determinant of the attitudes and the reactions of the members of the organization. The impact of hierarchical level on individual influence is very great in the management of the organization as a whole. Furthermore, hierarchical level to a large extent defines the qualities of a job and, consequently, the opportunities for creative and interesting work.

At the same time, a number of aspects of the attitudes and the reactions of organization members do not appear to be affected very much by hierarchical level. For example, members at different levels do not differ very much from one another with respect to:

   a. their attitudes toward the plant leadership and their perceptions of the style and personal qualities of their immediate superior
   b. their assessments (real and ideal) of the consequences of good and bad performance by a member
   c. their perceptions of the criteria for getting ahead in the organization
   d. their aspirations for advancing within the enterprise
   e. their satisfaction with aspects of the enterprise's activities

3. Subjective measures are not always adequate to study the issues related to hierarchy. Time budgets, we believe, provide an objective approach to assessing aspects of the enterprise's activities, but this approach is not widely accepted. Our application of this method in ten industrial enterprises in Bulgaria shows its potential. Possibilities are therefore at hand for combining subjective assessments with the more objectively defined measures of time that are important to understanding organizations. We believe that information collected in this way can be utilized to raise the efficiency of participation.

4. The improvement of the hierarchical structure can contribute importantly to a positive attitude by the members toward the enterprise and can help raise their level of participation; consequently, it can increase the effectiveness of their work. In order to achieve all of this, however, the structure should be simplified to the largest possible extent, so that workers may become familiar with

all of the activities of the enterprise and so that communication concerning these issues among the various levels may be facilitated. In both the large and some of the small enterprises that we investigated, there exists today an excessively complicated hierarchical structure, and hierarchies are unnecessarily tall. The setting up of an optimal hierarchical structure in industrial enterprises is therefore one of the problems of prime importance for the theory and practice of social management.

8

Romania

Ion Drăgan, Septimiu Chelcea, Petre Cristea, Pompiliu Grigorescu,
Stefan Stefănescu, and Cătălin Zamfir

Introduction

From the very beginning, the goal set by the socialist revolution
was not simply the industrialization of the country—that is, the
development of modern enterprises—but *socialist industrialization*—
that is, the development of a system of production based on socialist
principles of organization. To this end, the Romanian Communist
Party has elaborated on and attempted steadily to perfect a socialist
system of organization and management of industrial enterprises.
Therefore, Romanian enterprises are characterized not only by the
modernization of the technology but also by improvement of the
socialist forms of the organization of work.

We will review briefly the main features of the socialist system
of organization in Romania.

The Unitary Management of Social and Economic Life
According to a National Plan

The role of the market as the general regulator of production
has been taken over, to a great extent, by the national plan, which
controls and directs all socioeconomic activity in the nation.
Enterprises are part of a national system.

The industrial system of Romania is organized at four levels:

1. *Enterprises*, which are the basic economic units and which, according to law, are charged with administering their property
   with maximum efficiency, fulfilling their production plan, up-
   dating their technology, increasing the productivity of their
   labor, reducing their production expenses, and raising the
   quality of their products. It is within the enterprise that
   workers exercise directly their prerogatives as owners and
   producers, participating directly in the management of their

production activity.

2. *Industrial centrals*, which are highly integrated enterprises or systems of enterprises that produce similar or related products. Industrial centrals were designed to coordinate the production among enterprises and to promote technological progress and scientific research. Centrals ensure specialization and cooperation among their member enterprises.

3. *Ministries*, each of which coordinates the centrals within a single industry (for instance, within the machine-building, chemical, or iron and steel industries).

4. At the *national level* an economic plan is formulated. This planning function is assumed by the Supreme Council for Economic and Social Development and by the State Planning Committee. The planning is done in collaboration with ministries, industrial centrals, and enterprises. After being voted by the Supreme National Assembly (Romania's parliament), the national plan has the status of law.

The Principle of Democratic Participation

Enterprises maintain a certain autonomy even though they are integrated into the system of national economic planning. Furthermore, they have a participative role in the development of the national plan. Romania is attempting to add economic democracy to traditional political democracy. All working people may participate in the management of the national economy and of social life through their participation in their work and departmental group, their enterprise, the Union of Communist Youth, the Communist Party, and trade unions. Thus, in their twofold capacity as collective owners of the means of production and as producers, the working people have the right and duty to take an active part not only in the goal-setting process but also in decision making at all levels of the society.

The supreme decision-making body of the enterprise is the General Assembly of Working People. It decides about the general economic and social problems of the enterprise. It elects a Council of Working People (CWP) in which all categories of personnel are represented. The Council, made up of managerial personnel, representatives of the political and social organizations of the enterprise, elected representatives of the workers, and technical experts, is the managerial body of the enterprise. Such democratic institutions have been set up in all enterprises and centrals. They have the power to decide the socioeconomic issues of their unit.

Recently, at the initiative of Romania's president, Nicolae

Ceausescu, Secretary General of the Romanian Communist Party, a series of measures have been taken to increase the role of the Councils of Working People and the General Assemblies in the management of enterprises. The number of workers and of other personnel in the managerial councils was increased (75 percent of the council members are now workers and foremen), as was the number of issues to be considered by the councils.

New national bodies have been established to ensure the participation of the workers through their representatives in the leadership of society. Thus, new permanent bodies have been set up: the National Council of Working People (which convenes periodically), the Congress of the Councils of Working People, the Legislative Chamber of the People's Councils, the Congress of County People's Councils, the National Council for Agriculture, and the Congress of the Management Councils of Socialist Agricultural Units of the Whole Peasantry. As pointed out by President Nicolae Ceausescu at the National Conference of the Romanian Communist Party of December 1977,

> We may say that we have an organizational frame—both at the level of socioeconomic units, towns, communes, and nationwide—unique in its kind, which ensures the direct participation of all the categories of working people, regardless of nationality, in the management of the economy and of the social life of society as a whole.

A major component of the socialist program is the promotion of a participative style in the interpersonal relationships between superiors and subordinates. Participation at the interpersonal level is consistent with and complements participation at the collective level. Along with the collective participative structures, it contributes to a culture of participation.

The formal structures of the industrial system are partly a realization of the above principles and partly an expression of the realities of contemporary society, such as the education level and skills of the work force as well as the cultural context. Romanian industry has experienced a succession of organizational forms. The country's leadership has attempted to find more adequate and more fully participative forms of organization as technological, economic, social, and cultural conditions have changed. Thus, since we began this investigation, substantial changes have taken place in enterprises to broaden economic democracy and workers' self-management.

Characteristics of Plants Studied

The field work for the present study was conducted during the years 1972–73 in eight enterprises. Table 8.1 provides information about the size, sex composition, and types of industry of each enterprise.

Table 8.1

CHARACTERISTICS OF PLANTS

Industry	Number of Employees	Sex (Percentage Female)
Foundry	7,000	8.8%
Chemical	2,000	31.9
Plastics	1,400	28.6
Canning	1,100	35.5
Textile	4,300	80.0
Electrotechnical	1,800	28.3
Machine building	3,100	15.7
Furniture	3,000	28.0

The investigation covers only big enterprises, since these are characteristic of Romania's industry. The Romanian policy of industrialization aimed mainly at creating big, modern, state-owned units. As a rule, cooperatives are the only industrial organizations that are small.

Three hierarchical levels were studied: top management (the director and his immediate managerial staff); middle management (managerial staff and supervisory personnel); and rank and file (workers who have no subordinates). The definition of top management in this chapter differs from that in the other chapters since the top group here includes the director's immediate managerial staff; in the other chapters, it includes only the director.

The sample consists of 361 subjects. Table 8.2 shows the distribution of subjects by the three hierarchical levels.

Correlates of Hierarchy

Economic and Demographic Characteristics

In order to understand the psychological and social consequences of hierarchy, it is necessary to see how persons at different levels may differ with respect to education, seniority in the plant, remuneration, and sex.

Table 8.2

HIERARCHICAL DISTRIBUTION OF SUBJECTS

Hierarchical Level	Number of Subjects	Percentage
Rank and file	168	46.6%
Middle management	159	44.0
Top management	34	9.4
Total	361	100.0

We have not collected data concerning remuneration, but we can, nonetheless, describe with confidence the distribution of income within the plant, since the distribution of income within the nation as a whole is fixed by law. The ratio between minimum and maximum payment within the nation is 1:6. Remuneration is not negotiable at the plant level; it is set within the framework of the national norms, which results in a ratio of 1:2 or 1:3 between average remuneration at the bottom and the average at the top.

There are two principles underlying the system of remuneration in Romania. The first concerns the quantity and quality of the work performed. Differences between hierarchical groups in the quantity of their work cannot be defined, but quality can be defined by the complexity of the work, the training required, and the responsibility that it entails. In principle, the quality of work is higher at upper than at lower levels of the hierarchy; remuneration, therefore, is greater at upper than at lower levels.

The second principle, social equality, is aimed at reducing income differences between the members of society, ensuring each person satisfactory living conditions. This principle acts, therefore, to limit the effects of differentiation implied by the hierarchy.

Table 8.3 shows that persons at upper levels have more education than do those at lower levels. The character of work at upper levels requires persons who have the special skills that are acquired through education. A formal degree, therefore, serves as an indication of qualification; it has become an important basis for selecting persons to serve as organizational leaders.

The distribution of seniority does not conform to the simple notion that persons at the top will have more seniority than do those below.

Table 8.3 shows that the proportion of women decreases with

Table 8.3

DEMOGRAPHIC CHARACTERISTICS

	Top Management	Middle Management	Rank and File
Education[a] (average years)	5.5	3.9	3.3
Plant seniority[b] (average years)	5.8	6.1	5.5
Sex (percentage female)	12.0	14.0	21.0

[a]Education is measured on a scale where 1 = less than 4 years, 2 = 4 to 6 years, 3 = 6 to 8 years, 4 = 8 to 10 years, 5 = 10 to 12 years, and 6 = more than 12 years of education.

[b]Plant seniority is measured on the following scale: 1 = under 6 months, 2 = 6 months to 1 year, 3 = 1 to 2 years, 4 = 2 to 3 years, 5 = 3 to 6 years, 6 = 6 to 10 years, 7 = 10 to 20 years, and 8 = 20 years or more.

hierarchical ascent. Traditionally, top positions have been preferentially accessible to males. Since the revolution, Romania has had a policy of sex equality and the emancipation of women, which has as its goal the integration of women into all the economic and social activities of the nation. The realization of this objective, however, takes time not only because of the change in attitude that is required but also because of the need to provide facilities, such as day-care centers, mass-produced food services, and shopping centers, that free women to commit themselves to a career in industry. Subsequent to the time when the data of this study were collected, the Romanian party and state leadership issued firm directives designed to encourage the promotion of women in management jobs at all levels.

Role Characteristics

Hierarchy implies differences not only in the demographic characteristics of role incumbents but also in its intrinsic characteristics: the authority, influence, participation, and control associated with different positions.

Authority and influence. An index of authority/influence was constructed by averaging the results of two questions that were asked of each respondent:

Q.1g. In your work, to what extent can you have authority over
other people?

Q.26d. How much influence do you personally have on what happens in the plant?

Both questions were answered by checks on a five-point scale.
In addition to the above index of "actual" authority/influence, we
used a parallel index designed to measure "preferred" authority/
influence (Q.2g and 27d). Figure 8.1 shows the hierarchical distribution of these indices.

The data indicate that authority/influence is unevenly distributed in the hierarchy, with top levels reporting higher values
than bottom levels. Furthermore, the preferred amount of
authority/influence is higher than the actual amount at each level.

We assume that the uneven distribution of authority/influence in
the hierarchy of organizations is universal. Organization inevitably
requires that persons at upper levels exercise more authority and
influence than persons below. The extent to which hierarchical differences are large or small depends on a number of technoeconomic
and sociopolitical factors. These might lead to the creation of two
basic types of hierarchy: the authoritative, in which the differences
are large, and the democratic or participative, in which the differences are small. In Romania, an effort is being made to encourage the
development of participative hierarchies.

The index of preferred authority/influence is an indicator of important tendencies in hierarchy. Normally, one would expect that
persons prefer to have more authority/influence than they perceive
themselves to have. This expectation is founded on an image of the
organization in which participants aspire to increase their control
over events. Preference by members for an amount of authority/
influence that is less than the actual amount implies either (a) that
the members have been assigned responsibilities they cannot cope
with or (b) that they are apathetic towards the organization. These
two instances represent, however, exceptional situations, and the
amount of influence members prefer to exercise is therefore likely to
be higher than the actual amount.

It also seems reasonable that the preferred distribution of
authority/influence is similar to that of the actual distribution.
Aspirations ordinarily tend to be close to actualities. People are
realistic in this sense; they aspire to more of something they would
like, but not too much more than they have. They may also sense
the realities of organization. Organization requires a hierarchical
distribution of control; people therefore express aspirations consistent with this reality. The result is a preferred distribution that is
somewhat higher than and parallel to the actual distribution. The

Figure 8.1
HIERARCHICAL DISTRIBUTION OF AUTHORITY/INFLUENCE
BASED ON SELF-REPORTS

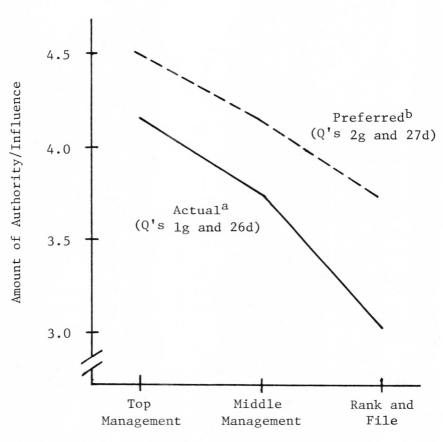

--Position in Hierarchy--

[a]Differences between each of the three
   hierarchical levels are significant at the
   .01 level of confidence.

[b]Differences between each of the three
   hierarchical levels are significant at the
   .05 level of confidence.

data of Figure 8.1, which show a somewhat more participative preferred than actual distribution of authority/influence, are one indication of support for the development of democratic hierarchy.

Distribution of control (control graph). The data of the previous section are based on the reports of each respondent about his or her personal authority and influence. In this section, we present data in which persons from all groups jointly report about the influence of each group. The results are shown in Figure 8.2. The implications of these data are very much like those of the previous section, although the control curves of Figure 8.2 are a bit higher and perhaps flatter than the corresponding curves of Figure 8.1. The present curves are based on questions about the influence of groups, while the previous ones refer to the authority and influence of only the respondent. In any event, we believe that respondents answered these questions in terms of the aspects of control in the plant that are most meaningful to them. For example, workers have a substantial guarantee of security; it is unlikely that they will be fired or transferred against their will. As a further illustration, workers may have significant input with respect to how bonuses are allocated among the members of their work group; the group is assigned a bonus and the members decide how it is to be divided. Within this context, workers undoubtedly see themselves as having substantial control over issues such as placement, promotion, discipline, hiring/firing, and transfer.

Questions about control touch on issues that are important in the conception of the work organization as described by communist ideology, which advocates control by the workers. Respondents may be answering the questions partly in terms of these ideological ideals. This effect may be especially apparent in the high values and relatively flat distribution of preferred control shown in Figures 8.1 and 8.2.

Bases of superior's power. We expected to find hierarchical differences in the bases of power of leaders. These bases were measured in terms of the reasons that subordinates give for doing what their superior asks of them. We assume that the six bases of power proposed by French and Raven (1959) describe the types of motivation that underlie conformity to the requests made by one's superior, and that these six types can be divided into two categories—*organic* and *external*. The organic bases of power rely on one's own decision to participate in a common activity. The respondent does what his or her superior asks because it is necessary for the good of the organization, it is the respondent's duty, or he or she respects the superior's competence and experience. The external bases rely on rewards and penalties. In these cases, the

Figure 8.2
DISTRIBUTION OF CONTROL AS REPORTED BY ALL MEMBERS

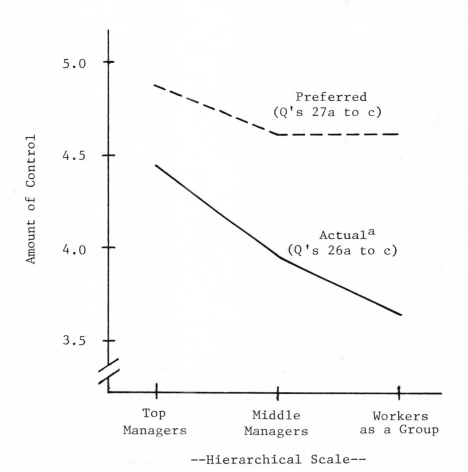

--Hierarchical Scale--

[a]Differences between each of the three
hierarchical levels are significant at the
.05 level of confidence.

respondent does what his or her superior suggests because the superior can be helpful or can penalize or is a nice person. The distinction is not absolute, but in general, we expect that the organic bases are more likely to be consistent with a participative hierarchy and the external bases with an authoritarian hierarchy.

Table 8.4 presents the data concerning the bases of the superior's power as reported by persons at the bottom and middle levels. In general, the organic bases appear to be more prominent than the external, but the data do not offer much support for the hypothesis that the hierarchy may be somewhat more organic at upper levels than at lower levels.

Table 8.4

BASES OF THE SUPERIOR'S POWER AS REPORTED BY SUBORDINATES

Q.47. When you do what your immediate superior requests you to do on the job, why do you do it?	Middle Management	Rank and File
I respect his competence and judgment.	3.9	4.1
He can give special help and benefits.	3.9	3.7
He's a nice guy.	3.5	3.5
He can penalize or otherwise disadvantage me.	2.8	3.1
It is my duty.	4.7	4.6
It is necessary if the organization is to function properly.	4.7	4.4

Enriching qualities of the job. Democracy implies not only equalization of power in the organization but also equalization of the "human quality" of work. In principle, work in a democratic hierarchy should provide intrinsic satisfaction at all levels, although it is not likely that the quality of work can be entirely equalized throughout the hierarchy.

In order to assess the human quality of work, we resorted to two indices. The first concerns opportunities that a job provides, for example, for a member to use his or her skills and abilities, to learn new things, to do interesting work, and to set his or her own work pace. The second index concerns the physical qualities of the job— for example, whether it is dirty or clean, physical or mental, and dangerous or safe.

Figure 8.3 shows the data concerning an index, computed on a five-point scale, of the enriching qualities that members perceive in their jobs (averaging all of the qualities they perceive), along with an index of the qualities members would like to have in their jobs. The picture presented by the distribution of these enriching qualities is not unlike that for the distribution of authority/influence discussed in earlier sections. The enriching qualities provided by the job show some hierarchical differentiation, and members generally indicate a preference for more enriching qualities than they perceive themselves to have.

Physical qualities of the job. Table 8.5 presents an index that averages the physical qualities of work scaled in terms of their "favorableness." (For example, clean, mental, and safe are scaled as more favorable than dirty, physical, and dangerous.) Again, we see the implications of hierarchy, at least with respect to the differences between the bottom level and the others. Although the differences are small, they are significant statistically.

Reactions and Adjustments

In this section we shall analyze the impact of hierarchy on the reactions and adjustments of members—their morale, motivation on the job, psychological adjustment, and perceptions of their organization.

Morale

We had intended to include a description in this section of job satisfaction, satisfaction with pay, and attitude toward the company as components of morale, but due to an error in data processing we are unable to include data about job satisfaction. Satisfaction with pay was measured through a direct question about the member's satisfaction with his or her pay, which was answered on a five-point scale (Q.59). Attitude toward company management was measured in terms of an index based on an average of responses to three questions:

Q.24. Do you think the responsible people here have a real interest in the welfare of those who work here?

Q.25. Do the responsible people in this plant improve working

Figure 8.3
ENRICHING QUALITIES OF THE JOB BASED ON SELF-REPORTS

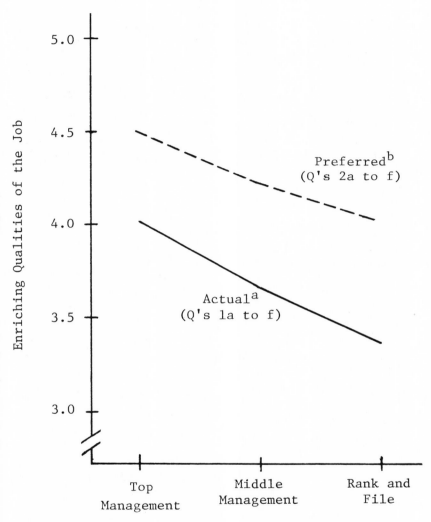

--Position in Hierarchy--

[a]Differences between each hierarchical
level are significant at the .01 level
of confidence.

[b]Differences between the rank and file
and the middle management level are
significant at the .05 level of confidence.

Table 8.5
PHYSICAL QUALITIES OF THE JOB

	Top Management	Middle Management	Rank and File
Tiring (1) — not tiring (6)	2.4	2.8	2.8
Unhealthful (1) — healthful (6)	3.6	3.6	3.5
Physical (1) — mental (6)	4.9	4.5	2.5
Dirty (1) — clean (6)	4.4	4.2	3.1
Heavy (1) — light (6)	2.8	3.1	2.8
Same tasks during the day (1) — different tasks during the day (6)	4.8	4.3	3.2
Dangerous (1) — safe (6)	4.3	3.8	3.4
Average (Q.3)[a]	3.9	3.8	3.0

[a]The difference between the middle-management and rank-and-file levels is significant at the .05 level of confidence.

conditions only when forced to?

Q.28. When a worker in this plant makes a complaint about something, is it taken care of?

Table 8.6 provides information concerning these aspects of morale, neither of which shows very sharp hierarchical differentiation.

Table 8.7 shows the results of multiple regression analyses used to explore the possible determinants of satisfaction with pay and of attitude toward plant leadership.

We did not compute significance tests for these regression analyses. It is interesting, nonetheless, to see that the pattern of results is similar to that in other countries. For example, job qualities rank first in importance as a predictor of satisfaction with pay in the Federal Republic of Germany (Chapter 3) and Bulgaria (Chapter 7) as well as here in Romania. Similarly, authority/influence ranks first as a predictor of attitude toward company

Table 8.6

MORALE

	Top Management	Middle Management	Rank and File
Satisfaction with pay[a] (Q.59)	3.6	3.1	3.1
Attitude toward plant leadership (Q.24, 25, 28)	3.7	3.5	3.5

[a]Differences between middle and top management levels are significant at the .05 level of confidence.

Table 8.7

THE RELATIVE IMPORTANCE OF THE PREDICTORS OF MORALE[a]

Multiple R	Satisfaction with Pay .24		Attitude toward Plant Leadership .28	
Predictors	Beta	Rank	Beta	Rank
Enriching job qualities	−.02	4.5	.06	4.5
Authority/ influence	−.02	4.5	.22	1
Physical job qualities	.22	1	.16	2
Education	−.01	6	.01	6
Plant seniority	−.14	2.5	−.06	4.5
Level in hierarchy	−.14	2.5	−.15	3

[a]Several variables employed in the other chapters are not included here either because we did not collect the data or because of errors in calculation: age, length of hierarchical chain, remuneration, and job satisfaction. The first three of these variables, which were meant to be predictors in the regression analyses, are therefore excluded from the above regression analyses as well as from those that follow.

management in these three countries. Tannenbaum and others (1974) explain the importance of job qualities for satisfaction with pay that they found in an earlier study in five countries:

> The importance of physical qualities of the job (in the United States and Italy) or of opportunities provided by the job (in Yugoslavia) for satisfaction with pay suggests a curious relationship between satisfaction with job and with pay in some countries at least. Money per se does not make a job satisfying in any country . . . even though it may contribute to satisfaction with pay. Nonetheless, many persons, if given the opportunity, choose jobs and careers on the basis of the money offered. They may regret the choice, however, because they are not likely to be satisfied with their job simply because it pays well. But if they choose a job where conditions are congenial or opportunities for self-actualization are available, then they are likely to be satisfied with their pay *as well as* with the job itself. The moral is that one who seeks high satisfaction with pay might further this objective by choosing a job on the basis of pay, but he risks being dissatisfied with his job. On the other hand, he might very well achieve satisfaction with pay as well as satisfaction with job by choosing work that is congenial or that provides opportunities for self-actualization. (Tannenbaum et al., 1974, p. 145)

Motivation

The following aspects of a member's work motivation were studied:

a. *Sense of responsibility* was measured by a three-item index— the degree to which one feels responsible for the work of one's own work group, one's department, and the enterprise as a whole (Q.11).

b. *Motivation* was measured through the question, "In your kind of job, is it usually better to let your superiors worry about introducing better or faster ways of doing the work?" (Q.6).

c. *Initiative* was measured through the question, "How often do you try out on your own a better or faster way of doing the work?" (Q.7).

d. *Mobility aspirations* were measured by asking respondents whether or not they would accept a higher position even if such advancement brought difficulties like frequent criticism, problem employees, more worries, sacrifices in order to acquire higher skills, and additional obligations and responsibilities (Q.48). The items were given a score of 1 if the response was no and 2 if the response was yes; the scores are averaged for the respective groups in Table 8.8. Thus, the score of 1.4 for the managers indicates that 40 percent of the managers answered these questions affirmatively, on the average, while the score of 1.5 for the rank and file indicates a corresponding percentage of 50 for that group.

The regression analyses of Table 8.9 indicate some of the fac-

Table 8.8

MOTIVATIONAL ASPECTS

	Top Management	Middle Management	Rank and File
Responsibility for the system[a] (Q.11a, b, c)	4.1	3.9	3.7
Motivation on the job[b] (Q.6)	3.4	3.0	2.5
Initiative[c] (Q.7)	4.3	4.0	3.6
Mobility aspirations[d] (Q.48)	—	1.4	1.5

[a]Differences between middle and bottom levels and between top and bottom levels are significant at the .05 level of confidence.

[b]All differences are significant at the .01 level of confidence.

[c]Differences between top and bottom levels and between middle and bottom levels are significant at the .05 level of confidence.

[d]These scores are based on an index composed of items answered by respondents in terms of a dichotomous scale. The numbers, therefore, indicate that 50 percent and 40 percent of the rank-and-file workers and middle managers, respectively, answered the questions affirmatively and that mobility aspirations are therefore higher among workers than among middle managers (see text). We found this difference significant statistically at the .05 level of confidence.

tors that predict our measures of motivation. The importance of authority/influence as a determinant of sense of responsibility, suggested by this table, is consistent with the rationale frequently offered for democratizing organizations; it is also consistent with the results of earlier studies in a number of countries (Tannenbaum et al., 1974). In fact, authority and influence are the means through which responsibility is fulfilled. It may be difficult to behave responsibly without the ability also to behave influentially.

Enriching qualities of the job, along with authority and influence, also appear to play a role in determining the responsibility and initiative of members. These qualities, along with authority and influence, are in effect (or they provide) opportunities to take initiative and to behave responsibly.

Table 8.9

THE RELATIVE IMPORTANCE OF THE
PREDICTORS OF MOTIVATIONAL ASPECTS

Multiple R	Responsibility for System .40		Motivation .34		Initiative .38	
Predictors	Beta	Rank	Beta	Rank	Beta	Rank
Enriching job qualities	.13	2	.18	1	.22	1
Authority/ influence	.28	1	.07	5	.18	2
Physical job qualities	.01	6	.03	6	.00	6
Education	.03	5	.14	3	.09	3
Plant seniority	.12	3	−.15	2	.03	5
Level in hierarchy	−.04	4	.10	4	.04	4

Personal Adjustment

We are concerned in this section with measures of psychological adjustment and alienation. Psychological adjustment was measured by having the respondents indicate reactions such as the extent to which they feel discouraged, bored, that they work well, that they do not get what they deserve, and that they do well what they do. A high score on some of these items indicates a positive adjustment; on others it implies a negative adjustment. The items were combined, however, so that in the resulting index a high score implies positive adjustment. These scores, averaged for the hierarchical groups, are shown in Table 8.10. Persons at upper levels appear, from this table, to have a better psychological adjustment than do those at lower levels.

By "alienation," we mean here the psychological lack of integration of persons into their work place. Alienation defined in this way has a number of sources, the most important of which, according to Marx, is man's relationship to the means of production. There are also secondary sources of alienation, such as technology, work organization, and personal relationships. Socialist revolution has eliminated the main objective source of alienation—the private

Table 8.10

PSYCHOLOGICAL ADJUSTMENT[a]

	Top Management	Middle Management	Rank and File
Psychological adjustment (Q.49)	3.0	2.7	2.6
Alienation (Q.52)	2.4	2.7	3.0

[a]The differences in psychological adjustment and alienation between the rank and file and middle management are significant at the .05 level of confidence.

ownership of the means of production and capitalist exploitation. The development of a socialist society will bring with it the progressive elimination of the secondary sources of alienation, too.

We attempted to measure the following components of alienation, which we combined into an index: powerlessness, meaninglessness, normlessness, self-estrangement, and social isolation (Dean, 1961; Seeman, 1959). Table 8.10 shows the results with respect to this index. High scores imply high alienation. Persons at lower levels are somewhat more alienated than are those at upper levels. These data suggest that hierarchy, with its uneven distribution of control and other qualities of work, creates an uneven distribution in psychological adjustment and alienation.

Table 8.11, which presents regression analyses that predict our measures of adjustment, provides some indication of the possible implications for psychological adjustment and alienation of job qualities and authority/influence.

Perceptions

In this section we are interested in determining whether persons in different positions differ in their perceptions of important aspects of organizational functioning. Therefore, we shall compare persons at the respective levels with respect to their perceptions of decision making, control, the rewards and sanctions that persons may receive for good or bad performance, the criteria for advancement, and the benefits of high position in the organization.

Decision making. We asked three sets of questions about decision making in the plant. The questions are not concerned with the decision making of the respondent himself or herself, but rather

Table 8.11

THE RELATIVE IMPORTANCE OF THE
PREDICTORS OF PERSONAL ADJUSTMENT

Multiple R	Psychological Adjustment .29		Alienation .34	
Predictors	Beta	Rank	Beta	Rank
Enriching job qualities	.03	4.5	−.05	4.5
Authority/influence	.03	4.5	−.18	2
Physical job qualities	.29	1	−.21	1
Education	−.05	2.5	−.07	3
Plant seniority	.05	2.5	−.05	4.5
Level in hierarchy	.00	6	.03	6

with decision making in the plant generally. Therefore, we are able to determine how persons at different levels perceive this general aspect of plant functioning. The perceptions of the three hierarchical groups in response to these questions are presented in Table 8.12. We also asked questions designed to measure the preferences of members; these measures are shown along with the corresponding data.

We do not find differences between hierarchical groups with respect to their perceptions of decision making as measured by these questions. We do find, however, that the preference with respect to decision making as measured by one of the questions does differ significantly between the groups. Persons at lower levels, more than persons at upper levels, prefer that members who are affected by decisions be asked their opinions about these decisions.

Distribution of control. We discussed in the second section of this chapter the distribution of control as reported by all respondents jointly (see Figure 8.2). We shall analyze here how persons at different levels perceive this distribution. We will also present their preferences with respect to the distribution of control. Figure 8.4 shows the actual distribution as perceived by the three hierarchical groups (Q.26a-c); Figure 8.5 shows the distributions that the respective groups prefer (Q.27a-c). The differences between groups in both figures are small, although upper-level persons tend to perceive a more equalized distribution of control than do lower-level

Table 8.12

PERCEPTIONS AND PREFERENCES ABOUT THE PARTICIPATIVENESS IN
THE PLANTS, MEASURED IN TERMS OF LIKERT'S MODEL

	Perceptions by:[a]		
	Top Management	Middle Management	Rank and File
Q.34. Actual participation by workers in job decisions	2.8	2.8	3.0
Q.35. Preferred participation by workers in job decisions[b]	3.2	3.6	3.7
Discrepancy Q.35 − Q.34	0.4	0.8	0.7
Q.36. Actual participation by workers in plant decisions	2.9	2.5	2.7
Q.37. Preferred participation by workers in plant decisions	3.3	3.4	3.5
Discrepancy Q.37 − Q.36	0.4	0.9	0.8
Q.39. Actual extent to which opinions are asked of those who are affected by decisions	2.7	2.6	2.8
Q.40. Preferred extent	3.5	3.5	3.6
Discrepancy Q.40 − Q.39	0.8	0.9	0.8

[a]The data presented in this table are averages for the respective groups on a four-point scale where 4 implies a high degree of participation.

[b]The difference between top management and the rank and file is significant at the .05 level of confidence.

persons, which indicates a hierarchical effect on how members view the distribution of control in their organization.

Each curve of Figure 8.6 shows the perceptions by persons in one hierarchical group of the discrepancy between the preferred and actual control exercised by each hierarchical level. All groups report that the control exercised by each hierarchical group should be greater than it is, but the discrepancy as perceived by all hierarchical groups is lower at the top of the hierarchy than at the bottom. Furthermore, the trend of increasing discrepancy perceived for lower compared to upper groups (slope of line) decreases with hierarchical ascent.

Rewards and Sanctions

In order to maintain performance at a high level, organizations use various types of rewards for good work and penalties for bad work. The actual rewards and penalties an organization uses, as well as the rewards and penalties its members prefer, can be used as significant indicators of the social and cultural profile of that organization. Respondents were asked to check as many rewards (for good work) and penalties (for bad work) as applied from the lists shown in Tables 8.13 and 8.14.

These tables present the percentages of respondents who indicated the respective items as actual or preferred consequences of good work (Table 8.13) or of bad work (Table 8.14). Perceptions of actual rewards and penalties do not seem to vary significantly between the three hierarchical levels. However, there is a slight but systematic tendency for top managers to estimate less frequently an association between the quality of work and the various types of rewards and penalties. The most interesting finding in our data is the difference between the consequences respondents say follow and *should* follow good (or bad) work.

Two important types of reward and penalty result from the attitude of the superior: (1) praise or criticism and (1) a high or a low opinion of the member. In all four cases (the first and eighth items from Tables 8.13 and 8.14), the preferred frequency is lower than the actual. This tendency is found at all hierarchical levels. In other words, people at all hierarchical levels think that exercising organizational power in interpersonal relationships through praising, criticizing, or having a high or low opinion of another is done more than it should be, even though it might be effective. Is it possible that our respondents do not approve generally of the mixing of personal relationships with work problems? Other items suggest a negative answer to this question. The respondents think that co-

Figure 8.4
DISTRIBUTION OF CONTROL AS REPORTED BY
PERSONS AT THREE HIERARCHICAL LEVELS

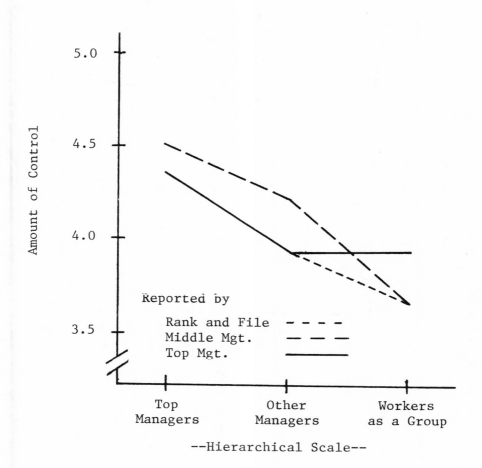

--Hierarchical Scale--

Figure 8.5

PREFERRED DISTRIBUTION OF CONTROL AS REPORTED
BY PERSONS AT THREE HIERARCHICAL LEVELS

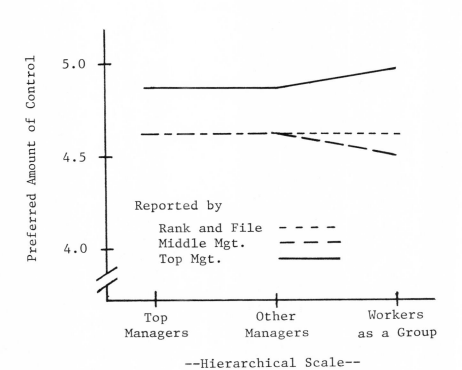

Figure 8.6
DISTRIBUTION OF DISCREPANCY BETWEEN
PREFERRED AND ACTUAL CONTROL AS REPORTED
BY PERSONS AT THREE HIERARCHICAL LEVELS

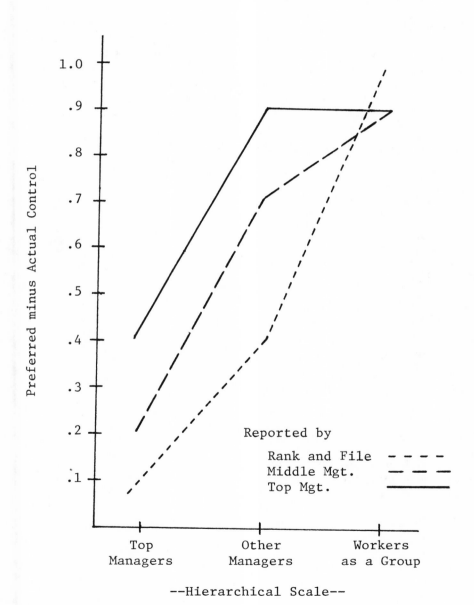

--Hierarchical Scale--

Table 8.13

ACTUAL AND PREFERRED CONSEQUENCES OF GOOD WORK

Q.12/13. In your opinion, what happens (should happen) if a member in this organization does an especially good job in his work?	Percentage of Respondents Checking the Response					
	Top Management		Middle Management		Rank and File	
	Actual	Pre-ferred	Actual	Pre-ferred	Actual	Pre-ferred
His superior will praise him.	51%	43%	68%	55%	72%	60%
His co-workers will praise him.	31	37	46	48	51	55
His co-workers will criticize him.	6	3	8	3	5	7
He may be offered a better job at the same level.	22	20	29	39	32	38
He will be given a bonus or higher wage.	40	66	47	78	51	80
His co-workers will have a high opinion of him.	51	43	48	54	45	44
He will have a bet-ter opportunity for advancement.	60	49	45	53	50	57
His superior will have a high opinion of him.	54	51	60	57	50	40
Nothing will hap-pen.	9	3	9	2	15	9

Table 8.14

ACTUAL AND PREFERRED CONSEQUENCES OF POOR WORK

Q.14/15. In your opinion, what happens (should happen) if a member in this organization does very poor work?	Percentage of Respondents Checking the Response					
	Top Management		Middle Management		Rank and File	
	Actual	Pre- ferred	Actual	Pre- ferred	Actual	Pre- ferred
His superior will criticize him.	74%	57%	83%	62%	76%	51%
His co-workers will criticize him.	49	60	57	66	54	58
His co-workers will support him against criticism.	14	3	10	4	3	8
He will be given an inferior job.	23	34	31	36	28	29
His salary will be reduced.	54	40	74	58	77	54
His co-workers will have a low opinion of him.	34	40	45	36	43	30
He will have a less good opportunity for advancement.	54	46	49	46	47	37
His superior will have a low opinion of him.	37	23	46	26	44	30
Nothing will hap- pen.	11	17	4	1	5	9

workers should praise good work or criticize bad work more than they actually do. But in the relationship with co-workers there is no formal or organizational power, only informal and social power.

Quite another attitude is expressed about the benefits and sanctions the organization can provide for good and bad work (wages, bonus, promotion). Respondents tend to prefer the positive incentives to the negative ones.

Advantages of advancement. Many members desire advancement in the hierarchy because of the social and psychological benefits advancement entails. Therefore, we were interested in learning how members at each hierarchical level perceived these benefits. From a list of potential benefits (see Table 8.15), respondents were asked to select, in order of their preference, the three most important ones. A score of 3 was assigned to the item that was considered most important, 2 to the item second in importance, and 1 to the third most important item. All other items were scored 0.

The data of Table 8.15 show some commonalities as well as some differences in the way the respective groups view the benefits of advancement. For example, none of the groups attach much importance to social contacts or influence outside of the plant. But top managers attach more importance to variety in work and to decision-making opportunities than do the workers. On the other hand, workers attach importance to prestige and salary as advantages that accrue from high position. The social status and prestige that are associated with higher positions in an organization have traditional importance in Romania. The difference in importance attached to salary may reflect the salary scale, which provides increments between jobs of different rank—increments that are a larger fraction of the salaries of members at lower levels than of salaries at upper levels.

Criteria for advancement. Table 8.16 presents data concerning members' perceptions about the criteria for promotion in the plant. The table is marked more by agreement between levels than by disagreement, although workers may perceive quantity of work (if not quality) and the superior's opinion of the worker to be somewhat more important than managers perceive these criteria to be. Having friends in management is given the same relative ranking by all groups, but workers rate this as a more important criterion than do managers. On the other hand, managers more than workers see initiative and outstanding ability to work with others as relatively important criteria for advancement.

Table 8.17 shows members' preferences with respect to criteria for promotion. Differences between groups are not very great, and

Table 8.15

PERCEIVED ADVANTAGES ASSOCIATED WITH HIGH POSITION

Q.55. What do you think are the main advantages of moving into a higher position in this plant?[a]	Top Management		Middle Management		Rank and File	
	Score[a]	Rank[b]	Score	Rank	Score	Rank
Prestige or esteem	0.9	3	0.8	3.5	1.2	2
Variety of work	1.1	1	0.8	3.5	0.4	6
Independence	0.4	6	0.4	7	0.3	7
Social contacts	0.1	8.5	0.2	8	0.1	8.5
Opportunity to make decisions	1.0	2	0.5	6	0.5	4.5
Opportunity to enlarge skills	0.6	4.5	1.0	2	0.8	3
Opportunity to enlarge knowledge	0.6	4.5	0.7	5	0.5	4.5
Influence people outside the plant	0.1	8.5	0.1	9	0.1	8.5
Higher wages	0.2	7	1.2	1	1.5	1

[a] Scores reported here are averages of the responses of all respondents.

[b] Items are ranked according to their relative importance, based on the responses of all respondents.

the preferred pattern is similar to the actual pattern.

Conclusions

The main objective of our analysis was to explore the question of the larger research of which this is a part: Does hierarchy have general features and sociopsychological consequences in addition to the specific features and consequences that are attributable to socialist organizations?

The data of the Romanian study help provide some answers to

Table 8.16

ACTUAL CRITERIA FOR ADVANCEMENT

Q.16. How important is each of the following factors for getting ahead in this company?	Top Management		Middle Management		Rank and File	
	Score	Rank	Score	Rank	Score	Rank
Quality of work done	4.3	2.5	4.3	2.5	4.4	1
Quantity of work done[a]	4.0	7.5	4.2	5	4.4	1
Superior's opinion[b]	4.1	5.5	4.3	2.5	4.3	4
Dependability	4.3	2.5	4.2	5	4.1	6
Creativeness, inventiveness	3.9	9	3.8	10	3.5	10
Seniority in the plant	3.5	10	4.0	8	4.2	5
Having friends in higher management[c]	2.4	12	2.8	12	2.9	12
Having good professional knowledge	4.4	1	4.4	1	4.4	1
Taking initiative[d]	4.0	7.5	4.2	5	3.8	8.5
Having outstanding ability to work with people[e]	4.1	5.5	4.1	7	3.8	8.5
Loyalty to the company	4.2	4	3.9	9	4.0	7
Recommendations of political nature	2.9	11	3.5	11	3.1	11
Elbowing one's way to get ahead	2.1	13	2.3	13	2.2	13

Note: Significant level differences are reported for the following factors:

[a]Middle management vs. rank and file, $p > .05$.

[b]Top management vs. rank and file and middle management vs. rank and file, $p < .05$.

[c]All differences, $p < .05$.

[d]Top management vs. middle management and middle management vs. rank and file, $p < .01$.

[e]Top management vs. rank and file and middle management vs. rank and file, $p < .01$.

Table 8.17
PREFERRED CRITERIA FOR ADVANCEMENT

Q.17. How important *should* each of the following factors be for getting ahead in this company?	Top Management		Middle Management		Rank and File	
	Score	Rank	Score	Rank	Score	Rank
Quality of work done	4.8	1	4.6	3.5	4.7	1.5
Quantity of work done[a]	4.2	8	4.6	3.5	4.7	1.5
Superior's opinion	3.9	9	4.0	9	4.1	8.5
Dependability	4.5	6	4.4	7	4.3	4.5
Creativity, inventiveness[b]	4.5	6	4.3	8	4.1	8.5
Seniority in the plant[c]	3.8	10	3.7	10	4.0	10
Having friends in higher management	1.8	12	1.7	12	1.9	12
Having good professional knowledge	4.7	2	4.7	2	4.6	3
Taking initiative[d]	4.6	3.5	4.5	5.5	4.2	6.5
Having outstanding ability to work with people[e]	4.6	3.5	4.5	5.5	4.2	6.5
Loyalty to the company	4.5	6	4.9	1	4.3	4.5
Recommendations of political nature	2.6	11	3.0	11	2.8	11
Elbowing one's way to get ahead	1.2	13	1.4	13	1.3	13

Note: Significant differences have been found as follows:

[a]Top management vs. rank and file and middle management vs. rank and file, $p < .01$.
[b]Middle management vs. rank and file and top management vs. rank and file, $p < .05$.
[c]Top management vs. rank and file and middle management vs. rank and file, $p < .05$.
[d]Top management vs. rank and file and middle management vs. rank and file, $p < .01$.
[e]Top management vs. rank and file and middle management vs. rank and file, $p < .01$.

this question. We see support in our data for a number of general propositions that have been formulated on the basis of earlier research in a number of countries. Our analysis indicates that hierarchical position is associated in significant ways with a number of important objective as well as subjective characteristics of organization members:

1. Persons at upper levels of the hierarchy compared to those below are more likely to have higher education and (to some extent) more seniority, to be male, and to receive a relatively high salary.

2. The authority/influence and control that members exercise are greater at upper levels than at lower levels, as are the opportunities and positive qualities provided by jobs. To some extent, this uneven distribution is also found for the preferences (or ideals) expressed by organization members. We did not find, however, that the interpersonal participativeness of superiors as reported by subordinates varied with hierarchical levels.

3. We have also found the effect of hierarchy extending to the subjective reactions of members—their morale, psychological adjustment, satisfaction with payment, sense of responsibility, motivation, and initiative. Our measures show increasing values with hierarchical ascent for each of these variables.

4. Regression analyses suggest that the authority and influence that members feel they exercise is an important correlate of many of their subjective reactions (psychological alienation and attitude of members toward the leadership of the plant). We take this as an indication that the amount of authority and influence that members have in the organization is an important determinant of their adjustment in the organization. This finding supports the idea that increasing the participativeness of the organization has important and positive consequences.

5. We have not found that members' perceptions of aspects of their organization differ as a function of hierarchical position. Even though persons in different hierarchical positions differ in many subjective reactions to their role, they nonetheless agree about what their organization is like; for example, with respect to its level of participativeness and its distribution of control. There are some differences, however, in their perceptions of the benefits that are associated with advancement in the organization and in the criteria that determine such advancement.

   Our analysis was not designed to provide a complete picture of the specifics of the Romanian work organization; nonetheless, it does provide some basis for understanding the social reality of the Romanian organization. A great social experiment is under way in our country. New forms of organizing work are being introduced. The main objective of these forms is the achievement of economic democracy and the participation of working personnel at all levels. It is necessary to remember that the data of this chapter were collected in 1972. Since then, many things have probably changed in the social and psychological aspects of our enterprises. For example, a great emphasis has been put on deepening the participative character of managing enterprises, and the authority of the General Assemblies and of the Councils of Working People have been substantially enlarged. Enterprises have been given more responsibility and autonomy. This orientation is expressed in the principle of self-management. Some recent research suggests that these changes in political orientation as well as in the formal structures of organizations are already reflected in the social and psychological reality of our enterprises.

9

Summary and Conclusions

Arnold S. Tannenbaum and Tamás Rozgonyi

Culture and political system differ radically among the six countries of this research and the five of the earlier study, but the modern work organization represents a common denominator among them. Furthermore, all work organizations share similar features; therefore, they are likely to elicit similar reactions among members in all societies. We summarize here the commonalities documented in this research that may apply broadly to organizations everywhere.

Hierarchical Gradients

The organizational world of persons at upper levels of the work organization is predictably different—physically, socially, and psychologically—from that of persons at lower levels. At the top more than at the bottom, it is a world in which persons have authority and exercise influence. The world at the top is also more rewarding economically and psychologically; it is more interesting and "enriching," more congenial and comfortable, more satisfying, and less alienating. Organization members in all of the societies we have studied, whether socialist or capitalist, developing or developed, provide evidence for these differences.

Some features that are common to all work organizations are intentional by design and are deemed everywhere to be essential. The hierarchical distribution of authority is one such universal feature, even though it is a source of ambivalence in many places. The hierarchical distribution of wages illustrates a second feature that is designed into organizations, but one that does not have the absolute universality of the hierarchical distribution of authority. The unusual work organizations of the kibbutz demonstrate that wages need not be distributed hierarchically. Wage differentials exist in each of the other societies of this research, although the differentials are smaller in the socialist societies than elsewhere.

Not only are wages clearly hierarchical in all of the societies where wages are paid, but workers in all of these societies view high wages as among the most important advantages or rewards of high rank. For example, in each of the five countries of the present study where data are available on this issue, rank-and-file workers (but not top managers) cite high salary as the most important of nine possible advantages of high rank. Workers in the different countries also agree essentially with one another in their ordering of the other advantages, which include prestige, variety in work, independence, and opportunity to make decisions. Thus, workers in these countries appear to be more alike than different in their evaluation of these advantages—and high wages are indisputably the most important of the advantages in each place. Furthermore, in their judgment about pay and other advantages of high rank, workers in one culture may be more like those in another culture than they are like their own managers.

Like authority and wages, demographic characteristics of members are correlated with hierarchical position. Some of these correlations are purposely built into the organizational design. Seniority, age, and education, for example, which are associated with rank, are generally considered to be among the grounds for advancement. They may also be correlated with technical competence or taken as criteria of technical competence and, therefore, as bases for advancement. Hence, on the average, persons at upper levels compared to those below are older, have more seniority, and have more years of formal education. The kibbutz factory again proves an exception, however, with regard to one of these characteristics, education. Members of the kibbutz, unlike members of other societies, do not differ very much from one another in years of formal education, nor do managers differ from workers in this respect.

Sex is among the most striking demographic correlates of rank in all societies: The female manager is a very rare person. Principles of organization do not formally argue for a hierarchical gradient of sex in any of the countries; on the contrary, official ideology in a number of the societies explicitly rejects the inegalitarianism of such a gradient. Yet it persists as a manifest fact of organization; the likelihood of an organization member being male rather than female increases substantially with hierarchical ascent everywhere.

Organizations in all societies appear to be characterized by other gradients that are not usually designed into the organization or intended by managers. These gradients, in fact, would seem to contravene rational principles of organizational design. If organizational designers were to have their way, for example, *everyone* in the organization would be satisfied with his or her job and would feel a sense of commitment and responsibility to the organization. However, it is persons at the top, more than those at the bottom, who are likely to feel this way. In this sense, organizations are designed better at the top than they are at the bottom.

It should not be surprising that there is evidence for the universality of a hierarchical distribution of authority and reward in the work organization and of the accompanying gradients of satisfaction, motivation, and alienation. This evidence is encouraging methodologically, because it provides at least a modest form of construct validity for the measures. The results of this research go beyond the documentation of hierarchical gradients, however; they suggest facts and relationships that, like those concerning the gradients themselves, may have broad generality in organizations.

Authority and Influence as Values

A first generalization concerns the value that members attach to the exercise of authority and influence in organizations. On the average, members in each country indicate that they *want* to have authority and influence; and in general, they report wanting to have more than they perceive themselves to have. Members thus experience what Porter (1962b) has referred to as a perceived deficiency with respect to authority-related needs. Furthermore, in all countries the felt deficiency is greater at the bottom of the organization than it is at the top—consistent with the general principle of hierarchical gradients.

The deficiency in authority and influence and the hierarchical distribution of this deficiency imply several additional facts. First, most members perceive the exercise of authority and influence to be directly or indirectly rewarding. By definition, persons who exercise influence can affect conditions within their organization. Therefore, organizational life is likely to be more congenial to persons who have influence than to persons who do not. Furthermore, as Treiman (1977) argues, authority and influence are sources of prestige in all societies. Those who exercise authority thus enjoy a degree of respect, deference, or esteem greater than that enjoyed by persons who do not exercise authority.

The hierarchical gradient of perceived deficiency in personal influence can be broken into two constituent gradients—the gradient composed of the influence individuals at different levels perceive themselves to have and the gradient composed of influence they would prefer to have. The latter gradient is flatter and, on the average, higher than the former. Thus, in all countries, members'

responses imply that they would prefer an "ideal" organization that
is more egalitarian than is the "actual" organization.

The preference for a more equalized distribution of influence is
apparent in members' responses to several other questions in addition to those concerning their *own* authority and influence. For example, control graphs drawn on the basis of members' responses to
questions about the influence actually exercised by the hierarchical
groups (from the rank-and-file workers to the managers) and the influence these groups *should* exercise again show that members in all
countries prefer a more egalitarian distribution than they perceive
exists. Furthermore, these data are in agreement in essential
respects with those from a number of earlier studies, which suggests their broad generality. For example, they agree perfectly
with the summary of studies reviewed by Smith and Tannenbaum
(1963):

> A negatively sloped distribution of control occurs [in all the industrial] or-
> ganizational units studied. It is also apparent that the ideals which mem-
> bers have concerning the pattern of control differ from the actual pattern
> in almost all cases. The ideal distribution of control is more positively
> sloped than the actual and the ideal level of total control is higher than
> the actual level in a large percentage of the organizational units. While
> members desire a more positively sloped distribution of control than they
> perceive, they do not wish to achieve this by reducing the control exer-
> cised by other levels. They are more inclined to increase the control exer-
> cised by most groups, especially their own. (Members desire an increase
> in the control exercised by the rank-and-file group in 99 percent of the or-
> ganizational units examined.) This results in a higher level of ideal than
> actual total control in most organizations. It also results in the actual
> curve approaching more closely that of the ideal near the upper levels of
> the organization. It is at the level of the rank-and-file member that the
> greatest discrepancy between actual and ideal control, as reported by
> members, occurs. (pp. 306–307)

Worker Participation

The seemingly universal preference for increasing the influence
of lower-level participants and for a more egalitarian distribution of
influence is consistent with the current advocacy of worker participation. Many countries now legally mandate participative
procedures (IDE, 1981; Schregle, 1970; Tannenbaum, 1976), although the amount of control that workers actually exercise through
these procedures may be only nominal. Laws of "codetermination"
in a number of countries, for example, reflect a norm that supports
the idea, if not the substantial practice, of participation. Similarly,
even though managers express support for the idea of participation,
many of them feel some ambivalence about its actual practice.
Haire, Ghiselli, and Porter (1966), in a study of managers in 14
countries, found prevailing support among managers for the idea of

worker participation, although managers seem to have reservations about the feasibility of such participation, questioning the capability of workers to participate effectively.

This ambivalence on the part of top managers expresses itself indirectly, in the present study, in the responses to questions concerning workers' participation in decision making. Managers as well as workers in all of the countries report favoring such participation. Furthermore, while neither this expressed support for participation nor the perception of actual worker participation is consistently different at the top than at the bottom of the hierarchy among the countries, the *discrepancy* between the preferred and perceived level of participation is consistently greater at the bottom than at the top in every country. (In Romania, one of the three pairs of questions designed to measure this discrepancy proved an exception, not yielding a difference in the discrepancy score between the top and bottom. But two of the three pairs are consistent with this generalization.) Thus managers, like workers, say participation is a good thing, but managers indicate that the enterprise is already as participative as it should be, or almost so. Insofar as managers are concerned, the organization should continue to operate more or less at the level of participation at which it is operating. Workers, on the other hand, are unequivocal in reporting that the enterprise is not working the way it should; in the view of workers in all of the countries, the enterprise should be substantially more participative than it is.

Authority and Responsibility

One might suspect that the expressed preference by workers for more authority and influence and for greater opportunity to participate in decision making is a purely egoistic reaction reflecting the belief that the exercise of authority and influence is personally rewarding, whatever consequences it may have for the organization. Persons who exercise authority and influence, however, are likely also to feel a sense of responsibility in as well as a favorable attitude toward the company. First of all, the reports of persons at upper and lower levels show that persons at upper levels—who have more authority and influence than persons at lower levels— feel more responsible in and favorable toward the company than do persons at lower levels. In addition, regression analyses indicate, in nine of the ten countries where these analyses were performed (including those of the earlier study), that persons who have authority and influence are more likely to report feeling responsible in and favorable toward the company even when hierarchical level is controlled.

Both the feeling of responsibility and the feeling of alienation show hierarchical gradients, although of opposite slope. In general, however, even members at the bottom of the hierarchy are not entirely alienated and disaffected; nor are they without some feeling of responsibility in their company. Moreover, they do not take a revolutionary view of the distribution of authority and influence in their company. They want to increase their own influence, but they do not propose to undo the influence of the organizational leadership. Most respondents implicitly take a "constructive," nonzero sum view, assuming that the influence of workers can be enhanced without a corresponding decrease in the influence exercised by other groups in the hierarchy. Thus, the "ideal" distribution of control in all of the countries implies a greater total amount of control than does the actual distribution as members perceive it. Control in organizations has legitimacy for members (Tannenbaum, 1986).

Responses to questions concerning the "bases of superior's power" (French & Raven, 1959)—why members accede to the influence attempts of their superior—are a further indication of norms that imply the legitimacy of organizational control and that are shared widely by all members in all of the countries. Of the six possible reasons that members might endorse for acceding to the influence of their superior, two—legitimacy and functional necessity—rate substantially ahead of the others in all ten countries where these questions were posed. Members report doing what their superior asks of them because they see it as their "duty" and because it is "necessary if the organization is to function properly." On the other hand, members in all countries report that they are least likely to accede to the influence of their superior because their superior can "penalize or otherwise disadvantage" them. Nor do they attach much importance to the possibility that the superior can provide special help or benefits. Thus, the order of importance members attribute to the six bases of power is virtually identical in the ten countries, despite the substantial social and political differences between them. Power based on legitimacy or functional necessity is at the top of the list; coercive power is at the bottom, everywhere. If respondents are simply reporting stereotypes, those stereotypes are nonetheless very widely shared.

Members' Perceptions and Preferences
Concerning Their Organization

Members differ from one another in their perception of how their organization functions and in how they would like it to function. There are two general reasons to expect such differences as a function of hierarchy. First, persons in different positions, because they are located differently in "organizational space," have correspondingly different perspectives concerning aspects of that space. Because their vantage points differ, members differ from one another in what they see of the organization and in what they feel is necessary or desirable for the organization. Second, and more specifically, persons at the top, who are relatively highly rewarded and who identify with and are loyal to the organization, are likely to have a correspondingly positive image of the organization; they must have, if they are to maintain a positive image of themselves. They are thus likely to see or interpret their organization in terms of a favorable, socially approved stereotype. On the other hand, persons at the bottom, who are relatively disadvantaged and disaffected, are likely to interpret the organization in less favorable terms. Thus, managers' rationalizations about their organizations are likely to be supportive of the system, with which they identify, while workers' rationalizations, relatively speaking, are likely to find fault with the system, which they experience as frustrating and alienating.

While all of the differences in perception between levels, as indicated by our data, are not large or consistent among countries, a number of such differences support the above arguments. For example, when asked how persons get ahead in their company, managers and supervisors in all of the countries studied were more likely than workers to report socially acceptable criteria like creativity, initiative, and ability to work with people. Workers in most countries, however, were more likely than managers to take a less sanguine view, seeing "pull" or "elbowing one's way" as the bases of advancement. Furthermore, the discrepancy between a person's perception of how the organization functions and his or her preference concerning how it should function is likely to be smaller for persons at the top than for those at the bottom of the hierarchy. For example, in all countries, managers as well as workers report that their organization should be more participative than it is. But the discrepancy between the way it is and the way it should be is greater for workers than for managers. For higher-level managers, the organization comes closer to being as participative as it should be.

Explaining the Effects of Hierarchy

Similarities among the countries apply not only to aspects of hierarchy but also to relationships among variables that may help explain the psychological effects of hierarchy. For example, in most of the countries of this research and of the earlier one, regression analyses were performed in which hierarchical rank along with measures of authority and reward, salary, qualities of a job, and a number of demographic characteristics were used as predictors of the reactions and adjustments of members. The analyses in some countries do not include all of the predictors and dependent variables, but there is sufficient overlap in the content of the analyses to provide some basis for gauging the possible generality of relationships. As a guide to that generality for a predictor of a given dependent variable, we simply count the number of countries in which the magnitude of the beta associated with the predictor is among the three largest positive or negative betas of the approximately nine betas in each analysis. We assume that the analysis in each country can be considered an independent replication of the analyses in the other countries and that results indicating similar relationships in a high proportion of the countries therefore suggest a relationship that has broad generality. For example, in seven countries, regressions were performed in which a member's salary was included among the predictors of his or her satisfaction with pay. Salary was among the first three positive predictors of satisfaction with pay in *all seven* of these countries. In *none* of the countries, however, was salary among the first three predictors of *satisfaction with the job*. Thus, understandably enough, pay predicts satisfaction with pay in all societies, socialist and capitalist, where these analyses were done; but it does not predict satisfaction with the job in any of these societies. On the other hand, an index composed of certain physical qualities of the job (e.g., dirty vs. clean, tiring vs. not tiring, and physical vs. mental) predicts satisfaction with the job (in six of eight countries) as well as satisfaction with pay (in seven of eight countries). Other things being equal, therefore, members are likely to be more satisfied with their wages *and* with the job itself when they are doing work that is congenial than when they are doing work that is difficult or unpleasant.

The educational level of organization members also has implications for satisfaction with pay as well as for satisfaction with the job and a favorable attitude toward the company (in at least seven of nine countries). In these cases, however, the effect is *negative*. Relatively educated members are likely to be less favorable toward the company than are their less educated co-workers. A second characteristic of members, their seniority in the company, also contributes negatively to members' attitudes toward the company (under the controlled conditions of the regression analyses). The more senior the person, the less favorable he or she is likely to be toward the company (in nine of nine countries). Theories of social comparison and of equity (Adams, 1963; Lawler, 1971; Patchen, 1961) would suggest that persons who are relatively senior or relatively more highly educated (and who therefore *should* be higher in rank, salary, and other benefits) will feel some dissatisfaction in comparison to persons who are less senior or less highly educated, if the persons being compared are at the same rank, receive the same pay, and are otherwise equated on the variables that are controlled in the regression analysis.

From a value standpoint, however, the effects of education are not all negative. Relatively well-educated members are likely to take more initiative in "introducing better or faster ways of doing the work"; they are also less likely to feel alienated than less-educated members (in seven of ten countries). Education thus has conflicting implications in terms of commonly held values, in that it contributes to the positive outcomes of initiative and reduced feelings of alienation on the one hand and to the negative outcomes of dissatisfaction with pay and work and unfavorable attitudes toward the company on the other. These relationships emphasize the distinction between alienation and dissatisfaction. "Alienation" refers to a sense of powerlessness and normlessness, and like dissatisfaction, implies negative affect. But to be dissatisfied is not necessarily to be alienated, and the causes of one of these psychological reactions can be different from the causes of the other. Education may be one cause that, under the controlled conditions represented in our regression analysis, reduces the feeling of alienation while it increases the sense of dissatisfaction.

Other factors also have the effect of reducing alienation. Enriching qualities of a job, such as the opportunity the job provides to learn new things, to use one's own ideas, and to set one's own work pace, appear to have this effect (in seven of ten countries). Unlike education, however, these qualities of work are related positively to job satisfaction and favorable attitudes toward the company. Marx argued that the nature of work in mechanized industry is a source of alienation and frustration for workers because the machine "mutilates the worker into a fragment of a human being, degrades him to become a mere appendage of the machine, makes his work such a torment that its essential meaning is destroyed" (Marx, 1967, p. 713). Marx argued that ownership of the means of production is a root cause that determines the very development and the utilization of mechanized industry. Nonetheless, the nature of work in mechanized industry can itself be alienating, because it limits the opportunity to learn, to use one's own ideas and skills, and to set one's own pace.

Hierarchy and Participation

In nine of ten countries, regression analyses suggest a positive relationship between the amount of authority and influence members perceive themselves to have and the sense of responsibility they feel in their company. Thus, the traditional administrative injunction against assigning responsibility without authority appears to have a psychological counterpart: Members are not likely to *feel* responsible if they are not given authority.

Schemes of worker participation that are designed to broaden the authority of workers in their organization are gaining popularity throughout the industrial world. The rationale for these schemes often includes the argument that broadening the authority of workers encourages a sense of responsibility on the part of lower-level personnel. The data of this research are consistent, as far as they go, with this argument. However, participative schemes are not always effective in providing workers with real authority and influence in their organization. Part of this failure may be because many managers are cautious about participation and are implicitly, if not explicitly, opposed to it. This caution is illustrated by the "reassuring" remarks by a prominent German business leader printed in a business newspaper. "There aren't any problems with [codetermination] . . . because the workers haven't any real power to force their views. Where the workers' advice is good, it is listened to. Otherwise the shareholders' directors vote them down." While many managers endorse the idea of participative decision making, most of them maintain that rank-and-file workers are incapable of leadership and prefer to be directed and to avoid responsibility: "The apparent enlightened democratic beliefs of managers with respect to organizational government are merely a superficial cover to the basic negative beliefs about human capabilities" (Haire et al., 1966, p. 103). If so, contemporary managers are in essential agreement with the arguments of Robert Michels (1959) that led him to assert the inevitability of oligarchy in organizations.

Michels' assertion may or may not be correct, but the assumptions—that workers are basically apathetic and prefer to be directed and to avoid responsibility—that underlie his "iron law" do not find support in this research. Persons in all countries, in general, want more opportunity than they perceive themselves to have to learn new things and to use their ideas, skills, and abilities. In all countries, workers are clear in expressing the desire to participate and to have more authority and influence than they already have in their organization. Especially at the bottom of the hierarchy, members feel the need to increase their opportunities to learn, to use their skills and abilities, and to enhance their authority and influence; and to the extent that members have authority and influence, they are likely to feel a sense of responsibility in their organization. Nor do workers approach these issues in ways that imply an intentional challenge to the control managers exercise; in general, workers accept the legitimacy of managerial control.

The ostensibly positive attitudes of workers toward participation are not in themselves a guarantee that participation will prove to be a practical form of governance in the work organization. If there are valid arguments against worker participation, however, they are not that workers want to be led or to avoid responsibility, or that they are inherently antagonistic toward the company. Nonetheless, given the nature of hierarchy, workers may very well seem to managers to have such traits, which are inconsistent with effective participation. Compared to the managers at the top of the hierarchy, workers at the bottom do feel less responsible, less motivated, and less favorable toward the company; and they do feel more alienated. Managers, therefore, see "evidence" that workers do not have the right attitudes for effective participation. Thus, hierarchy is partly responsible for the problems of motivation and attitude that call for participation but that also seem to provide evidence that participation will not work.

Appendix A

History of the Project

Gunilla Vyskovsky

We describe here some of the events and decisions of this project that were significant for the development and coordination of the research and that might interest persons who intend to engage in international research collaboration.

The Origin

In 1970 the Board of the Vienna Centre accepted for inclusion in the Centre's coordination program a research project on the effects of organizational hierarchy on the reactions of organization members. This study was proposed by Arnold S. Tannenbaum (Institute for Social Research, The University of Michigan, Ann Arbor), who was asked to act as project co-director. Kazimierz Doktor (Institute of Philosophy and Sociology, Polish Academy of Sciences, Warsaw) was appointed in 1972 as co-director from Eastern Europe and served in that capacity until 1975, when Tamás Rozgonyi (Institute of Sociology, Hungarian Academy of Sciences, Budapest) became co-director.

Contacts with prospective project participants were established, and a first general meeting was held in Vienna in January 1971. This meeting was attended by researchers from six countries: Austria, Italy, the United States, Yugoslavia, the Federal Republic of Germany, and Poland. The scientists from the first four of the above countries had taken part earlier in a similar research study (Tannenbaum et al., 1974). The main issues of this meeting were to explore the possibility of linking the "new" study with the earlier one and to recruit additional participants into the new project.

Implementation of the Research and Data Analysis

A second general meeting was held in Yugoslavia in July 1971. This conference was attended by participants from three groups of

countries:
1. Italy, the United States, and Yugoslavia, where analyses had already started on the data of the earlier research.
2. Bulgaria and Hungary, where field work had commenced on the present research.
3. Algeria, Brazil, the Federal Republic of Germany, Ireland, Poland, and Romania, where some preparatory activities had been carried out, such as translation of the questionnaire.

In addition, British and Mexican scientists had shown interest in the project but were unable to attend the meeting.

One decisive agreement was that participants wished to preserve, to a great extent, the research design of the earlier study.

The choice of industrial branches was agreed upon, and an option was given to draw an additional sample at the rank-and-file level.

In December 1972, a meeting was held in Poland. As data collection had been completed in several countries, this meeting aimed at the preparation of a plan for the data analysis. The participants planned to have separate centers for data processing for Eastern and Western Europe and Latin America. In addition, it was agreed that a common book was to result from the project, and a list of items for comparative analysis was established. However, this plan was changed subsequently since some national teams preferred to analyze their own data and to write separate national reports.

In 1973, data collection had been completed in Brazil, Bulgaria, the Federal Republic of Germany, Hungary, Ireland, Mexico, Poland, and Romania. Algeria carried out a pretest but dropped out of the project.

Publication

In Autumn 1974, at a meeting in Bucharest, a common data analysis plan was established to serve as a guide for the writing of national reports. In 1975, at a project meeting in Hungary, this plan was closely reviewed and partly revised as a result of experiences of the participants during data analysis. A common form for the presentation of the text was also agreed upon. It was decided that each national report was to become one chapter in the proposed publication and that one chapter would be written by the researchers of the earlier study summarizing the results of that study. The publication would also contain introductory and synthesis chapters.

Reports from Brazil, Bulgaria, the Federal Republic of Germany, Hungary, Ireland, Mexico, and Romania were discussed and commented on at the last general meeting, in Wuppertal, the Federal Republic of Germany, in January of 1976.

Project Coordination and Specific Problems of the Study

At the end of 1980, the international research cooperation was concluded and work on the final manuscript started. Six national chapters were available, but a Polish national report was not written and a final version of the Brazilian contribution was not completed. Chapters based on the data of these countries, therefore, are not included in the present volume.

The project took considerably more time than anticipated because of difficulties in coordinating the efforts of persons separated geographically, reconciling conceptual differences between participants based on differences in culture and ideology, and communicating in several languages. During the course of the study, the following persons were Vienna Centre project coordinators: Risto Kolari (1970–71), Helmut Ornauer (1971–74), and Gunilla Vyskovsky (1975–80).

Project participants decided not to nominate an editor or editorial committee, but agreed that Arnold Tannenbaum should provide linguistic editing. There were a number of bilateral contacts between Tannenbaum and the respective participants. Gunilla Vyskovsky also helped with the editing, especially with regard to headings, references, and tables.

Appendix B

Questionnaire

As you know, this research concerns the life of people in industry. We begin by asking you some questions about your work.

1. In your work, to what extent can you:
   (Circle one number on each line across.)

	Not at all	A little	Some-what	Quite a bit	Very much
a. Learn new things?	1	2	3	4	5
b. Use your own ideas?	1	2	3	4	5
c. Do interesting work?	1	2	3	4	5
d. Use your skills, knowledge, and abilities?	1	2	3	4	5
e. Talk with other people during work time?	1	2	3	4	5
f. Decide your own pace of work?	1	2	3	4	5
g. Have authority over other people?	1	2	3	4	5

We have just asked questions about certain characteristics of your work. Now we would like to know something about your aspirations concerning these characteristics.

2. In your work, to what extent *would you like to*:
   (Circle one number on each line across.)

	Not at all	A little	Some-what	Quite a bit	Very much
a. Learn new things?	1	2	3	4	5
b. Use your own ideas?	1	2	3	4	5
c. Do interesting work?	1	2	3	4	5
d. Use your skills, knowledge, and abilities?	1	2	3	4	5
e. Talk with other people during work time?	1	2	3	4	5
f. Decide your own pace of work?	1	2	3	4	5
g. Have authority over other people?	1	2	3	4	5

3. Mark with a cross (X) along the following lines more or less near to the end that most closely describes your work.

tiring	|__|__|__|__|__|	not tiring
unhealthful	|__|__|__|__|__|	not unhealthful
physical	|__|__|__|__|__|	mental
dirty	|__|__|__|__|__|	clean
heavy	|__|__|__|__|__|	light
same tasks during the day	|__|__|__|__|__|	different tasks during the day
dangerous	|__|__|__|__|__|	safe
alone	|__|__|__|__|__|	together with others
dependent on others	|__|__|__|__|__|	independent of others

4. Are there real possibilities for people like you to advance in this plant? (Circle one number.)

   1. No possibilities at all
   2. Few possibilities
   3. Some possibilities
   4. Many possibilities
   5. Very many possibilities

5. Do you think that at some time in the future you will have a position in this plant higher than your present position? (Circle one number.)

   1. Not at all probable
   2. Slightly probable
   3. Somewhat probable
   4. Very probable
   5. Almost certain

6. In your kind of job, is it usually better to let your superiors worry about introducing better or faster ways of doing the work? (Circle one number.)

   1. Strongly agree
   2. Agree
   3. Uncertain
   4. Disagree
   5. Strongly disagree

7. How often do you try out on your own a better or faster way of doing the work? (Circle one number.)

   1. Very often
   2. Often
   3. Sometimes
   4. Rarely
   5. Never
   6. In my work it is not possible.

8. How much satisfaction do you get from your job in the plant compared to what you can do after leaving the plant? (Circle one number.)

  1. I get much more satisfaction from my job than from my other activities.
  2. I get a little more satisfaction from my job.
  3. I get about the same satisfaction from my job as from my other activities.
  4. I get a little more satisfaction from my other activities.
  5. I get much more satisfaction from my other activities than from my job.

9. Do you like working for this company? (Circle one number.)

  1. It's not a very good company to work for.
  2. It's all right.
  3. It's a fairly good company.
  4. It's a good company.
  5. It's a very good company.

10. Do you like the work you are doing in this plant? (Circle one number.)

  1. I like it very much.
  2. I like it quite a bit.
  3. I like it somewhat.
  4. I like it only a little.
  5. I do not like it at all.

11. To what extent do you feel really responsible for the success of: (Circle one number on each line across.)

		Not at all	A little	Some- what	Quite a bit	Very much
a.	Your own work group	1	2	3	4	5
b.	Your department	1	2	3	4	5
c.	The whole plant	1	2	3	4	5

12. What happens if a member in this organization does an especially good job in his work? (Circle *all that apply.*)

    1. His superior will praise him.
    2. His co-workers will praise him.
    3. His co-workers will criticize him.
    4. He may be offered a better job at the same level.
    5. He will be given a bonus or higher wage.
    6. His co-workers will have a high opinion of him.
    7. He will have a better opportunity for advancement.
    8. His superior will have a high opinion of him.
    9. Nothing will happen.
    10. Other (write in) _____

13. In your opinion, what *should* happen if a member in this organization does an especially good job in his work? (Circle *all that apply.*)

    1. His superior should praise him.
    2. His co-workers should praise him
    3. His co-workers should criticize him.
    4. He should be offered a better job at the same level.
    5. He should be given a bonus or higher wage.
    6. His co-workers should have a high opinion of him.
    7. He should have a better opportunity for advancement.
    8. His superior should have a high opinion of him.
    9. Nothing should happen.
    10. Other (write in) _____

14. What happens if a member in this organization does a very poor job? (Circle *all that apply.*)

    1. His superior will criticize him.
    2. His co-workers will criticize him.
    3. His co-workers will support him against criticism.
    4. He will be given an inferior job.
    5. His salary will be reduced.
    6. His co-workers will have a low opinion of him.
    7. He will have a less good opportunity for advancement.
    8. His superior will have a low opinion of him.
    9. Nothing will happen.
    10. Other (write in) _____

15. In your opinion, what *should* happen if a member of this organization does a very poor job? (Circle *all that apply*.)

    1. His superior will criticize him.
    2. His co-workers will criticize him.
    3. His co-workers will support him against criticism.
    4. He will be given an inferior job.
    5. His salary will be reduced.
    6. His co-workers will have a low opinion of him.
    7. He will have a less good opportunity for advancement.
    8. His superior will have a low opinion of him.
    9. Nothing will happen.
    10. Other (write in) _____

16. How important is each of the following factors for getting ahead in this company? (Circle one number on each line across.)

		Not at all	Slight	Moderate	Great	Very great
a.	Quality of work done	1	2	3	4	5
b.	Quantity of work done	1	2	3	4	5
c.	His supervisor's opinion of him	1	2	3	4	5
d.	Dependability	1	2	3	4	5
e.	Creativeness, inventiveness	1	2	3	4	5
f.	Seniority in the plant	1	2	3	4	5
g.	Having friends in higher management	1	2	3	4	5
h.	Having good professional knowledge	1	2	3	4	5
i.	Taking initiative	1	2	3	4	5
j.	Having outstanding ability to work with people	1	2	3	4	5
k.	Loyalty to the company	1	2	3	4	5
l.	Recommendations of a political or religious nature	1	2	3	4	5
m.	Elbowing one's way to get ahead	1	2	3	4	5

17. How important *should* each of the following factors be for getting ahead in this company? (Circle one number on each line across.)

		Not at all	Slight	Moderate	Great	Very great
a.	Quality of work done	1	2	3	4	5
b.	Quantity of work done	1	2	3	4	5
c.	His supervisor's opinion of him	1	2	3	4	5
d.	Dependability	1	2	3	4	5
e.	Creativeness, inventiveness	1	2	3	4	5
f.	Seniority in the plant	1	2	3	4	5
g.	Having friends in higher management	1	2	3	4	5
h.	Having good professional knowledge	1	2	3	4	5
i.	Taking initiative	1	2	3	4	5
j.	Having outstanding ability to work with people	1	2	3	4	5
k.	Loyalty to the company	1	2	3	4	5
l.	Recommendations of a political or religious nature	1	2	3	4	5
m.	Elbowing one's way to get ahead	1	2	3	4	5

18. How good is your immediate superior in his relations with the people he supervises? (Circle one number.)

  1. He is very good at this.
  2. He is good at this.
  3. He is fairly good at this.
  4. He is *not* good at this.
  5. He is poor at this.

19. How good is your immediate superior in organizing the work of your group? (Circle one number.)

    1. He is very poor.
    2. Poor
    3. Fair
    4. Good
    5. Very good

20. How adequate are the technical and professional skills of your immediate superior? (Circle one number.)

    1. Poor
    2. Fair
    3. Good
    4. Very good
    5. Excellent

21. Do you like your immediate superior as a person? (Circle one number.)

    1. Very much
    2. Quite a bit
    3. Somewhat
    4. A little
    5. Not at all

22. How well does your immediate superior do in reconciling the interests of your work group with that of other groups in the plant? (Circle one number.)

    1. He is very good at this.
    2. He is good at this.
    3. He is fairly good at this.
    4. He is *not* good at this.
    5. He is poor at this.

23. All in all, does your immediate superior do a good job as a superior? (Circle one number.)

    1. He does a poor job.
    2. He does a fair job.
    3. He does a good job.
    4. He does a very good job.
    5. He does an excellent job.

24. Do you think the responsible people here have a real interest in the welfare of those who work here? (Circle one number.)

    1. They have no interest at all.
    2. They have a little interest.
    3. They have some interest.
    4. They have quite a bit of interest.
    5. They have a very great interest.

25. Do the responsible people in this plant improve working conditions only when forced to? (Circle one number.)

    1. They improve working conditions *only* when they are forced to.
    2. They *seldom* try to improve working conditions without being forced to.
    3. *Sometimes* they try to improve working conditions without being forced to.
    4. *Often* they try to improve working conditions without being forced to.
    5. They *always* try to improve working conditions without being forced to.

26. How much influence do the following groups or persons actually have on what happens in this plant? (Circle one number on each line across.)

	Very little influence	Little influence	Some influence	Quite a lot of influence	A very great deal of influence
a. Plant manager and his executive board	1	2	3	4	5
b. All other managerial or supervisory personnel	1	2	3	4	5
c. The workers as a group	1	2	3	4	5
d. You, personally	1	2	3	4	5

27. In your opinion, how much influence *should* the following groups or persons have on what happens in this plant? (Circle one number on each line across.)

	Very little influence	Little influence	Some influence	Quite a lot of influence	A very great deal of influence
a. Plant manager and his executive board	1	2	3	4	5
b. All other managerial or supervisory personnel	1	2	3	4	5
c. The workers as a group	1	2	3	4	5
d. You, personally	1	2	3	4	5

28. When a worker in this plant makes a complaint about something, is it taken care of? (Circle one number.)

1. It's never taken care of.
2. It's rarely taken care of.
3. It's sometimes taken care of.
4. It's usually taken care of.
5. It's always taken care of.

29. Please rank in the order of their importance the following characteristics that are necessary for a person in the position of your immediate superior. (Place a "1" in the space next to the most important characteristic; a "2" next to the second most important, etc.)

___ Good in relations with people
___ Good in organizing the work of his group
___ Good in technical and professional aspects of the work
___ Good in reconciling the interests of his group with that of other groups
___ A good person in general

30. Suppose your immediate superior told you that you did some job badly. How much would it bother you? (Circle one number.)

   1. Not at all
   2. A little
   3. Somewhat
   4. Quite a bit
   5. Very much

31. Suppose some of your co-workers told you that you did some job badly. How much would this bother you? (Circle one number.)

   1. Not at all
   2. A little
   3. Somewhat
   4. Quite a bit
   5. Very much

32. What are the attitudes of the company members toward plant management? (Circle one number.)

   1. Attitudes are strongly opposed to the management.
   2. Attitudes are somewhat opposed to the management.
   3. Attitudes support the management.
   4. Attitudes strongly support the management.

33. What do workers communicate to their superiors? (Circle one number.)

   1. They communicate all relevant information accurately.
   2. They communicate mainly what their superiors like to hear.
   3. They communicate *only* what their superiors like to hear.
   4. They distort all information.

34. Do workers participate in making important decisions related to their work? (Circle one number.)

   1. Not at all.
   2. They never participate but they are sometimes asked for their opinions and suggestions.
   3. They jointly decide about many important things concerning their work.
   4. They jointly decide about all important things concerning their work.

35. *Should* workers participate in making important decisions related to their work? (Circle one number.)

   1. Not at all.
   2. They should never participate but they should sometimes be asked for their opinions and suggestions.
   3. They should jointly decide about many important things concerning their work.
   4. They should jointly decide about all important things concerning their work.

36. Do workers participate in making important decisions related to general plant problems? (Circle one number.)

   1. Not at all.
   2. They never participate but they are sometimes asked for their opinions and suggestions.
   3. They jointly decide about many important things concerning their work.
   4. They jointly decide about all important things concerning their work.

37. *Should* workers participate in making important decisions related to general plant problems? (Circle one number.)

    1. Not at all.
    2. They should never participate but they should sometimes be asked for their opinions and suggestions.
    3. They should jointly decide about many important things concerning their work.
    4. They should jointly decide about all important things concerning their work.

38. In this plant, are decisions made by the persons who have the most adequate and accurate information? (Circle one number.)

    1. Rarely
    2. Sometimes
    3. Often
    4. Always

39. When decisions are being made, are the people affected asked for their opinions and suggestions? (Circle one number.)

    1. They are almost never asked for their opinions and suggestions.
    2. They are sometimes asked.
    3. They are usually asked.
    4. They are almost always asked for their opinions and suggestions.

40. In your opinion, when decisions are being made, *should* the people affected be asked for their opinions and suggestions? (Circle one number.)

    1. They should almost never be asked for their opinions and suggestions.
    2. They should sometimes be asked.
    3. They should usually be asked.
    4. They should almost always be asked for their opinions and suggestions.

41. Does your immediate superior ask your opinion when a problem comes up that involves your work? (Circle one number.)

    1. He always asks my opinion.
    2. Often asks
    3. Sometimes asks
    4. Seldom asks
    5. He never asks my opinion.

42. Is your immediate superior inclined to take into account your opinions and suggestions? (Circle one number.)

    1. Not at all
    2. A little
    3. Somewhat
    4. Quite a bit
    5. Very much

43. Is your immediate superior friendly and easily approached if there are problems? (Circle one number.)

    1. Not at all
    2. To a very little extent
    3. To some extent
    4. To a considerable extent
    5. To a very great extent

44. Does your immediate superior make people under him feel free to take their complaints to him? (Circle one number.)

    1. He makes them feel completely free.
    2. Quite free
    3. Fairly free
    4. Not too free
    5. Not at all free

45. Would you want to have your immediate superior changed? (Circle one number.)

    1. I am definitely opposed to having him changed.
    2. Somewhat opposed
    3. Indifferent
    4. Somewhat for having him changed
    5. Definitely for having him changed

46. Do you have trust in your immediate superior? (Circle one number.)

    1. Never
    2. Rarely
    3. Sometimes
    4. Almost always
    5. Always

47. When you do what your immediate superior requests you to do on the job, why do you do it? (Circle one number on each line across.)

	Not at all	To a very little extent	To some extent	To a consid- erable extent	To a very great extent
Because:					
a. I respect his competence and judgment.	1	2	3	4	5
b. He can give special help and benefits.	1	2	3	4	5
c. He's a nice guy.	1	2	3	4	5
d. He can penalize or other- wise disadvantage me.	1	2	3	4	5
e. It is my duty.	1	2	3	4	5
f. It is necessary if the or- ganization is to function properly.	1	2	3	4	5

48. Imagine you were offered the following possibilities within this plant. Would you accept them or not? (Circle one number on each line.)

		Yes	No
a.	Move to a higher level position that has considerably more obligations and responsibilities for you	1	2
b.	Move to a higher level position that requires training that entails many sacrifices on your part	1	2
c.	Move to a higher level position where you may be frequently criticized	1	2
d.	Move to a higher level position in which you would have a group of "problem" employees working for you	1	2
e.	Move to a higher level position in which there are more worries than you now have connected with the work	1	2

49. How true are the following statements? (Circle one number on each line across.)

		Very true	Some-what true	Neither true nor untrue	Some-what untrue	Very untrue
a.	I feel depressed.	1	2	3	4	5
b.	Other people are always more lucky than I.	1	2	3	4	5
c.	I usually do a good job.	1	2	3	4	5
d.	I often feel bored.	1	2	3	4	5
e.	I seem not to get what is coming to me.	1	2	3	4	5
f.	Usually everything I try seems to fail.	1	2	3	4	5
g.	Things seem hopeless.	1	2	3	4	5
h.	I feel resentful.	1	2	3	4	5
i.	Almost every week I see someone I dislike.	1	2	3	4	5
j.	I sometimes feel that my life is not very useful.	1	2	3	4	5
k.	It seems to me that I am a failure.	1	2	3	4	5
l.	When I do a job, I do it well.	1	2	3	4	5

50. During the last 30 days, did you have any pain in your stomach?

    1. Yes
    2. No

    (If no, go to question 51)

    If yes:

    a. Did these pains come on before eating, while eating, right after eating, a couple of hours after eating, or when?

       1. Before eating
       2. While eating
       3. Right after eating
       4. Two or three hours after eating
       5. Not associated with eating

    b. Was this pain relieved by eating, drinking milk, bicarbonate of soda or other antacid, or by anything else?

       1. Eating
       2. Drinking milk
       3. Bicarbonate of soda or other antacid
       4. Anything else
       5. Nothing

    c. Did the stomach pain wake you up or keep you up at night?

       1. Yes
       2. No

    d. Thinking still about this past 30 days, on how many days would you think you had this pain for at least part of the day?

       _____ Days

51. Have you ever had an ulcer?

    1. Yes
    2. No

52. How true are the following statements? (Circle one number on each line across.)

		Very true	Some-what true	Neither true nor untrue	Some-what untrue	Very untrue
a.	It is not possible to rely on others.	1	2	3	4	5
b.	Today it is practically impossible to find real friends because everyone thinks only of himself.	1	2	3	4	5
c.	Men like me cannot influence the course of events; only men in high positions can have such influence.	1	2	3	4	5
d.	I have never had the influence over others that I would have liked.	1	2	3	4	5
e.	Public affairs are so complicated that one cannot help but be confused by them.	1	2	3	4	5
f.	Despite the many advances science has made, life today is too complicated.	1	2	3	4	5
g.	I can never do what I really like because circumstances require that I do otherwise.	1	2	3	4	5
h.	Life is so routinized that I do not have a chance to use my true abilities.	1	2	3	4	5
i.	Life seems to be moving on without rules or order.	1	2	3	4	5
j.	Nowadays it is hard to know right from wrong.	1	2	3	4	5

53. Do you know how your present job fits into the functioning of this plant? (Circle one number.)

   1. I don't know at all.
   2. I know slightly.
   3. I know somewhat.
   4. I know quite well.
   5. I know completely.

       a. Are you satisfied with your level of knowledge? (Circle one number.)

          1. Not at all
          2. A little
          3. Somewhat
          4. Quite a bit
          5. Very much

54. By which of the following ways do you get information about what is going on concerning the functioning of the plant? (Please choose the two most important and place the number "1" before the first most important and "2" before the second most important.)

   ___ From my immediate superior
   ___ From my subordinates
   ___ From the management
   ___ From written announcements
   ___ From worker meetings called by the management
   ___ From meetings called by the union
   ___ From my co-workers
   ___ From persons not working in the plant
   ___ Other (write in)_____

55. What do you think are the main advantages to moving into a higher position in this plant? (Please choose the three most important and place the number "1" before the first most important, "2" before the next most important, and "3" before the third most important. If you think there are no advantages at all to moving into a higher position in this plant, please check the last item in the following list.)

_____ Greater prestige or esteem
_____ Greater variety of work
_____ Greater independence
_____ Greater number of social contacts
_____ Greater opportunity to make decisions
_____ Greater opportunity to enlarge one's skills
_____ Greater opportunity to enlarge one's knowledge
_____ Greater influence with people outside the plant
_____ Higher wages
       _____ There are no advantages

56. What is the year of your birth? (Write in)

_____

57. How many years of school did you finish? (Circle one number.)

    1. Less than four years
    2. Four to six years
    3. Six to eight years
    4. Eight to ten years
    5. Ten to twelve years
    6. More than twelve years

58. Have you ever been a union officer or a member of a union committee in this plant? (Circle one number.)

    1. Yes
    2. No

59. Are you satisfied with your wages? (Circle one number.)

    1. Very dissatisfied
    2. Dissatisfied
    3. Neither satisfied nor dissatisfied
    4. Satisfied
    5. Very satisfied

Bibliography

Adams, J. S. (1963). Toward an understanding of inequity. *Journal of Abnormal and Social Psychology*, 67, 422–436.
Adams, J. S. (1965). Inequity in social exchange. In L. Berkowitz (Ed.), *Advances in experimental social psychology* (Vol. 1) (pp. 267–300). New York: Academic Press.
Anthes, J., Blume, O., et al. (1972). *Mitbestimmung, Ausweg oder Illusion?* Hamburg: Rowohlt.
Argyris, C. (1964). *Integrating the individual and the organization.* New York: Wiley.
Argyris, C. (1973). Personality and organization theory revisited. *Administrative Science Quarterly*, 18(3), 141–167.
Bartölke, K. (1969). *Überlegungen zu den Grundlagen der Planung von Betriebsorganisationen.* Berlin: Duncker & Humblot.
Bartölke, K. (1972a). Probleme und offene Fragen der Leistungsbeurteilung. *Zeitschrift für Betriebswirtschaft*, 42(9), 629–648.
Bartölke, K. (1972b). Anmerkungen zu den Methoden und Zwecken der Leistungsbeurteilung. *Zeitschrift für betriebswirtschaftliche Forschung*, 24(6), 650–665.
Bartölke, K. (1974). Die Gestaltung der Arbeitsstelle als Determinante der Personalpolitik — Ein Problemaufriss. *Wirtschaftswissenschaftliches Studium*, 3(7), 309–313.
Bartölke, K. (1975). *The importance of membership in top, middle, and bottom groups in selected plants in the GFR.* Arbeitspapiere des Fachbereichs Wirtschaftswissenschaft der Gesamthochschule Wuppertal No. 6, Wuppertal.
Bartölke, K., Flechsenberger, D., & Wilfer, R. F. (1976). Technologie, Hierarchie und Entfremdung. In H. J. Engeleiter (Ed.), *Unternehmen und Gesellschaft.* Herne-Berlin: Verlag Neue Wirtschaftsbriefe.
Bartölke, K., & Nieder, P. (1975). Sur Frage nach der Leistungswirksamkeit von Führungsstilen. *Zeitschrift für betriebswirtschaftliche Forschung*, 27(6), 449–460.
Bartölke, K., & Wächter, H. (1974). Mitbestimmung und betriebswirtshaftliche Organisationstheorie. In N. Koubek, H.-D. Küller, and I. Scheibe-Lange (Eds.), *Betriebswirtschaftliche Probleme der Mitbestimmung.* Frankfurt: Fischer Athenäum.
Bass, B. M., & Barrett, G. V. (1972). *Man, work, and organization.* Boston: Allyn and Bacon.
Becker, H. S. (1970). Whose side are we on? In W. J. Filstead (Ed.), *Qualitative Methodology.* Chicago: Markham.
Béla, C. N. (1971). *Magyar gazdaságpolitika* [Hungarian economic policy]. Budapest: Kossuth Könyvkiadó.
Béla, S. (1972). A helyi ipar fejlesztéséröl, a kis- és középüzemekröl [On development of local industry, about the small- and middle-size factories]. *Valóság*, No. 4.
Bendix, R. (1956). *Work and authority in industry.* New York: Harper and Row.
Blau, P. M. (1974). *On the nature of organizations.* New York: Wiley.

Blauner, R. (1964). *Alienation and freedom*. Chicago: University of Chicago Press.

Böhme, H. (1968). *Prolegomena zu einer Sozial- und Wirtschaftsgeschichte Deutschlands im 19. und 20. Jahrhundert*. Frankfurt: Suhrkamp.

Bruggemann, A., Groskurth, P., & Ulich, E. (1975). *Arbeitszufriedenheit*. Bern: Huber.

Bundesminister für Arbeit und Sozialordnung (Ed.) (1974). *Qualität des Arbeitslebens*. Bonn: Institut für Angewandte Sozialwissenschaften.

Burns, T. (1967). The comparative study of organizations. In V. H. Vroom (Ed.), *Methods of organizational research*. Pittsburgh: University of Pittsburgh Press.

Cartwright, D. (1965). Influence, leadership, control. In J. March (Ed.), *Handbook of organizations*. Chicago: Rand McNally.

Central Statistical Office (1966). *Az ipar koncentrációja Magyarországon* [Concentration of the industry in Hungary]. Budapest: Author.

Changley, I. (1973). *Trud* [Labor]. Moscow: Nauka Publishers.

Child, J., & Kieser, A. (1975). *Organization and managerial roles in British and West German companies—an examination of the culture-free thesis*. Berlin: Institut für Unternehmensführung der FU Berlin (Arbeitspapiere 7/75).

Coch, L., & French, J. (1948). Overcoming resistance to change. *Human Relations, 1*, 512–532.

Crozier, M. (1971). *The world of the office worker*. Chicago: University of Chicago Press.

Dahrendorf, R. (1969). On the origin of inequality among men. In A. Béteille (Ed.), *Social inequality*. Harmondsworth: Penguin.

Davis, L. E. (1972). The design of jobs. In L. E. Davis & J. C. Taylor (Eds.), *Design of jobs*. Baltimore: Penguin Books.

Dean, D. G. (1961). Alienation: Its meaning and measurement. *American Sociological Review, 26*(5), 753–758.

Deppe, F., von Freyberg, J., Kievenheim, C., Meyer, R., & Werkmeister, F. (1970). *Kritik der Mitbestimmung, Partnerschaft oder Klassenkampf?* (2nd ed.). Frankfurt: Suhrkamp.

Economic Research Institute of the Central Bureau of Statistics (1971). *Industrial concentration: An international comparison*. Budapest: Author.

Emery, F. E., & Phillips, C. (1976). *Living at work*. Canberra: Australian Government Publishing Service.

Emery, F. E., & Thorsrud, E. (1969). *Form and content in industrial democracy*. London: Van Gorcum.

Engelstad, P. H. (1972). Socio-technical approach to problems of process. In L. E. Davis & J. C. Taylor (Eds.), *Design of jobs*. Baltimore: Penguin Books.

European Economic Community (EEC) (1975). Employee participation and company structure. *Bulletin of European Communities, 8*.

Evans, W. E. (1963). Indices of the hierarchical structure of industrial organizations. *Management Science, 9*(3), 468–477.

Fitting, K. (1974). Grundzüge der Betriebsverfassung. In A. Christmann, W. Hesselbach, M. Jahn, & E. W. Mommsen (Eds.), *Sozialpolitik*. Cologne: Verlag Wissenschaft und Politik.

Follett, M. P. (1942). Dynamic administration. In H. C. Metcalf & L. F. Urwick (Eds.), *Dynamic administration, the collected papers of Mary Parker Follett*. New York: Harper.

Fox, A. (1971). *Sociology of work in industry*. London: Collier-Macmillan.

French, J. R. P., Jr., & Raven, B. H. (1959). The bases of social power. In D. Cartwright (Ed.), *Studies in social power* (pp. 150–167). Ann Arbor: Institute for Social Research, The University of Michigan.

Friend, E. K., & Burns, L. R. (1977). Sources of variation in job satisfaction: Job size effects in a sample of the U.S. labor force. *Personnel Psychology, 30*, 589–605.

Fromm, E., & Maccoby, M. (1970). *Social character in a Mexican village*. Englewood Cliffs, N.J.: Prentice-Hall.

Granick, D. (1972). *Managerial comparisons of four developed countries.* Cambridge, Mass.: MIT Press.

Gurin, G., Veroff, J., & Feld, S. (1960). *Americans view their mental health.* New York: Basic Books.

Gyenes, A., & Rozgonyi, T. (1974). *Hierarchia a gazdasági szervezetekben* [Hierarchy in economic organizations]. Budapest: MTA Szociológiai Kutató Intézet [Sociological Research Institute of the Hungarian Academy of Sciences].

Gyenes, A., & Rozgonyi, T. (1981). *Az alá- es fölérendeltzégi viszonyok a szervezetekben* [Subordination and superordination in organizations]. Budapest: Akadémiai Kiadó.

Habermas, J. (1973). *Legitimationsprobleme im Spätkapitalismus.* Frankfurt: Suhrkamp.

Hackman, J. R., & Oldham, G. R. (1976). Motivation through the design of work: Test of a theory. *Organizational Behavior and Human Performance, 16,* 250–279.

Hagen, E. E. (1962). *On the theory of social change.* Homewood, Ill.: Dorsey Press.

Haire, M., Ghiselli, E. E., & Porter, L. W. (1966). *Managerial thinking: An international study.* New York: Wiley.

Hartmann, H. (1959). *Authority and organization in German management.* Princeton: Princeton University Press.

Herbst, P. G. (1976). *Alternatives to hierarchies.* Leiden: Martinus Nijhoff.

Herzberg, F. (1966). *Work and the nature of man.* Cleveland, Ohio: World.

Hillery, B., & Kelly, A. (1974). Aspects of trade union membership. *Management,* April.

Hofstede, G. H. *Nationality and espoused values* (Working Paper No. 74–8). Brussels: European Institute for Advanced Studies in Management.

Hurley, J. (1973). Frustration and occupational level. Unpublished masters thesis, University College, Dublin.

Industrial Democracy in Europe (IDE) International Research Group (1981). *Industrial democracy in Europe.* Oxford: Clarendon Press.

Inkeles, A., & Rossi, P. H. (1956). National comparisons of occupational prestige. *American Journal of Sociology, 61,* 329–339.

Inkeles, A., & Smith, D. H. (1974). *Becoming modern: Individual change in six developing countries.* Cambridge, Mass.: Harvard University Press.

Israel, J. (1972). *Der Begriff Entfremdung.* Reinbek: Rowohlt.

Jenkins, D. (1973). *Job power.* Baltimore, Md.: Penguin.

Katz, D., & Georgopoulos, B. (1972). Organizations in a changing world. In J. M. Thomas & W. G. Bennis (Eds.), *Management of change and conflict.* Harmondsworth: Penguin.

Katz, D., & Kahn, R. L. (1966). *The social psychology of organizations.* New York: Wiley.

Katz, D., & Kahn, R. L. (1978). *The social psychology of organizations* (2nd ed.). New York: Wiley.

Kaufmann, K. (1974). Verhalten in Organisationen. In K. G. Specht, K. Kaufmann, K. Zeidler, & R. Wenzel (Eds.), *Soziologie im Blickpunkt der Unternehmensführung.* Herne-Berlin: Verlag Neue Wirtschafts-Briefe.

Kavčič, B., & Tannenbaum, A. S. (1981). A longitudinal study of the distribution of control in Yugoslav industrial organizations as perceived by members. *Human Relations, 34*(5), 397–417.

Kennedy, K., & Bruton, R. (1975). The Irish economy. *EEC Studies: Economic and Industrial Series,* No. 10, Table VI.2.

Lawler, E. E., III (1971). *Pay and organizational effectiveness: A psychological view.* New York: McGraw-Hill.

Lawler, E. E., III. (1973). *Motivation in work organizations.* Monterey, Cal.: Brooks/Cole.

Lewin, K., & Lippitt, R. (1938). An experimental approach to the study of autocracy and democracy. *Sociometry, 1,* 292–300.

Likert, R. (1961). *New patterns of management.* New York: McGraw-Hill.

Likert, R. (1967). *The human organization.* New York: McGraw-Hill.
Locke, E. A., & Schweiger, D. M. (1979). Participation in decision making: One more look. In B. M. Staw (Ed.), *Research in organizational behavior, Vol. 1.* Greenwich, Conn.: JAI Press.
Luhmann, N. (1975). *Macht.* Stuttgart: Enke.
Mann, F. C. (1953). *A study of work satisfaction as a function of the discrepancy between inferred aspirations and achievement.* Unpublished doctoral dissertation, The University of Michigan.
Marenco, C. (1959). *Employés de banque.* Paris: Conseil Supérieur de la Recherche Scientifique.
Marx, K. (1967). *Capital* (Vol. 1). New York: International Publishing Co.
Michels, R. (1959). *Political parties.* New York: Dover.
Morse, N. C. (1953). *Satisfaction in the white-collar job.* Ann Arbor: The University of Michigan Press.
Morse, N. C., & Reimer, E. (1956). The experimental change of a major organizational variable. *Journal of Abnormal and Social Psychology, 52*(5), 120–129.
Murphy, T. (1969). *Joint consultation in practice.* Irish Productivity Committee.
Naschold, F. (1973). *Organisation und Demokratie* (3rd ed.). Stuttgart: Kohlhammer.
Neuberger. O. (1974). *Theorien der Arbeitszufriedenheit.* Berlin: Kohlhammer.
Nick, F. R. (1974). *Management durch Motivation.* Stuttgart: Kohlhammer.
Nunnally, J. G. (1967). *Psychometric theory.* New York: McGraw-Hill.
Oetterli, J. (1971). *Betriebssoziologie und Gesellschaftsbild.* Berlin: de Gruyter.
Orpen, C., & Ndlovu, J. (1977). Participation, individual differences, and job satisfaction among black and white employees in South Africa. *International Journal of Psychology, 12*(1), 31–38.
Patchen, M. (1961). *The choice of wage comparisons.* Englewood Cliffs, N.J.: Prentice-Hall.
Porter, L. W. (1962a). Job attitudes in management: Perceived deficiencies in need fulfillment as a function of job level. *Journal of Applied Psychology, 46*(1), 23–51.
Porter, L. W. (1962b). Job attitudes in management: A perceived deficiency in need fulfillment as a function of job levels. *Journal of Applied Psychology, 46*(6), 375–384.
Presse- und Informationszentrum des Bundestages (Ed.) (1972). *Zur Sache.* Bonn.
Quinn, R. P., Staines, G. L., & McCullough, M. R. (1974). *Job satisfaction: Is there a trend?* (Manpower Research Monograph No. 30). Washington, D.C.: U.S. Government Printing Office.
Rosenberg, M. (1968). *The logic of survey analysis.* New York: Basic Books.
Rousseau, D. M. (1977). Technological differences in job characteristics, employee satisfaction, and motivation: A synthesis of job design research and sociotechnical systems theory. *Organizational Behavior and Human Performance, 19,* 18–42.
Rousseau, D. M. (1978). Measures of technology as predictors of employee attitudes. *Journal of Applied Psychology, 63*(2), 213–218.
Rubenowitz, S. (1974). Experiences in industrial democracy and changes in work organizations in Sweden. *Psykologiska Institutionen* (Goteborgs Universitet), *2*(1).
Rüthers, B. (1973). *Arbeitsrecht und politisches System.* Frankfurt: Fischer Athenäum.
Sarapata, A. (1974). Occupational prestige hierarchy studies in Poland. Paper presented at the 8th World Congress of Sociology, Toronto.
Sarapata, A., & Wesolowski, W. (1961). The evaluation of occupations by Warsaw inhabitants. *American Journal of Sociology, 66,* 581–591.
Schneider, D., & Kuda, R. F. (1969). *Mitbestimmung: Weg zur industriellen Demokratie?* Munich: DTV.
Schregle, J. (1970). Workers' participation in management. *Industrial Relations,*

9, 117–122.

Secretariat of Information of the SFR of Yugoslavia Assembly. (1977). *Associated Labour Act.* Ljubljana: Dopisma Delavska Univerza.

Secretary of Health, Education, and Welfare (Ed.) (1973). *Work in America.* Cambridge, Mass.: MIT Press.

Seeman, M. (1959). On the personal consequences of alienation in work. *American Sociological Review, 24*, 783–791.

Skinner, B. F. (1974). *About behaviorism.* New York: Knopf.

Smith, C. G., & Tannenbaum, A. S. (1963). Organizational control structure: A comparative analysis. *Human Relations, 30*(4), 299–316.

Srivastva, S., Salipante, P. F., Jr., Cummings, T. G., Notz, W. W., Bigelow, J. D., & Waters, J. A. (1975). *Job satisfaction and productivity.* Cleveland, Ohio: Department of Organizational Behavior, Case Western Reserve University.

Staikov, Z. (1973). *Byudgetat na vremeto* [Time budget]. Sofia: Partizdat.

Statistisches Bundesamt (Ed.) (1974). *Statistisches Jahrbuch für die Bundesrepublik Deutschland 1974.* Stuttgart: Kohlhammer.

Steinmann, H. (1969). *Das Grossunternehmen im Interessenkonflikt.* Stuttgart: Poeschel.

Strauss, G. (1974). Workers: Attitudes and adjustments. In J. M. Rosow (Ed.), *The worker and the job.* Englewood Cliffs, N.J.: Prentice-Hall.

Strauss, G., & Sayles, L. R. (1972). *Personnel: The human problem of management* (3rd ed.). Englewood Cliffs, N.J.: Prentice-Hall.

Szabó, B. (1972). On local industry development, small and middle factories. *Valóság,* No. 4 (in Hungarian).

Talmon, Y. (1972). *Family and community in the kibbutz.* Cambridge, Mass.: Harvard University Press.

Tannenbaum, A. S. (1966). *Social psychology of the work organization.* Belmont, Cal.: Brooks/Cole.

Tannenbaum, A. S. (1968a). Control in organizations. In A. S. Tannenbaum (Ed.), *Control in organizations.* New York: McGraw-Hill.

Tannenbaum, A. S. (1968b). The distribution of control in formal organizations. In A. S. Tannenbaum (Ed.), *Control in organizations.* New York: McGraw-Hill.

Tannenbaum, A. S. (1968c). Control in organizations: Individual adjustment and organizational performance. In A. S. Tannenbaum (Ed.), *Control in organizations.* New York: McGraw-Hill.

Tannenbaum, A. S. (1976). Systems of formal participation. In G. Strauss, R. Miles, C. Snow, & A. S. Tannenbaum (Eds.), *Organization behavior: Research and issues.* Belmont, Cal.: Wadsworth.

Tannenbaum, A. S. (1980). Organizational psychology. In H. Triandis & R. Breslin (Eds.), *Handbook of cross-cultural psychology* (Vol. 5, pp. 281–334). Boston: Allyn and Bacon.

Tannenbaum, A. S. (1986). Controversies about control and democracy in organizations. In R. N. Stern & S. McCarthy (Eds.), *The organizational practice of democracy.* New York: John Wiley & Sons.

Tannenbaum, A. S., & Cooke, R. A. (1979). Organizational control: A review of studies employing the control graph method. In C. J. Lammers & D. J. Hickson (Eds.), *Organizations alike and unlike* (pp. 183–210). London: Routledge & Kegan Paul.

Tannenbaum, A. S., Kavčič, B., Rosner, M., Vianello, M., & Wieser, G. (1974). *Hierarchy in organizations.* San Francisco: Jossey-Bass.

Tausky, C. (1970). *Work organizations.* Itasca, Ill.: Peacock.

Treiman, D. J. (1977). *Occupational prestige in comparative perspective.* New York: Academic Press.

U.S. Department of Labor (1971). *Survey of working conditions: Final report of univariate and bivariate tables* (Document No. 2916–0001). Washington, D.C.: U.S. Government Printing Office.

Vilmar, F. (1971). *Mitbestimmung am Arbeitsplatz.* Neuwied-Berlin: Vichterhand.

Vroom, V. H. (1970). Industrial social psychology. In V. H. Vroom & E. L. Deci

(Eds.), *Management and motivation*. Harmondsworth: Penguin.

W. E. Upjohn Institute for Employment Research (1973). *Work in America*. Cambridge, Mass.: MIT Press.

Wächter, H. (1973). *Grundlagen der langfristigen Personalplanung*. Herne-Berlin: Verlag Neue Wirtschafts-Briefe.

Weaver, C. N. (1977). Occupational prestige as a factor in the net relationships between occupation and job satisfaction. *Personnel Psychology*, *30*, 607–612.

Weber, M. (1964a). *The theory of social and economic organization*. New York: Free Press.

Weber, M. (1964b). *Wirtschaft und Gesellschaft*. Cologne/Berlin: Kiepenheuer und Wikesch.

Whyte, W. F., & Williams, L. K. (1963). Supervisory leadership: An international comparison. Symposium B3, paper B3c, CIOS XIII.

Woodward, J. (1965). *Industrial organization: Theory and practice*. New York: Oxford University Press.

Yadov, V. A., & Zdravomislov, A. G. (1967). *Tchelovek i evo raboty* [Man and his work]. Moscow: Misl Publishers.

Zdravomyslov, A. G., & Iadov, V. A. (1964). An attempt at a concrete study of attitude toward work. *Soviet Sociology*, *3*, 3–15.

Ziegler, H. (1970). *Strukturen und Prozesse der Autorität in der Unternehmung*. Stuttgart: Enke.